Weathered by Miracles

Weathered by Miracles

A HISTORY OF PALESTINE
FROM BONAPARTE AND
MUHAMMAD ALI TO
BEN-GURION AND THE MUFTI

Thomas A. Idinopulos

Ivan R. Dee
CHICAGO 1998

Frontispiece photograph by permission of Rafi Safieh, Authentic Photographs, Jerusalem.

Library of Congress Cataloging-in-Publication Data:
Idinopulos, Thomas A.
    Weathered by miracles : a history of Palestine from Bonaparte and
 Muhammad Ali to Ben-Gurion and the Mufti / Thomas A. Idinopulos.
        p.   cm.
    Includes bibliographical references and index.
    ISBN 1-56663-189-0 (alk. paper)
    1. Palestine—History—1799–1917.   2. Palestine—
 History—1917–1948.   3. Jewish-Arab relations.   4. Palestine—
 Ethnic relations.   I. Title.
 DS125.I35   1998
 956.94'03—dc21   98-14411

To the memory of

Yitzhak and Shoshana Spector

and Mahmoud al-Dajani

. . . whose lives graced the land

Contents

Acknowledgments

FOR RESEARCH GRANTS to support the writing of this book, I wish to thank Miami University's Faculty Research Committee and Dr. Karl Mattox, Dean of the College of Arts and Sciences.

I am indebted to several libraries: Yad Ben-Zvi, Hebrew University, and École Biblique in Jerusalem, and to Dana Fredrickson and Rick Hedrick at Hebrew Union College in Cincinnati.

My work is sustained by friendships with Brit Harwood, Edward Tomarken, Laurie Harwood, Wayne Elzey, Annette Tomarken, Marilyn Elzey, Jack and Nancy Sommer, Abe and Molly Miller, Gila Safran-Naveh, Charles Winquist, Dan Noel, John King-Farlow, Marshall Breger, Austin Wright, Dallas Wiebe, Yechiel and Miriam Ilsar, Jackie and John Drucker, Mira Harel, Bill Dean, Ari Rath, Jan and John Looman, Shalom Norman, and Michal, Shoshana, and Nasser.

Within my family, David, Michael, Lissa, and Kat enrich my life in ways that exceed words.

I am grateful for the encouragement and critical opinion of A. Weinberg and Professor Steven Bowman, who read portions of the manuscript. Professor Harold Forshey helped me understand the map of historic Palestine. Vickie Dearwester's skills were needed to prepare the original manuscript. Ivan R. Dee, my editor and publisher, smoothed a rough manuscript. Whatever problems remain in the printed text are my fault entirely.

Above all this book is for Lea mou, also known as the White Rabbit, who loves the land and yearns for its peace as much as I do.

Preface

THIS IS A BOOK about Palestine in the 150 years that began with Napoleon Bonaparte's invasion of the Middle East in 1798 and culminated in 1948 with David Ben-Gurion's proclamation of the Jewish state of Israel and the ensuing Arab-Jewish wars. It is the story of a diseased and wasted land that experienced an extraordinary reclamation.

This is the story of Muslims, Christians, and Jews confronting one another in a tiny place on the globe at a unique moment in history: the final muscular exercises of European empires and the first drawn breaths of Arab and Jewish nationalisms. For that reason this is necessarily a tale of political conflict between Christian and Muslim, between Arab and Jew—conflict whose seeds were sown in otherwise noble efforts to reclaim a wasted land.

Looking back, it seems inevitable that conflict would have followed the reclamation of Palestine. For despite their many good works, the presence and power of Western Christians provoked Muslims against them. Later, Muslim resentment fixed on the Zionists, who were seen as an instrument of foreign domination of a country that belonged to Arabs and Islam. The irony of Palestine in these 150 years is that the reclamation of the country planted the seed for the larger, bloodier conflict that would follow in the second half of the twentieth century.

BONAPARTE'S INVASION of Egypt in 1798, and of Palestine one year later, was truly a pivotal moment in the history of East-West relations. Not since the medieval Crusades had a Western power sought to conquer a part of the Middle East. But where the Franks had bled and burned Palestine to enrich themselves, Bonaparte was repulsed in Palestine by a combined Anglo-Turkish force that in 1801 drove the French out of Egypt altogether. Nonetheless Bonaparte had opened the East's door to the West. Going through that door for the next 150 years were a myriad of Westerners, "peaceful crusaders," one might call them—adventurers and archaeologists; artists, writers, and photographers; merchants, missionaries, and diplomats. Scarcely one of them entered Palestine without experiencing the spiritual feeling associated with the words "Holy Land."

To speak of the Holy Land is to point to the abiding paradox of this country. Palestine is blessed to be the birthplace of Judaism and Christianity and the nurturing soil of Islam. But Palestine also has had the bad fortune to be on the crossroads of world conquest. The world map shows this tiny portion of the Fertile Crescent to be at the intersection between Asia and Africa, serving as a corridor from Syria and Iraq in the northeast to Egypt and the Red Sea in the south. At different times many of the world's conquerors have marched through this corridor, some headed for glory, others for oblivion. Thus the historic significance of Palestine derives as much from the events of world conquest as from the religious imagination.

Over centuries, pilgrimages deepened the holiness of the Holy Land. Once a year the Hajj caravan would assemble at Damascus and make its way under armed guard down the desert road east of the Jordan River, one hot dry dusty mile after another, heading for Mecca. When it reached Mount Nebo, where Scripture says the prophet Moses spied the Promised Land, groups in the caravan would break off for a side trip to Jerusalem. It was a *ziyara*, a "visitation" to the large outcropping of limestone in Jerusalem where Islamic tradition placed Muhammad's Night Journey and Ascent to Heaven. On this site the earliest Muslim rulers of Palestine built the handsome octagonal shrine known as the Dome of the Rock. The building stands to this day as a beacon to pilgrims and a symbol of Islamic reverence for the city and the land blessed by Muhammad's miraculous presence.

To Christians, Palestine is the Holy Land which gave birth to Jesus Christ and fathered the church and inspired the New Testament's stories of witness and wonder. A few decades after the completion of the Gospels, cave-dwelling monks appeared on the cliffs of the Judean sandhills, sanctifying the land by their presence. After them an unending stream of pilgrims poured into Palestine, arriving just before Christmas and departing after Easter after having retraced what they believed to be Jesus' footsteps. Thus was created a Christian geography of the country, a geography further glorified by the construction of churches, monasteries, and convents over sacred sites. Protestants, who had little passion for "holy places," compensated for their skepticism by educating the ignorant, feeding the poor, healing the sick, and preaching a spiritual gospel to any Jew and Muslim in Palestine who would listen.

For Jews, the word *Palestine* had to be an alien word, referring to Israel's ancient enemy, the Philistines. This land could have but one legitimate Hebrew name, *Eretz Yisrael*, the Land of Israel. Here was the land that Yahweh promised to Abraham for a nation to live under Covenant Law. In this land David united the Israelite tribes; Solomon built the Temple of Jerusalem; the prophets foretold of Exile, Restoration, Final Judgment, and Messianic Redemption. From this land the people Israel—the Jews, as they came to be called—were exiled; and to this land they would return to live under foreign rulers while awaiting the Redemption. While in exile the memory of this land and its sacred capital, Jerusalem, would unite in the word *Zion*. And that word, resonating with mystically felt pride and power, would be bestowed on the modern movement of national restoration called Zionism.

Here then, in this land, is the home of three distinct yet intimately connected religious peoples. Here is the land where the One God of the three religions revealed his law, appointed his prophets, sent his messiah, and announced to the world the Final Days of Deliverance.

But Palestine could not conceal its tragic and sorrowful aspects. Jews, Christians, and Muslims, who shared the vision of the One God, could not (and seemingly cannot) agree on the practical, religious application of that vision. Profound questions divided the peoples: Whose prophet is the true voice of God? Who is the real messiah? To whom did God give this land? Behind these questions lies the recorded history of Palestine: a dismal chronicle of conquest and reconquest, of unceasing desecration, of the rise and fall of nations, races, and religions. From the time the original Canaanite inhabitants of this land were confronted in battle by invading Israelites, Palestine has witnessed the wars of Assyrians, Babylonians, Persians, Greeks, Romans, Byzantines, Arabs, Egyptians, Mongols, and, in our own century, Turks, Englishmen, Israelis, and Palestinians.

How does one explain this land where so much sanctification and strife have occurred hand in hand? In searching for an answer I was led to the explosive combination of power and religion that characterizes Palestine's history. In this country people go to war not in spite of their ideals but precisely because of them. At the root of the Muslim belief in *jihad*, and the Christian concept of holy war, the crusade, lies the ancient Hebrew practice of *herem*, the punishment of God's unbelieving enemies. Thus in the very ideals of Jews, Christians, and Muslims is enmeshed the obligation to oppose, punish, even destroy the unbelievers.

Power and religion shaped Palestine's history during those 150 years that began with Bonaparte's invasion of the Arab East and concluded with the establishment of the Jewish state. This was an age that saw Christian conquest and humiliation, Jewish return and resurgence, Muslim resentment and reaction. Palestine was transformed from a forgotten backwater of the vast Ottoman Empire and propelled onto a world stage where empires clashed and new nations were born. Not since the medieval Crusades had so many empires, so many nations, cultures, and religions, come into contention over Palestine. Its smallness mocks the enormity of the ambitions that collided there.

Weathered by Miracles

PART ONE

The Land Wasted

CHAPTER ONE

Land Weathered by Miracles

S o much history for such a small place with an uncertain name.
When Israelites were not referring to this land as Canaan, after
its original inhabitants, they called it after themselves, Eretz Yisrael.
The Romans were the first to name the land Palaestina, after the
Philistines, the nemesis of the Israelite tribes before King David defeated them and united the Israelites under his own banner. The Romans divided this land into three sectors: Palaestina Prima and
Secunda, which applied to the area west of the Jordan River, and
Palaestina Tertia, which referred to Transjordan, east of the river. It
was during the Middle Ages that the land west of the Jordan began
to be referred to in Latin as Terra Santa, the Holy Land.

The Arab conquerors of the land in the seventh century had no
proper name for it and considered it merely the southern region of
bilad al-Sham, the vast region of Syria stretching east from the
Mediterranean Sea to the Jordan River and then across the great
desert expanse to the banks of the Euphrates River. The land was divided between two provinces or pashaliks, one of which ran from
Nablus to Hebron and included Transjordan, with its capital in
Damascus; the other included the western sea coast, whose capital
was Acre. Possession of Acre meant domination of the whole country.[1]

The Arab conquerors adopted the Latin, Palaestina Prima, and
moved the capital from the exposed Caesarea on the coast to the
more central inland town of Lydda.[2] Until the twentieth century the
word *Palestine* held little if any meaning for Arabs. It was not a distinct geographical area with its own cultural tradition. Palestine was
merely a Latin-based word that referred to the southern portion of
the Syrian land mass. Under Ottoman rule from the sixteenth to the
twentieth centuries, the administrative centers of this land were the
capitals of the pashaliks of Damascus, Aleppo, Tripoli, and Sidon,

with its capital at Acre. Jerusalem was declared an independent province only in 1854, its pasha reporting directly to Istanbul. The growing Christian influence in late-nineteenth-century Palestine, and mass Jewish immigration beginning after 1860, had a sobering effect on the majority Muslim population, who in the first decade of the twentieth century began to speak of Filastin as *their* country.

But it was the British, ruling Palestine during the three decades from 1917 to 1948, who elevated Jerusalem as the capital of Palestine. The Palestine of the British mandate lay between the Jordan Valley and the Mediterranean Sea, south of the Lebanese mountains, on the western edge of the Syrian desert, north of the vast desert expanse of the Negev-Sinai. Thus the natural boundaries of Palestine were the desert and the sea, the river and the mountains. Palestine, west of the Jordan River, comprised 6.5 million acres, less than a third of which was fertile. The rest consisted of rocky hills, sand dunes, scrub land, water courses, and marshes.[3]

The climate of Palestine has not changed greatly since biblical times: a hot, dry, sparse country, with two months of rainfall. The chief crops—grain, citrus, vines, olives—have always been grown. Sand dunes and marshes in the coastal Plain of Sharon are the consequence of a centuries-old neglect of drainage, which in turn brought malaria. Because of Bedouin raiding throughout much of the nineteenth century, most of Palestine's population was not to be found in the exposed coastal areas but in the naturally protected central hill country of Judea, Samaria, and the upper Galilee.

For so small a country (about the size of Wales), Palestine had a number of cities, the largest of which were the old walled fortresses of Jerusalem, Acre, Haifa, Jaffa, and Tiberias, and the unwalled towns of Nablus, Hebron, Beersheba, Gaza, Nazareth, Bethlehem, Jericho, Ashkelon, and Ashdod. Within each town were square houses of stone and clay, each with its own wall and gate, built around an inner courtyard, usually containing a cistern for the collection of water. The houses were cooled by their distinctive rounded domes, built with bricks and mortar because of a lack of wood to construct flat roofs. Down the middle of every street was a drainage canal that served as a sewage system, which often became an overflowing cesspool in the winter.

Statistics point to the extraordinary demographic changes that occurred in Palestine in the period from Bonaparte to Ben-Gurion.

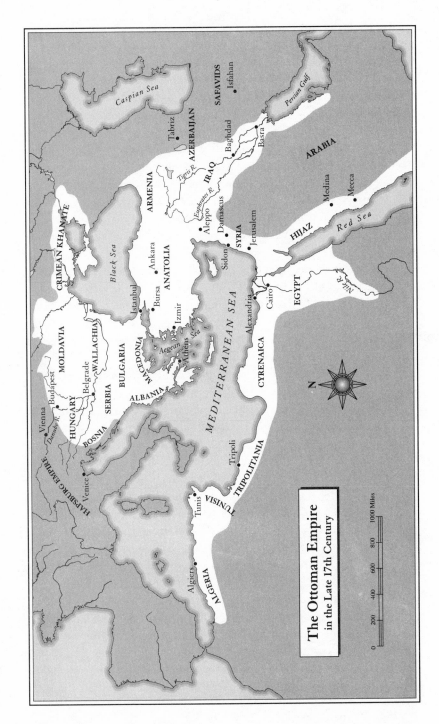

The Ottoman Empire
in the Late 17th Century

At the beginning of the nineteenth century fewer than 300,000 people lived in Palestine, more than 90 percent of them Muslim and the balance mostly Christian. Jews numbered only 5,000. By 1914, on the eve of World War I, there were 700,000 inhabitants, including 70,000 Jews. By 1948, before the outbreak of war, Palestine's population had reached 1.5 million, and the Jewish population had grown to 600,000.

As the Jewish population of the country increased dramatically, particularly in the 1930s, the Arab population, both Muslim and Christian, also grew notably. Arabs from surrounding lands entered the country because of work opportunities. After 1917 greater physical security, economic growth and prosperity, the improvement of community health and education—all contributed to the revitalization of Palestine.

This resurgence was due in great part to the vision, industry, and investment of Christians. To say this does not mean to ignore the ample evidence of Christian bias and bigotry. The old medieval Crusader zeal for conquest, domination, and exploitation was in some respects perpetuated by new Western Christian travelers and settlers in Palestine. And Western Christians persisted in their "orientalist" distortion of the Islamic and Arab peoples and culture as exotic, sensuous, irrational, lazy, and corrupt.[4]

But we must also recognize the quality of commitment in the Western Christian attitude. Throughout the nineteenth century Westerners came to Palestine to explore an unknown land, associated in their minds with the triumphs of Israelite kings and the prophecies of the Bible. Westerners walked the land, dug the ground for remainders of the past, searched into villages, learned Arabic and Hebrew, mastered the teachings of Judaism and Islam. They did this in the belief that Palestine, the Holy Land, had much to teach them about themselves. Far from the "zealous intruders" they are often depicted as, they are more accurately seen as earnest adventurers, eager to search out the spiritual roots of their own lives and culture in the soil of this ancient country.[5]

Such earnest adventurers were the explorers Clarke, Seetzen, and Burckhardt; the archaeologists Robinson, Clermont-Ganneau, Wilson, and Tyrwite; the painters Roberts and Holman Hunt; the surveyors Conder and Kitchener; the writers Volney, Chateaubriand, Kinglake, and Mary Rogers. To Westerners, Palestine had the feeling of "the beginning." They were drawn to this country as one is always drawn to the living sources of one's own being. Even Mark Twain, who made a feast of parodying the ugly and absurd in this country, was emotionally moved by it and admitted so.

What Westerners found in the Palestine of the nineteenth and early twentieth centuries was a disaster. One of the first to experience that disaster and write about it accurately and eloquently was Comte de Volney, the French nobleman. In 1783, fifteen years before Napoleon's invasion of Egypt, Volney traveled through Syria, Palestine, and Egypt and recorded his impressions in a journal that remains one of our most compelling accounts of life in Palestine at the close of the eighteenth century.[6]

Arabs, Volney wrote, have a "a grave and phlegmatic exterior, a flayed and almost listless deportment, and a serious, nay, even sad and melancholy countenance." The reason is that "in such a country, where the subject is perpetually watched by a despoiling government, [a person] must assume a serious countenance for the same reason that he wears ragged cloths, and makes a public parade of eating cheese and olives."[7]

Volney's "despoiling government" was embodied in the person of the Ottoman sultan, an oriental despot, for whom Palestine, as all of the other twenty imperial provinces, existed to be exploited. The better word is *fleeced*. Appropriately enough, the non-Muslim Christian and Jewish subjects of the realm were called *raya* or sheep.

The fleecing of both Muslim and non-Muslim subjects began in Istanbul and took the form of a system of taxation that relied on the entire bureaucracy of the empire, beginning with the twenty-six pashas or provincial governors. The Ottoman tax system was a snake whose head was in Istanbul and whose tail touched every town and village of the empire. Sometimes the tail was stronger than the head. Uncertain of the amount of revenue he could collect from each province, the sultan preferred quick returns. Each year he would auction off to the highest-bidding pasha the tax farm for Palestine. The bidding was fierce because the position was lucrative. None bid higher than Pasha Ahmad al-Jazzar, who was governor of western Palestine and the northern Galilee for almost thirty years (1773–1803), and would gain a place in world history by repulsing Bonaparte's invasion.

Auctioning off the taxing rights for the province of Palestine initiated the taxing system. The pasha bought the tax right for one million piastres, let us say. In turn he would lease the tax right to his deputy governor for two million piastres; and the deputy governor would then farm out the tax collection for appropriately high sums to village sheiks and other lesser despots. Not surprisingly, two-thirds of Palestine's agricultural produce went toward the payment of taxes. "Everything is taxed," wrote W. J. Stracey, a contemporary observer, "every fruit tree, so none are planted; every cow or horse . . . every vegetable sold out of a private garden. Every eighth egg is not taxed but taken by the government."[8]

The incentive to cultivate crops was destroyed when one knew that any surplus would be taken for taxes or simply confiscated by the pasha's army for its own use. Peasants crippled their farm animals in order to keep them from being seized by the army. Roads to villages were damaged or left unrepaired by peasants who hoped to prevent the entry of soldiers or tax collectors.[9] Food was hoarded and hidden. Hunger was common. Volney observed that villagers "were reduced to a little flat cake of barley ordourra, to onions, lentils, and water."[10] When these were gone, they roasted acorns. As soon as the corn turned yellow it was picked and hidden in mountain caves.[11] During periods of drought there were reports of cannibalism. Hunger and other deprivations had reduced a population of more than a million in previous generations to 300,000 at the start of the nineteenth century. Sometimes a peasant would make a gift of his land to the Muslim religious trust, which could not be taxed, and then he would live off the produce. Occasional tax rebellions that occurred in the towns of Nablus, Gaza, and Damascus were ruthlessly suppressed.

There were three main Ottoman taxes: *salyna*, the annual tribute paid to the Noble Porte, the Ottoman government; *miri*, the crown tax collected from all who lived on the Sultan's land; and *cizye*, the head tax paid only by Christians and Jews, an emphatic symbol of the inferiority of non-Muslims in the House of Islam, meaning the state. Additional taxes could be ordered at any time by a pasha who needed money for his army or who had simply run out of cash. Nor was the haughty pasha above selling a taxing concession to lowly Christians. The monks of Nazareth once bought the right to collect taxes from the villages surrounding their monastery.

Added to these regular taxes were the special taxes levied on pilgrims: one to enter the country, another to pass through Jerusalem's gates, still another in the form of a fee for every holy site visited. To assure one's safety, bribes were paid to the Bedouins and other brigands who awaited the pilgrims on the road from Jaffa to Jerusalem.

Pashas used their taxing power to gain monopolies, particularly on Palestine's largest export products of cotton and soap. Peasants were required to sell these to the pasha at below-market prices. Crippling taxes also forced Palestine's peasants to borrow money at interest rates from 20 to 50 percent in order to cover their taxes, thus plunging them further into debt. Wealthy urban families often paid the taxes of peasants in order to gain control of land which the peasant would sign over to them as collateral for the loan. Throughout the nineteenth century and well into the twentieth, a handful of land-owning Muslim families in this way grew wealthy on the purchase of cheap farm land. Gradually peasants left the land and became part of an enlarging urban proletariat which was poor, ignorant, resentful, and ripe for revolution. The end result was the impoverishment of the land.

There was still more evidence of a "despoiling government." Volney notes in 1873 that along the entire coast of Palestine there was "no harbor capable of admitting a vessel of four hundred tons." No large usable road could be found anywhere, no canals to direct badly needed water, no bridges over rivers and streams—nothing that was needed to lift the country out of its malaise and mire. Concessions for the few exports of cotton, olive oil, and soap to Egypt were sold to Jews, Greeks, Armenians, and the French at reduced prices, with appropriate bribes to the pasha. As exports were sold cheaply, so imports—mainly luxury goods from Europe and India, "furs, laces, sugars, and shawls"—were bought dearly, a practice, says Volney, that served only "to increase the dissipation of the rich . . . and aggravate the wretched condition of the people."[12]

Upon receiving his annual revenue, the sultan left the pasha alone to govern his own province as if he were king. But the temptation to be king—to stay long in office, grow wealthy, feel independent of Istanbul, and forget the revenue due the sultan—was overwhelming. Frequently the sultan's vizier had to order out the imperial army to bring a rebellious pasha into line.

Compared to other regions of the empire in the late nineteenth century, Syria and Palestine were not profitable tax farms for the Noble Porte. Gone were the days when the two countries were part of the commercial overland route from the East to Mediterranean ports. The discovery of the sea route to India and Africa had diminished the economic importance of the Middle East as the land bridge to Asia. The decline of the Ottoman Empire in the nineteenth century shows up in lost revenue. The sultan was said to reap less than 25 percent of all tax revenue from his provinces in Egypt, Syria, and Palestine.

What the tax collector did not take from the peasant, the Bedouin took. Perched on the edge of the three desert regions of Arabia, Syria, and the Sinai, Palestine was a lucrative target for Bedouin looting. Outside the control of the pasha's army, Palestine was in the grip of large, powerful Bedouin tribes, which lived to make war on one another and to raid villages. The pashas might control the main provincial towns of Damascus, Tripoli, Sidon, Gaza, Acre, Jaffa, and Jerusalem, but the hinterland between the towns belonged to the Bedouins.

Equipped with the latest weapons, fighting in familiar terrain with the confidence of a warrior caste, raiding villages on camel or horseback, extorting money, stealing animals and food, preying on roads, pillaging caravans, the Bedouins were the bane of the peasants' existence. Even pashas were willing to pay bribes to Bedouin chiefs to be freed for a time from the ravages of the desert marauders. Bribes were also paid to protect the annual Hajj caravan which started from Damascus and traveled through the desert south to Mecca.

The strongest of the Bedouins was the confederation of tribes known as the Anaza, which had moved north from the tip of the Arabian peninsula and in the eighteenth century had become dominant in the area between the Euphrates and the Jordan rivers. Another powerful tribe east of the Jordan was the Banu Sakhr. Both tribes commonly raided Palestine, particularly in the areas of Nablus and Jerusalem, large towns that were nonetheless ill-protected from raiders. East of Jerusalem in the area between Hebron and the Dead Sea, the feared Ta'amra Bedouin held sway.

Villagers paid protection money to keep from being raided, or they found themselves pawns between warring Bedouin tribes vying to extract protection money from the same village. When they were

not victims of Bedouin raiding, peasants formed alliances to stage rebellions against the pasha's tax extortions.

Typical of a Bedouin raiding family was the all-powerful Abu
Ghosh, which guarded the road from Ramleh to Jerusalem's gate,
preying on Christian and Jewish pilgrims. The Jerusalem monasteries, whose economy depended on the annual pilgrimages, paid the
Abu Ghosh clan an annual fee.[13] So completely did the Abu Ghosh
dominate its area that the Turkish government in the mid-nineteenth
century decided it could save money by paying the clan an annual fee
to act as protector of Jerusalem.

In addition to taxes, pashas, and Bedouins that bedeviled the
peasants, natural calamities afflicted Palestine throughout the nineteenth century—earthquakes, droughts, and plagues of locusts. Out-
breaks of epidemic disease were not infrequent. Great stretches of
stagnant water made Palestine one great breeder of disease. The
most common afflictions were dysentery, cholera, malaria, typhus,
and bubonic plague. Visitors were required to undergo quarantine,
sometimes for weeks. Hot summer winds, which could easily raise
the temperature to 100 degrees Fahrenheit, were carriers of deadly
bacteria.

European travelers noted that however foul-smelling were the
streets of their own native towns, the streets of Palestine were still
worse. They observed that local peoples seemed oblivious to the
odors, and wondered if "the organs of sense have in the East the same
susceptibility as in the West."[14] The streets of mountain towns such as
Haifa and Safed ran their sewage down the mountain into the fields
below, where the foul waters would irrigate the crops.

No town was said to have more biting flies, fleas, and ticks than
Jerusalem.[15] For centuries this rock-dry city depended for water on a
vast number of underground cisterns. During the rainy season the
cisterns would fill with water, but they would also collect garbage
which was perpetually lying in the streets. An open sewer ran down
the middle of the street, overflowing with human and animal waste.
The rotting carcasses of dead animals were a common sight in
Jerusalem's streets, as were packs of tough dogs, unafraid to attack
humans who interfered with their foraging. Volney writes that "The
Turks, who shed the blood of man so readily, do not kill these dogs,
though they avoid touching them as unclean. They pretend they ensure the safety of the cities by night. . . ."[16]

No qualified doctor resided in Palestine until the Christian missionaries sent one in the early 1800s. When people found that the doctor could cure the sick, they flocked to him, including Jews who risked the censure of their rabbis. For reasons of health, winter was a preferred season because the cold diminished the chances of spreading disease. An outbreak of cholera in 1813 took one-quarter of the population. Between 1836 and 1840 cholera epidemics drastically reduced the numbers of pilgrims to a few thousand each year.[17]

Was it the sickened air that made Palestine's peoples so disagreeable? "Romans, Greeks, Armenians, and Jews, all [hate] each other sincerely," wrote Alexander Kinglake, who made the Eastern tour in 1835.[18] The Christian communities were united only in being a common object of contempt for Muslims, who would not accept from a Christian nor return the salute of *Salam-alai-kam* (Peace to you). Anti-Christian contempt was written into law. A Christian could not strike a Muslim without risk of his life, but a Muslim might kill a Christian and escape for a stipulated price.[19] Christians were prohibited from riding horses in town; nor could Christians imitate Muslim dress by wearing yellow slippers, a white shawl, or the color green anywhere on their bodies.

Contemptible though they were, Christians were coveted for their income. Like peasants, they survived through bribes. Because of the prohibition against building a new church or repairing an old one, bribes were common in order to keep the churches from crumbling under the weight of the centuries or the devastations of earthquakes, fires, or floods. There were bribes to hold religious processions, and more bribes to allow the cross to be shown publicly. There were very large bribes by Catholics and Greeks and Armenians to maintain their proprietary rights of worship in the Bethlehem Church of the Nativity and the Jerusalem Church of the Holy Sepulchre, and always further bribes to Turkish officials in the hope that one Christian community might enlarge its presence in these churches at the expense of a rival community.

The Turks profited too from the annual Christian pilgrimage, which began in November and concluded in the spring, after Easter. The pilgrims, Catholics and Greek Orthodox from the Mediterranean countries and hordes of devout Russians, all sailing in the winter sea on tiny, cramped, leaky vessels, would arrive at Jaffa with some dead and others near dead. After setting foot on holy soil they would drop to their knees—and then dip into their purses to pay for a hundred and one needs, beggings, and extortions until their money, patience, and innocence were exhausted.

Volney, a true son of the French Enlightenment, could not hide his rationalist-skeptic disdain for those Christians who, with "superstitious zeal," threw themselves and their children naked into the Jordan River and fervently believed that pilgrimage absolved the sinner from "murder, incest, and pederasty."[20] With equal scorn he commented on the pious arrogance and superstition of Muslim religious practice. What was at the root of the immorality and incivility of Ottoman government in Palestine? It was Islam and its holy book, answered Volney.

> Whoever reads the Koran must be obliged to confess, that it conveys no notion, either of the relative duties of mankind in society, of the formation of the body politic, or of the principles of the art of governing. . . . [The Koran] is merely a chaos of unmeaning phrases; an emphatical declamation on the attributes of God, from which nothing is to be learnt; a collection of puerile tales and ridiculous fables. . . .[21]

Who was Muhammad? For Volney he was the first of a long line of oriental despots who were ultimately responsible for the debasement of the East. "[Muhammad] did not wish to enlighten men, but to rule over them; he sought not disciples but subjects; and obedience, not reasoning is required from subjects. It was to lead them the more easily that he ascribed all to God."[22]

Volney closes his travel account by commenting on the "orientals'" treatment of women—as slaves. "Since beasts of burden are not known to have souls, Men hold that women have no souls. Marriage occurs at the moment of puberty. It is not uncommon to see girls of ten married to boys of twelve." And because of polygamy, Arabs and Turks "are enervated early, and nothing is more common than to have men of thirty complaining of impotence."[23]

The last word on the subject of Arab men and women in Palestine is reserved for François René de Chateaubriand, the French poet-traveler, who thirty years after Volney journeyed to Palestine and observed that "Nothing about [Arab men] would proclaim them savage, if their mouths were always shut, but as soon as they begin to speak, you hear a harsh and strongly aspirated language, and perceive long and beautifully white teeth—like those of jackals. . . ." By contrast, Arab women are "taller in proportion than men," had dignified carriages, regular features, beautiful figures, and reminded one of "the statues of the priestess and of the Muses."[24]

Like Volney before him, Chateaubriand experienced in Palestine a vision both ideal and real. In speaking of Palestine as a country "weathered by miracles," he provides us with an accurate image of this country in the nineteenth century.

> When you travel in Judea, the heart is at first filled with profound disgust; but, when passing from solitude to solitude, boundless space opens before you, this disgust wears off by degrees, and you feel a secret awe, which, so far from depressing the soul, imparts life, and elevates the genius. Extraordinary appearances every where proclaim a land weathered by miracles. . . . Every hill re-echoes the accents of a prophet. God himself has spoken in the regions. . . .[25]

For Chateaubriand this was Bibleland, the scene of God's mighty acts, revelations, and wonders. But in his observations he also anticipated something concrete, visible, practical, and palpable about this country at the turn of the century. For the miracles that would ultimately reclaim Palestine were to come from human beings. Through the idealism, courage, and investment of countless Westerners, first Christians and later Jews, a transformation occurred that changed this land from an obscure, dangerous, and diseased place to one revitalized, safe, and healthy. By the mid-nineteenth century this wretched land ceased to be a backwater of the Ottoman Empire and became a center of world interest for Western empires and nations. To use Alex Carmel's metaphor, "At the time that 'sick man of the Bosphorus' was slowly dying, there were French, Russian, English, German and other 'doctors' busy injecting vitality into the veins of Palestine without even consulting the patient."[26]

This energy to transform Palestine came not from the Muslims who held sway over the country, nor from the old Greek and Latin Christian community leaders who held to their traditional privileges and powers; nor did it come from the tiny clusters of ritualized Orthodox Jews awaiting the Messiah. The energy came instead from European Christians, many of them English and German Protestants. But this should not surprise us if we remember that the abiding strength of Protestantism lies in its practical righteousness. If a person is persuaded that his deeds are reclaiming God's own land, he will work and sacrifice and accomplish much.

Not since the Crusades of the twelfth and thirteenth centuries had the West shown such interest in the Arabic-speaking, Muslim-dominated East. At the beginning of the nineteenth century came soldiers, priests, and missionaries; they were followed at midcentury by explorers, excavators, and mapmakers, who in turn showed the way to painters, photographers, tourists, and business agents. Once the British and French began roaming over Egypt, pilgrims, who had avoided the Holy Land when it was unsafe, came by the thousands: poor pilgrims from Russia, Poland, Italy, and Cyprus, wealthier ones from Britain, France, Germany, and America.

Virtually all who traveled here, it seems, recorded their impressions. Most published their words in hometown newspapers and magazines, a few in expensively bound books of impressions of a once-in-a-lifetime trip to the Holy Land. Among the writers were such greats as Flaubert, Melville, and Mark Twain. By the end of the nineteenth century thousands of published books had made Palestine the most written about place in the world.

In the path of pilgrims, tourists, and writers came the builders, who put up hotels, hospices, and hospitals, churches, convents, and monasteries, schools and orphanages. Dozens of scientific, cultural, religious, philanthropic, and ethno-national societies were founded to explore, excavate, and build, and to care for the people of Palestine. By the end of the nineteenth century almost every European nation had rediscovered the Holy Land and established a visible physical presence there.

Western Christians saw the malaise of Palestine for what it was and acted to reclaim the country. In this respect the transformation of Palestine was an act of human grace, a weathering of Palestine by miracles. But the transformation came at a price. Westerners also brought with them piety, arrogance, and imperial ambitions. No one better expressed the Western Christian sense of superiority than B. Walker, an English millenarian of the early nineteenth century. Faithful to his sense of the Divine Providence ruling over the Holy Land, Walker, like Volney and Chateaubriand before him, could explain the existence of the Arabs there only as an abortion of history, a rude interruption between the glorious days of God's chosen people and the new dispensation represented by the ingathering of Jews and Christ's Second Coming. Those "miserable, ignorant, half-wild Arabs, with their dirty villages and wretched hovels," Walker wrote, could not be the "fit successors and rightful heirs to the millions of intelligent, refined, highly-civilized, and well-governed subjects whom David and Solomon ruled over in the days of Israel's glory."[27]

Walker's attitude was of a type well known to Muslims. The successes of the Christians in building churches, establishing schools, and opening hospitals angered Muslim religious authorities. They could see that Christian medicine combated diseases and that Christian investment brought money to the country. But the medicine was practiced by proselytizing missionaries, and the investors seemed determined to purchase Palestine for Britain or France or Russia. Growing Christian involvement with Palestine simultaneously intensified Muslim fears that the country would be lost to the West. For this reason, for example, the Ottoman government delayed improving the harbor at Jaffa. Better that Western merchants go elsewhere. The essential Muslim feeling toward the Westerner was expressed by a Jerusalemite in the mid-nineteenth century: "When I have money to spare I lay it on a house, a slave, a diamond, a fine mare, or a wife; but I do not make a road up to [Jerusalem] in order to invite strangers to come that way. Jerusalem is the Jewel after which all Europeans are greedy; why should we facilitate access to the prize they aim at?"[28]

Behind this feeling lay age-old animosities born of religious rivalry and triumphalism. In the latter decades of the nineteenth century, Muslim anti-Christian hostility led to riots in Aleppo, Nablus, and Damascus. Muslims simply could not abide the growing presence and power of Christians, whom they considered theologically and socially inferior. Provocations were often caused by the growing power of a boastful Christianity in a country overwhelmingly Arabic and Muslim in language and culture.

And what of the Jews? Before the mass immigration of European Jews to Palestine, small clusters of Jews had for centuries lived in their recognized quarters in the towns of Safed, Tiberias, and Hebron, where patriarchs, sages, and saints were buried, and in the holy city of Jerusalem, site of the ancient Temple, the symbol of Jewish national unity and redemption. Years of loss had produced a ritualized memory of Jerusalem and a yearning for restoration to the city and the land. The religiously orthodox looked to God to bring the New Jerusalem into being. So long as these Jews comprised small, pious communities in a handful of towns, so long as they paid their taxes, deferred to Muslim authority, and made no show of their religion, they were tolerated and protected, if not always treated decently by Muslim governors and religious officials. That was to change when a "new kind" of Jew began arriving in numbers in the opening decades of the twentieth century.

HERE, THEN, was a Palestine rich with historic personalities, cherished ideals, dramatic decisions, arrogant assumptions, political passions—but also a fateful energy that moved events in unpredictable ways. An explosive combination of power and religion had shaped the country's history, from the time that King David transported the Ark of the Covenant to Jerusalem to symbolize and cement Israel's pride of place. Power and religion drove the Western nations to Palestine, there to confront an Islamic people which defended its soil. Power and religion were behind the policies of the Egyptian governors who introduced a radically new political framework for the peoples of Palestine.

The Western biblical tradition was a force that came into sharp conflict with the Arab Muslim East, just as imperialism and colonialism encountered regional ethnic nationalism. These forces finally exploded in Palestine in the period from 1798 to 1948. In doing so they prepared a stage for the succeeding Arab-Israeli conflict.

CHAPTER TWO

Conquerors, Explorers, Mapmakers, Artists

> From earliest childhood I had read of and studied the
> localities of this sacred spot; now I beheld them with
> my own eyes. And they all seemed familiar to me as if
> the realization of a former dream. I seemed to be
> again among the cherished scenes of a childhood,
> long unvisited, indeed, but distinctly recollected.
> —Edward Robinson, 1840s

Early in his career Napoleon Bonaparte made no secret of emulating the exploits of Alexander the Great. With the young Macedonian in mind, he confided to a friend, "We must go to the Orient; all great glory has always been acquired there."[1] So in 1798, fresh from his victories over the Papal States, Bonaparte invaded Egypt.

Within his grandiose vision of world conquest was a vastly more important strategic reason for invading Egypt. He was reluctant to attack mighty England in a cross-channel invasion. Talleyrand advised him that before attacking it would be wise to deprive England of her trade route to the wealthiest of her colonies in India and the Far East. This was not a new idea. French kings had been advised for years that it was in France's interest to seize Egypt, excavate the Isthmus of Suez for a canal, and "bring about a revolution in world trade, that would assure France's predominance over the India route."[2]

Talleyrand also advised Bonaparte of France's delicate diplomatic relations with the Ottoman sultan, Selim III. Selim and his sultanic predecessors were France's oldest, most reliable friends in the Middle East. But Selim was an unstable friend. Throughout the eighteenth century, the mismanaged Ottoman Empire was slowly disintegrating. Egypt, one of its largest and richest provinces, was in fact ruled by regional Mamluk beys, who defied Istanbul by keeping for themselves the revenue they collected. An increasingly weakened sultan, Talleyrand reasoned, was a growing temptation to Western empires. Better that France plant her foot in Egypt lest Russia or Britain get there first.

With this decision, the pattern in East-West relations was set for the next hundred years. A weakened Ottoman Empire did indeed whet the appetites of Western powers. But any sign of expansionism, any too aggressive grab for Ottoman territory by any one Western power, might bring aggressive retaliation from the others. In turn, to retain his empire the sultan was prepared to make an alliance with any Western power willing to come to the defense of the Noble Porte in the event of external threat. In the first half of the nineteenth century this called for an alliance with Britain and Russia against the designs of France; at midcentury it led to an alliance with Britain and France to thwart Russia; and at the turn of the century it meant joining Germany to combat almost the entire West.

IN EARLY May 1798 Napoleon assembled a specially selected force of 34,000 at Toulon for the sea crossing to Alexandria. Expecting quick victory, France budgeted money to pay the troops for only four months. Excessive confidence explains how badly prepared were Bonaparte's troops for the battles that lay ahead. The territory of Egypt was unknown to the French, as were the customs of its people. The military leadership had no appreciation of the problems of desert fighting under the summer sun; no one thought of equipping the troops with water flasks.

Upon reaching Alexandria on July 1, 1798, the French fought bravely but stupidly. They seized Alexandria and were ordered on to Cairo. Men went mad from sunstroke and fell from thirst on the forced march through the desert. But the army held up and won battles against Mamluk forces at Shubra Kit and Enbaba on the left bank of the Nile River. The victory at Enbaba gave Bonaparte the victory that secured his fame throughout Europe. He had prevailed at the Battle of the Pyramids, as French army propagandists called it, comparing his exploits to Alexander the Great.

The conquest of Cairo on July 24 was the summit of Bonaparte's campaign in Egypt, from which he would plummet. A week later the French fleet at anchor in Abukir Bay at Alexandria found itself facing a squadron of English ships under the command of Admiral Horatio Nelson, who had been sent to frustrate Bonaparte's bid for Eastern conquest. Nelson destroyed the main French fighting ships, an event which alone decided the fate of the French army in Egypt. But more fighting lay ahead.

If there is reason to question Bonaparte's skills as a military strategist, no one should deny his talents as a propagandist. Just before his invasion he sent this proclamation to the Egyptian Muslim leadership.

> Cadis, sheiks, imams, tell the people that we are friends of the true Moslems. Is it not we who destroyed the Pope, who called for war against the Moslems? Is it not we who have destroyed the Knights of Malta [seized shortly before the invasion of Egypt], because these madmen believed God wished them to fight the Moslems? It is not we who have been through the centuries the friends of the Sultan (may God grant his desire) and the enemies of his enemies?[3]

The sultan was not fooled. He read Bonaparte's words as the blasphemy of an infidel who would stain Islam's soil with his unholy presence. Why should he not think so? The France he admired and trusted was the France of conservative, pious, friendly kings, a believer's France. This Bonaparte was the general of a new republican, atheistic France which practiced revolution and preached the equality of man. So the sultan issued his own counterproclamation, calling on the faithful to defend the empire against the infidel.

> Know that the French nation . . . are impious and iniquitous libertines. . . . They have confiscated the riches of their own churches and stripped them of their crosses and attacked their priests and monks. They claim that the [holy] book which prophets brought to mankind are manifest falsehoods; that the Koran, the Torah and the Gospel are nothing but perjury; that Moses, Jesus and Muhammad and others made false claims to being prophets. . . . And now

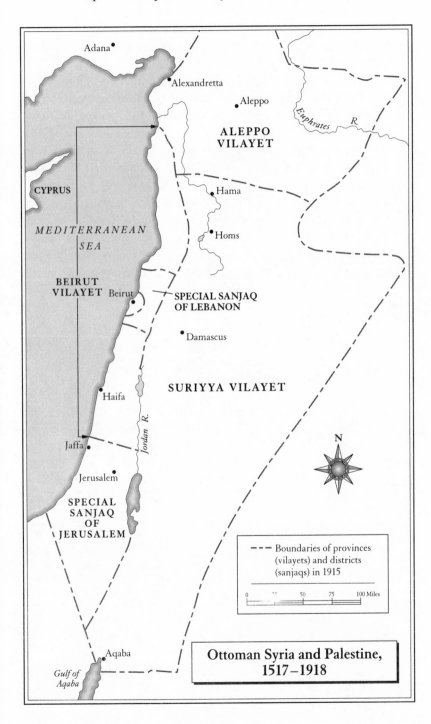

Adana

Alexandretta

Aleppo

ALEPPO
VILAYET

Euphrates R.

CYPRUS

Hama

*MEDITERRANEAN
SEA*

Homs

BEIRUT
VILAYET Beirut

SPECIAL SANJAQ
OF LEBANON

Damascus

Haifa

Jordan R.

SURIYYA VILAYET

N

Jaffa

Jerusalem

SPECIAL
SANJAQ
OF
JERUSALEM

- - - Boundaries of provinces
(vilayets) and districts
(sanjaqs) in 1915

0   25   50   75   100 Miles

Aqaba

*Gulf of
Aqaba*

Ottoman Syria and Palestine,
1517–1918

their mischief and evil intentions have reached the Muhammadan nation. . . . All you Muslims who believe in God and His Messenger . . . rise to fight this French nation. . . .[4]

And they did rise. None more than the sultan himself, who formed a military collaboration with England and assembled an army in Anatolia, which was ordered south to drive the French out of Egypt.

To avert crippling defeat, Bonaparte decided to attack first by invading Palestine. In the first week of February 1799 he led a force of thirteen thousand soldiers, two thousand camels, and three thousand mules and donkeys up the coast of Palestine. He met little resistance until he reached Jaffa, where a scarcity of food slowed his advance and an outbreak of bubonic plague ravaged his troops. Plague had always been the secret weapon of the East. The Hebrew Scriptures told that plague had prevented the Assyrians from invading Judah. Bonaparte, who knew his Bible, ignored its wisdom and pressed on. After seeing to the diseased—an act immortalized in Antoine Jean Gros's monumental painting "Napoleon Visiting the Plague Victims at Jaffa"—he left the wounded in Jaffa and ordered the army to move up the coastline for Acre, where fate awaited.

Bonaparte's force attacked Acre on March 18, 1799. The town's walls held through fourteen separate assaults. During the two-month siege, Ahmad al-Jazzar Pasha (known as "the Butcher"), the strongman of Acre and all northern Palestine, sat in his citadel paying out gold coins for every severed French skull brought to him. He had planned carefully for this siege and he was confident of the outcome. Offshore, British and Turkish naval guns fired at the oncoming French.

Acre's walls were finally breached, but a squad of fifty French soldiers entering the city were destroyed. The fight was over. In defeat Bonaparte was peevish, remarking to his subordinate, General Murat, "The fate of the East depends on that petty town."[5] A third of the original French force of thirteen thousand was killed or maimed in Palestine. Those who knew Bonaparte were not surprised. Another subordinate, General Kleber, had once said that to wage war Bonaparte needed a monthly income of ten thousand soldiers.[6]

The French remnant retreated slowly, in orderly fashion, down the coastline. Fearing the Turkish army behind them, they burned villages and towns. A continuous blaze could be seen from the Carmel mountains to Gaza. Fires were reported burning two years after the French left the country. Stopping at Jaffa, the army evacuated its wounded and diseased; for those too sick to move, Bonaparte ordered lethal injections of morphine—an order which his officers were reluctant to carry out.[7]

In retreating to Egypt Bonaparte wasted no time in exercising his genius for propaganda. On July 14 he entered Cairo as a conquering hero, with bands playing, trophies displayed, and prisoners paraded. Messages were sent to leaders in Paris informing them of resounding success in the Holy Land and a wounded and defeated Pasha Jazzar. The question came back: "Why did you not then capture Acre?" Bonaparte replied with more lies:

> Our spies, deserters, and our prisoners all reported that the plague was ravaging the city and that every day more than sixty persons were dying of it. . . . If the soldiers had entered the city they would have brought back into camp the germs of that horrible evil, which is more to be feared than all the armies in the world.[8]

A day after Bonaparte entered Cairo triumphantly, the music stopped. A Turkish armada sailed into Abukir Bay and destroyed what was left of the French fleet. A thorough realist, Bonaparte knew what he had to do. Secretly, with a few trusted aides, he sailed away at night to France, abandoning his army and navy to inevitable defeat in a land that had humiliated him but that had also served his ambitions.

Bonaparte's Eastern adventure of 1798–1799 had taught Britain a lesson. Under no circumstances would she ever again allow a military threat to the Ottoman Empire, which could put at risk Egypt and Palestine, the Middle Eastern land bridge to the Far East.

And what of Ahmad al-Jazzar, the Butcher of Acre? He was thought to be illiterate but had one of the two known libraries in Syria and Palestine, a mammoth collection of three hundred books. After Bonaparte's withdrawal, he began the restoration of Acre's city walls. He angered Admiral Sidney Smith, who commanded the Anglo-Ottoman armada, by ordering the execution of all pro-French Christians in Nazareth and Jerusalem who were accused of collaborating with the French. Smith, a devout Anglican, sent word to the pasha that "if a single Christian head should fall he would bombard

Acre and set it on fire."⁹ Taking his pride one step further after ousting the French at Acre, Smith held a victory march in the Christian quarter of Jerusalem, British flag flying—a display of Western power not lost on the Muslims, who had to wonder how they had benefited from the British defeat of the French.

Also worrisome to Muslims was Smith's success in persuading the Ottoman government to remove the limit on Jewish habitation in Jerusalem, set at two thousand. Without realizing it, Smith had sharpened a knife over Arab-Jewish relations. In the next 150 years the mere thought of the equality of Christians and Jews with Muslims would arouse the communities against one another in acts of bigotry and bloodshed.

Apart from establishing hospitals and schools during their brief stay in Egypt, French technicians did not effect that enlightened, progressive administration of which Bonaparte's sycophantic biographers boasted. But the general of fire and death did have a taste for culture and a sincere admiration for scholarship. In assembling his expeditionary force at Toulon, he added 170 scientists and artists who explored, studied, wrote about, and painted Egypt, Palestine, and Syria. Together they formed the Institut d'Egypte, which produced the multivolumed, richly illustrated *Description de l'Egypte* (1808–1829) and initiated Western cultural investigation of the Middle East. One of the Institute's singular achievements was the first scientific map of portions of Egypt and Palestine. Named "Jacotin's map" after its chief editor, an officer in Napoleon's army, it was the product of a survey of only those lands that had fallen under military control: the Palestine coastline from El Arish in the south to Tyre and Sidon in the north; the interior around the towns of Nazareth and Tiberias; and the Samarian hill country surrounding Nablus. The Jerusalem areas were also mapped, as was the territory east of Jerusalem down to Jericho and the Dead Sea.

Jacotin's map was filled with errors. Distances were misjudged; areas not surveyed were filled in with trees, villages, hills, rivers, and valleys. But this map, for all its errors, countered the dreamy, idealized image of the Holy Land, the "Heavenly Kingdom," depicted in medieval engravings of pilgrim maps.

Jacotin's map signaled the beginning of the Western rediscovery of Palestine, led initially by explorers. Their motives were mixed: love of travel, lure of the exotic, scientific curiosity, desire for fame and fortune, the sheer excitement of digging up and showing to the world the biblical evidence of God's presence on earth. What French sabers and muskets had failed to conquer was now seized by the surveyor's compass, the excavator's shovel, the painter's brush, the missionary's Bible. More than any other place on earth, Palestine in the nineteenth century was surveyed, dug up, mapped, painted and photographed, prayed over, and written about in more than two thousand books in all the Western languages.[10] It became so well known to Western readers of travel journals and scientific reports that the country took on the appearance of a cozy front yard in an English country cottage. One traveler, Randall Davidson, who would later become Archbishop of Canterbury, spoke directly of this familiarity after two visits in 1873 and 1876. He kept physically fit by daily riding around the countryside of Jerusalem until the area was, as he put it, more familiar to him than "any part of England or Scotland."[11]

The Westerner's fascination with Palestine sprang from major changes in the culture of the West in the eighteenth and nineteenth centuries. Rapid industrialization produced in British and American cities both material wealth and spiritual emptiness. The emptiness induced a nostalgic, spiritualized feeling about Palestine as the Holy Land, the place in which one's childhood innocence and faith might be recovered. Wealth spreading to a burgeoning middle class created a new tourist industry for Palestine, particularly after midcentury. The Protestant religious revival that swept Britain and America emphasized a scripturally based faith and inspired the "reborn" to visit the land of the Bible.

The intellectual upheaval caused by the publication of Charles Darwin's *Origin of Species*, which challenged the biblical account of Creation, curiously worked to provoke greater interest in the Holy Land. Darwin's book, together with Charles Lyell's *Principles of Geology*, introduced doubts about the earth's beginnings. And the Scriptures themselves were subjected to newer modes of intellectual scrutiny. A new breed of critical theologians had gained ascendancy at Germany's Tübingen University to challenge the historical authenticity of such biblical stories as Noah's Ark and the Exodus of the Israelites. In reaction to these intellectual innovations, Christian scholars and ordinary pietists alike were inspired to travel to Palestine in order to seek for themselves the evidence of the Bible's historical truth.

The exploration of Palestine began in 1799, in the very year that Napoleon returned to France from Egypt. Edward Daniel Clarke, mineralogist, geographer, Cambridge University don, and experienced traveler in Europe and Asia, was persuaded to undertake a journey to the region in which England had vanquished France. In just seventeen days of exhausting travel, he covered the land from Acre to the Galilee, down through Samaria to Jerusalem, from there into the Judean desert wilderness, and slowly back to Acre, where he shipped back to England a suitcase filled with notes.

Clarke produced the most exhaustive and accurate account of Palestine that had yet appeared.[12] He traveled with an armed guard provided by Acre's Pasha Ahmad al-Jazzar, a token of gratitude for British help in ousting Bonaparte. Clarke not only looked into the ground, he carefully observed the people walking on it. He made notes of the bitter interchurch quarrels in Jerusalem between Greeks, Armenians, and Latins, and of Muslim contempt for the local Jews. The "true spirit of the Gospel," he wrote, "is even less known in this Holy Land than in Caliphornia [sic] or New Holland."

Clarke was not reluctant to ask a number of provocative questions about the holy sites. Was Jesus really buried where the Latin and Greek churches said he was buried? And was he actually born in Bethlehem? Clarke was skeptical about Empress Helena's "inspired" discovery of Jesus' birthplace and tomb. He wondered if there were any factual basis for the holy sites associated with prophets and saints throughout Palestine. In pursuing these questions, Clarke undertook the first scientific exploration of the country.[13] In his footsteps would follow a host of archaeologists and explorers from England, France, Germany, Austria, Russia, and America.

Despite his preference for a secular means of investigation, Clarke was moved to explore Palestine chiefly because it was the biblical Holy Land. In his mind the pious reverence for Palestine shared by so many Englishmen was not in contradiction to scientific procedures of exploration and archaeology. The fact that Jesus might not be buried exactly where the Latin and Greek churches said he was buried did not make the Holy Land any less holy. Clarke's skepticism was not that of the disbeliever; it admitted more of an enlightened Anglican's intellectual disdain for the superstitions of the older church traditions in the Holy Land.

The story of Edward Clarke's seventeen days in the Holy Land inspired the pursuits of two of the most fascinating men ever to set foot in Palestine: Ulrich Seetzen, a German, who studied medicine but had his heart in Middle Eastern languages and religions; and Jean-Louis Burckhardt, a Swiss-born champion of Britain's empire, who set out to explore trade routes to Africa but found the Middle East much more captivating.

In 1802 Seetzen set sail for Istanbul and from there made his way to Syria, dressed for self-protection in Arab costume—a shabby one because he intended to pass as a beggar. The diary of his years of travel to Syria, Palestine, Arabia, and Egypt proved to be one of the earliest and most valuable accounts of the life, manners, and customs of life in the Middle East at that time. Seetzen's journey was paid for by the Duke of Saxe-Goeha and later by Tsar Alexander I, both of whom expected him to send them antiquities for their private museums.

But Seetzen was no mere collector of objects for his rich patrons. His unique love of travel combined adventure, danger, and scholarly learning, as evidenced by his mastering Hebrew and Arabic well enough to teach them. His knowledge of Islamic religion was the equal of Muslim teachers of Shari'a law. Later in his life many of his friends remarked that his habitually worn Muslim clothes were no longer a disguise because he had sincerely converted to the religion of Islam.

Above all Seetzen was a disciplined traveler who made elaborate preparations for his journey. Before reaching Palestine he spent a year studying maps of all the Arab lands. Then he went forth for three years of travel which took him first to the Persian Gulf area, where he studied and wrote about the Wahabis, the puritanical Islamic sect whose vision of Muhammad's teaching would later inspire the Saudi clan to seize control of the Arabian peninsula. From the Persian Gulf Seetzen returned to Damascus, and from there he journeyed to Palestine.

Wandering into the interior, Seetzen became the first explorer to travel completely around the Dead Sea. Later he traveled east of Lake Tiberias, along the Jordan River, and became the first European to stop in the Decapolis region, where he identified the cities of Gadara, Gerasa, and Philadelphia. He perpetually ran out of money and suffered hunger. But he kept moving, observing, taking notes, and learning languages, including local dialects in the Nile Valley, which were taught to him by a slave trader.[14]

Seetzen risked his life many times, no time more dramatically than when he traveled as a pilgrim to Mecca in his Arab disguise and defied official prohibiton by making a sketch of the Ka'ba, the black meteorite which is the sacred touchstone of Islamic faith. He died a young man, poisoned it was said by the Imam of Yemen, with whom he had a disagreement about a fine point of theology. His travel notes were slow to see publication; four volumes of them did not appear until 1854.[15] They comprised a magnificent record of Palestine's monuments and antiquities, offering information on minerals, plants, and animals, and accounts of the customs and folkways of desert tribesmen and town dwellers.

Jean-Louis Burckhardt, a friend of both Clarke and Seetzen, followed in Seetzen's footsteps, even to the extent of wearing an Arab burnoose. Where Seetzen had found it useful to go by the name of Sheik Mousa, Burckhardt chose for himself the name Sheik Ibrahim ibn Abdullah. From his family Burckhardt had acquired an intense hatred of Napoleon Bonaparte and Republican France, a feeling equaled by his admiration of the British, whose empire he hoped to serve. As Seetzen's travels had been funded by rich collectors of antiquities, so Burckhardt sought to pay for his journey by exploring (for the British-based commercial African Association) a northern route to the raw goods of Africa.[16]

After completing his oriental studies in Leipzig and Heidelberg, in 1809 (the year Seetzen stole into Mecca) Burckhardt left England for Aleppo in Syria, bound for Africa. But the Middle East immediately captivated him. Following the lead of Seetzen, he visited Mecca in Arab camouflage and wrote one of the first detailed accounts of the Islamic holy city. He was also one of the first to report on Palestine's Bedouins, who, despite their shabby treatment of him, he found to be honorable.[17]

Burckhardt's greatest act of exploration had to do with a city that had been much discussed but never seen. Many Europeans had heard tales of the awesome red rock city of the Nabateans, the desert tribes destroyed by the Roman army in the second century C.E. Where Seetzen had searched in vain for Petra, Burckhardt became the first European to discover and explore the hidden Nabatean capital, lying southeast of the Dead Sea, in a desert ravine of Transjordan. It was an awesome site of temples, houses, and tombs hewn into reddish copper sandstone: perfectly preserved timeless structures which spoke of a magnificent civilization.

Burckhardt complained about the labors of notetaking: "It is less fatiguing duty to perform travels than to write them down," he recorded in his journal. By one account he took notes while pretending to sleep.[18] Another story has it that in order to hide his notes from Bedouins who might suspect him of being a sorcerer, he would dismount, squat to urinate in Bedouin fashion, and then scribble words on a note pad hidden in the folds of his robes. Like Seetzen he successfully passed as a Muslim. Put to the test by a suspicious *cadi* (a Muslim religious judge) in Mecca, he responded to a rigorous oral examination in the Koran so successfully that the *cadi* asked him to join the evening prayers.

Burckhardt, no less than Seetzen, loved adventure and was driven by the mystery of the Middle East. Out of that love he was willing to bear the most abominable conditions of travel. He justified the filthy caravans he was often compelled to use with one simple remark: "I see things and hear things which remain unknown to him who travels in comfort."

The likes of Clarke, Seetzen, and Burckhardt—for courage, curiosity, and intellect—do not appear again until 1838 with the arrival in Palestine of Edward Robinson, the American Bible scholar. Robinson came to the country determined to deepen his knowledge of the Bible and to counter skepticism about its content and chronology. Academic skepticism introduced by the rationalist theologians at Tübingen had spread to the influential Harvard Divinity School. Robinson, like many theological conservatives, worried that this skepticism might influence the education of the entire Protestant ministry in America. Newly appointed to New York's Union Theological Seminary, Robinson saw himself on a grave mission to preserve the integrity of the Bible. Through geographic and archaeological research, he believed he could identify the connection between the Bible and the historical past. Postponing his classroom teaching, he embarked for the East and six months of exhaustive research across Palestine.

With his traveling companion, Eli Smith, the American missionary and Bible scholar from Beirut, Edward Robinson set out on March 12, 1838, from Cairo to cross the Sinai and from there to enter

Palestine. On the journey he visited Petra in Transjordan and crossed back into Palestine, south of the Dead Sea; from there he made his way north from Beersheba to Hebron and Jerusalem.

Robinson found nothing to confirm or deny the literal truth of the biblical stories; what he did find was solid evidence that the Bible contained a record of past events. He uncovered enough evidence to substantiate the existence of Israelite kings, of biblical towns built, destroyed, and rebuilt, of ceaseless warfare between the ancient tribal peoples of Palestine. With compass and walking stick, or aboard a camel, he traversed much of the country. He identified the remnants of ancient churches, synagogues, and dozens of biblical sites. He wrote new maps which advanced the cartography of Palestine. He surveyed the length and breadth of the Red Sea. He made major discoveries in Jerusalem, whose walls, gates, and water sources he surveyed. He found the ancient third city wall built in King Agrippas's time. He also discovered a great stone fragment of a monumental arch to the Temple Mount at the lower end of the town. His accomplishments in the archaeology, geography, and linguistics of Palestine have never been equaled. From his field work came a magisterial study, *Biblical Researches in Palestine, Syria, Arabia Petraea and Adjacent Region*, published in 1841, a work that won him a gold prize from the British Royal Geographic Society.

One of Robinson's greatest accomplishments, following clues from the writings of Seetzen and Burckhardt, was to prove that the ancient Hebrew biblical language had not vanished from Palestine. Hebrew was hidden in the form of Arabic place names. Robinson showed that the Arabic names of hundreds of villages and hills and other places were really Arabized Hebrew names, as in the village of Beitin, which in its original Hebrew form was the ancient biblical shrine of Bethel.

By contrast with Seetzen and Burckhardt, who for all their learning were amateur explorers, Robinson was a trained linguist and Scripture scholar who pioneered the field of biblical archaeology in Palestine. In his steps followed a series of scholarly excavators and geographers. From England came Charles Wilson and Charles Warren, who explored Jerusalem and provided a detailed account of the Temple Mount. From France came Claude Clermont-Ganneau, who gained fame when he exposed the treasure-hunting frauds of archaeology. As France and Britain competed in digging for antiquities, the excitement spread to Germany and Russia, which sent out their own teams of scholars and professional excavators. The discoveries of Edward Robinson had a powerful effect on American archaeological studies, inspiring George Reisner, whose advanced techniques of excavating and deciphering earth strata would later revolutionize archaeology.

Yet overall, excavations in the Holy Land proved to be a disappointment. Here was no Luxor or Karnak, no grand discoveries as at Nineveh. Nothing could be found to prove the historical truth of the Bible; no physical evidence confirmed the biblical miracles of Creation, the Exodus, or Jesus' Resurrection. Many devout Christians experienced a quickening of their faith merely by setting foot in the Holy Land; but after entering villages and towns, that faith was better sustained by closing their eyes rather than keeping them open to the sights of impoverishment all around.

At no place were Western Christians more prone to disappointment than at the Church of the Holy Sepulchre in Jerusalem. What they expected to see built over the tomb of Jesus was a church as grand as St. Peter's in Rome; instead they found a dark, drab, shapeless structure, a stony reminder of all the tragedies befallen Christianity in the Holy Land. The ugly Gothic-Romanesque building at the northwest corner of the old walled city was not the original church constructed by Emperor Constantine in the early fourth century, and named in Greek after Christ's Resurrection, *Anastasis*. The *Anastasis*, reported to be a lovely building of three parts, had been damaged in the Persian invasion of 618 and utterly destroyed by the mad Egyptian caliph Hakim in 1009. Not until the arrival of the Latin Crusaders at the end of the eleventh century did work begin on a new building which, combining the original form of the rotunda over Jesus' tomb, came to be called the Church of the Holy Sepulchre. Thereafter the church suffered from every battle in Jerusalem but survived until 1808, when a major fire destroyed much of the interior.

No battle proved more threatening to the Church of the Holy Sepulchre than the dispute over its claim to house Jesus' tomb. While most Protestant travelers were willing to accept the Greek and Latin veneration of the site of Calvary and Jesus' tomb within the church, archaeologists and Bible scholars had their doubts. Edward Robinson completely rejected the authenticity of the Holy Sepulchre and refused even to enter the church. He argued that the site lay within the walls of the first-century Jerusalem, where Jewish graves were prohibited by ritual law. Hence Jesus, a Jew, must be buried somewhere else, outside the city walls.

Protestant resentment deepened over profits made by monks from pilgrims in the Holy Sepulchre. The elaborate and unruly ceremonies conducted there, including the celebrated Holy Fire ritual, filled many Protestants with revulsion at the sight of so much raw piety and idolatrous veneration of icons and stone. Monks quarreled interminably over proprietary rights in every chapel, stairwell, and lamp stand in the church.

Even the most devout Protestants, recoiling at the practices of these bearded churchmen, were all too ready to believe that the Church of the Holy Sepulchre was a fraud. The matter was happily settled for them in 1883 with the visit of British General Charles Gordon, hero of Khartoum and devoted student of the Bible. Gordon, after a brief but inspired survey of the landscape outside Jerusalem, noted the similarity between the Gospel's account of Jesus' burial place, Golgotha (Aramaic for "place of the skull"), and a low hill north of Damascus Gate, where ancient tombs were located. Rising from his maps and prayers, Gordon (like Queen Helena in the fourth century) announced his "discovery" of the real tomb of Jesus. While no church was constructed at the site, the "Garden Tomb," as it came to be called, soon became Protestantism's most important shrine in Jerusalem. Today this shrine abounds with planted flowers and is suffused with a tranquil air. Overlooking the Arab bus station in East Jerusalem, it is a favored place of meditation and prayer in a city dominated by the loud and frenzied activity of commercialized pilgrimage.

AFTER THE 1840S, explorers and travelers to Palestine proliferated. The liberal policies toward foreigners enacted by Ibrahim Pasha's regime after 1831 were sustained by the new Ottoman rulers of Palestine. In 1854 the first steamships departing from Marseilles and Trieste had begun to dock at Jaffa port. Organized excursions to the Orient were planned by tourist companies for the wealthy and the middle class alike. Merchants began to see in Palestine a potentially rich new source of raw goods as well as a convenient bridge to the markets of the Far East.

And always, the fascination with Palestine as the Holy Land persisted, particularly in Great Britain and America where a religious revival was under way. Numerous Protestant ministers, singly or with groups, visited the land of Jesus' birth, often with the intention of gaining inspiration and new material for their preaching back home. And not a few travelers were motivated by a desire to investigate business possibilities in this land at the intersection of Europe, Asia, and Africa.

One of those who combined travel, adventure, religion, and commerce was an American naval lieutenant, William F. Lynch. In 1849 he undertook a major expedition to Palestine, aiming to survey the course of the Jordan River and chart the depths of the Dead Sea. Two Englishmen who had preceded him in that endeavor had perished from the suffocating heat in the Jordan River–Dead Sea valley. Lynch was determined to succeed where they had failed. He also hoped to see if the Jordan River could be used as a commercial route for goods passing from Syria to Egypt.

Lynch convinced the United States Congress and President James Polk to fund his expedition at substantial expense. He led a crew of ten, whom he ordered to swear off liquor for the duration of the expedition. He intended to navigate two specially made rowboats of copper and iron, the *Fanny Mason* and the *Fanny Skinner*, which were transported by ship to Acre and there carried overland on a wagon rig drawn by camels. The Americans rode on horseback. To protect the party from Bedouin bandits, Lynch paid for the services of the redoubtable chief of the Bani Huwara tribe, Akil Aga, who had begun to make a handsome living by providing his cavalry as guard for foreign visitors.

After eight days Lynch and his crew reached Lake Tiberias at springtime and immediately set their boats in the water and rowed into the Jordan River. He divided his men into two groups, one to navigate the river, the other to ride camels along the river bank, carry the provisions, and act as a guard. They were equipped with firearms, compasses for charting the course of the river, devices for sounding the depths of the water, and sketch pads for drawing pictures of the river banks and surrounding mountains.

After attaching American flags to each of the boat's sterns, Lynch set out. He found the Jordan winding and unpredictable. He encountered rapids in the area between the lake and the confluence of the Jordan with the Yarmuk River. In some places the water was deep, elsewhere the river was so shallow as to barely reach a man's shoulders. Despite myriad difficulties, Lynch succeeded. His map of the river was an important scientific advance, as was his later map of the Dead Sea.

In the course of surveying the Dead Sea, Lynch and his party were nearly overcome with heat exhaustion. Yet they learned something important from their expedition: the salinity of the Dead Sea is caused by condensation because of the extreme heat of the valley, the lowest known point on earth. Lynch's party searched for but never found the biblical towns of Sodom and Gomorrah, believed for centuries to be in the Dead Sea area.

Following the snakelike course of the Jordan from Tiberias to the Dead Sea, Lynch discovered that he traveled two hundred miles to traverse a distance of just fifty miles. Clearly a shipping route on the Jordan river was not feasible, as Lynch reported to his government upon his return to Washington. Learning of Lynch's account, American newspapers complained about the heavy expense of the expedition. But Lynch's scientific work was genuine and productive. He published two books on his expedition that were widely read and praised. That he was sensitive to criticism was shown in the preface to one of his books, in which he stated his hope to the American people that they "would not long condemn an attempt to explore a distant river, and its wondrous reservoir—the first teeming with sacred associations, and the latter, enveloped in a mystery, which had defied all previous attempts to penetrate it."[19]

EXPLORERS WERE NOT ALONE in risking their lives to learn the truth of this land and its peoples. There were also painters. One of the most gifted was the British artist David Roberts, who painted Palestine not as seen but as imagined. Visiting Egypt, Palestine, and Syria in 1838–1839, Roberts worked indefatigably and frequently found himself exhausted and sick: "Thirty miles a day, sitting on a camel, rather unfits me for sketching them."[20] At one point he bribed his way into Jerusalem's Mosque of Omar, agreeing not to use hog's hair brushes in painting his picture. In three short months he painted, drew, and sketched more than 140 works. These were made into colored and mounted lithogaphs and published as a handsome art book of three volumes (*The Holy Land, Syria, Idumea, Egypt, Nubia*, 1842–1849).

Roberts satisfied the British public's taste for the romance and mystery of the Holy Land. He drew an idealized Palestine as it existed in the minds of pious Christians who had never visited there: a timeless place, heavenly, dreamy, awesome, uplifting. In his depictions Roberts sought to substantiate the truth of the Bible no less than had the scholar Edward Robinson. For the land that God had chosen for himself had somehow to resound with the awe and wonder and majesty of God's sacred actions. In drawing Palestine, Roberts had in his mind the Exodus, the revealing of the Law, the teachings and healings of Jesus. Anyone who gazes upon his drawings cannot doubt that he found the physical settings for all God's wondrous acts in the stark and moving landscapes of the Sinai desert, in the Judean hills, in the River Jordan, and in the mountains of Lebanon.

But Roberts was not totally blind to the ruin of the country. Like Volney and Chateaubriand before him, he blamed this ruin on the laziness of the Arabs and the fanaticism inculcated by the Islamic religion. He noted in his journal: "Splendid cities once teeming with a busy population and embellished with temples and edifices, the wonder of the world, now deserted and lonely, or reduced by mismanagement and the barbarism of the Muslim creed to a state as savage as wild animals by which they are surrounded. Often have I gazed on them till my heart actually sickened within me."[21]

Not all the traveling artists similarly denounced Islam. Compare the words of Frederick Goupil-Fesquet, who was in the East at the same time as Roberts and was moved by the sight of Muslims praying in a Cairo mosque:

> A holy respect comes over the spectator in the presence of this silent gathering. The expression of humility and veneration imprinted on every face, which no distraction can alter, gives their features a stately grandeur that seems to harmonize with the building itself.[22]

It was a shock to Roberts and many Western travelers that the Holy Land was a land of Muslims, who, though lazy and barbaric, could also appear to be noble, exotic, colorful, and sensuous. Some, like the painters Horace Vernet and David Wilkie, believed that in the dress, carriage, and visage of the Arabs one could find the living link with the ancient Israelites of the Bible. In a totally romantic idealization called *Judah and Tamar*, Vernet painted those Hebraic personalities in the forms of an exotically veiled woman sitting alongside a desert sheik on a stone bench, his camel looming over them.

No doubt Roberts and the other artists who traveled to the East and to Palestine—William Holman Hunt, Beauteufriend, Bernatz, William Bartlett, Thomas Allon, Horace Vernet, and David Wilkie—were moved by the combination of elements they found there: remoteness, romance and exoticism, rich colors, the white light burning over the desert, and the memory of biblical glory. They were also excited by sights of public baths, private harems, veiled women, and the dizzying display of races and religions; above all they were attracted by the Arab bazaar. Roberts wrote vividly of Cairo's grand bazaar in words that would also describe Jerusalem's smaller version of the public market.

> These narrow, crowded streets render it very difficult to make drawings, for in addition to the curiosity of the Arabs, who, although they are picturesque in appearance, are ugly customers to jostle. I wish I could transport you for an hour into one of those bazaars. Such scenes! All the Eastern nations gathered together. Turks and Greeks in their picturesque costumes. The wild Arab, who never slept within walls, every tribe different in dress, and all armed. Then the motley groups of the lazzaroni lounging about; long strings of women sitting astride on mules or donkeys, all closely muffled up, going from one harem to another, attended by male and female black and white slaves on foot. Then the extraordinary variety of articles for sale, the gravity of the shopkeeper and his customer, smoking a pipe in front of the shop. The ladies smoke as the gentlemen, but the chaboukes of the former are more costly.[23]

In his art of Palestine, Roberts offered an image of an original order, perfect, unchanging, rising above the palpable evidence of decay, dirt, and disease (he was delayed in entering Jerusalem because of plague). His depiction of Palestine is that of an orientalized Eden filled with ripe, unspotted fruit. We recognize this Eden even in Roberts's picture of the town of Acre as Bonaparte's army is massing on the eastern plain, preparing for its assault. The troops are seen marching in close even ranks—all order, no commotion, no turmoil, no sense of the savagery that will be let loose on the town, no hint of blood or anything that will suggest the reality of the 1799 battle that occurred there.

Suddenly in the foreground we notice, set on the hilly ground above Acre, an Arabic-style metal water jug, tall, slim, a lovely vessel, with its softly rounded belly, its delicately shaped spigot and handle: a symbol of timeless indifference to the horror that will soon commence on the plain below. The metal jug works to orientalize the scene, to infuse it with the mystery and sensuousness of Arab Palestine as Roberts imagined it.

In similar fashion, Roberts posed small clusters of costumed Arabs in his landscapes to lend warmth and color to otherwise drab scenes. In Roberts's pictures Arabs are adornments to majestic landscapes. In many pictures they are shown lounging, as they do in the bazaar, smoking, chatting, making coffee, idling in the presence of ancient buildings whose pillars are fallen and broken. Here was Roberts's dramatic image of a broken Palestine waiting to be healed by the idealism and energy that could only come from the Christian West.

William Holman Hunt, unlike Roberts, did not idealize Palestine in his paintings. Founder of a school of painting called the pre-Raphaelite Brotherhood, he sought a quality of naturalistic truth, of humanistic realism. Like Edward Robinson before him, Hunt was driven to authenticate the truth of the biblical stories. He felt that "the painting of historically accurate biblical pictures was a distinctly Protestant endeavor ... an alternative to the decadent Italian tradition of Catholic devotional art."[24]

Hunt's passion was the artistic depiction of biblical scenes, particularly of the life of Jesus. To portray such scenes accurately, he traveled to Palestine for the first time in 1854 to see for himself what Jews really looked like—sometimes with dangerous results. At one point in his travels he was accused of "collecting the likeness of people to sell to the devil." Rabbis refused to provide models for a painter who made no secret of his conviction that the Christian religion had fulfilled Hebraic prophecy. But there was no denying Hunt's tenacity. His capacity to use naturalistic detail of people and places bore fruit in his arresting depiction of the New Testament's story of the young Jesus debating the Jerusalem Temple priests (Luke 2: 45–49), *The Finding of the Saviour in the Temple*.[25] To provide an accurate landscape for his painting of the sacrificial goat in *The Scape-goat*, he spent seventeen days on the torrid shore of the Dead Sea with a white goat as a model, surrounded by Arabs who so admired his bravery "that they offered to bestow on him the rank of sheik."[26] The white goat died from heat, to be replaced by a second who also perished. Hunt completed his picture in Jerusalem with a third goat standing in a pool of salt water in his studio.

CHAPTER THREE

A Taste of Equality

[Non-Muslims] shall be the object of our imperial
favors without exception.
—Sultan Mahmoud, 1839

During the Government of Djezzar and Abdallah
Pachas, a Christian could not appear in the streets
without great danger. In 1838 a Christian, wearing
the costume of his country, might go where he
would, not only in perfect safety but even without
being noticed as he passed.
—John Bowring, 1840

In 1831 Muhammad Ali Pasha, Egypt's viceroy, conquered Palestine and Syria, and welcomed Westerners through the door that Bonaparte had first opened. The event radically altered politics and society in the Middle East for the next 150 years.

Ali had been born in the lovely northern Aegean Greek seaport of Kavala, where his father was a tobacco merchant and commander of a battalion of fellow Albanian mercenaries. He succeeded his father as commander of the battalion, which he later led in the fight against Bonaparte, winning the respect of Turkish generals for his tactical skills.

Taking advantage of the disorder that followed the withdrawal of the French army from Egypt in 1801, Ali seized the Cairo citadel and in 1805 compelled the sultan to acknowledge him as governor of Egypt. He ruled for the next forty years as an enlightened despot, working energetically to modernize Egypt along Western lines—revising taxation, introducing cotton farming, and enlarging the gunpowder factories that Bonaparte had established. He recruited Christians for government administration and did not hesitate to promote them to high position over Muslims. His state monopolies over cotton, gum arabic, and indigo were intended to generate enough money to enlarge and equip the Egyptian army and navy, whose retraining he placed in the hands of French officers. Taking over projects that Bonaparte had planned, Ali completed dams, modernized irrigation works, planted new crops, and established new industries. Plans for the excavation of the Suez Canal, first laid in Bonaparte's time, were advanced by Ali and completed by his successors.[1]

Between 1811 and 1827 the Noble Porte could depend on Ali's strength to crush rebellion anywhere in the empire.[2] In 1811 he successfully quelled the revolt of the dissident Wahabi sect in west central Arabia (Hijaz), recapturing the holy cities of Mecca and Medina. And in the early 1820s he added his own army and navy to Turkish forces to put down the Greek rebellion in Crete, Cyprus, and the Morea area of southern Greece. In 1827 his son, Ibrahim Pasha, captured Athens. But in October of that year Ali experienced his first taste of defeat when the combined Egyptian-Turkish fleet was destroyed in Navarino Bay by a mixed British and French flotilla.

The defeat did nothing but embolden Ali. In three short years he rebuilt his navy, turned to French advisers to upgrade his army, and reaped sufficient funds from international trade arrangements to allow him to finance Egypt's breakaway from the sultan.

Egypt would not have gained her independence from Istanbul and Ali his fame as father of modern Egypt if Sultan Mahmoud II (who was determined to revitalize the Ottoman Empire with Western help) had not refused one of Ali's more audacious requests. To compensate him for continually rushing to the sultan's defense (which also included military aid in the Russo-Turkish War of 1827–1828), Egypt's viceroy asked the sultan for Syria and Palestine to be added to his domain. Why not? He badly needed money to continue modernizing Egypt. He expected substantial revenues from the timber resources of Lebanon, the coal and iron mines of Syria, and the silk production of Syria and Palestine. Wary of the sultan's jealousy of his growing power, Ali also wanted the territories as a buffer against a possible Turkish action to oust him from Egypt.

But the sultan's answer was a polite no. Mahmoud certainly needed military assistance from his energetic pasha, but he would not feed so ambitious a leader by ceding to him a region valuable to Istanbul as a shield against military threats from the Muslim East or the Christian West. No one had to remind Mahmoud that Bonaparte's forces could easily have reached Istanbul had they not been stopped at Acre. Indeed, no. Syria and Palestine were too valuable to relinquish to the pasha of Egypt.

There were also religious considerations. Ali already controlled the holy places in Arabia. If he were to come into possession of two of Islam's most treasured monuments, Jerusalem's Dome of the Rock shrine and the Al Aksa mosque, then he, not the sultan, might well be looked upon in the future as the caliph, the custodian of Islam's Holy Law. Possession of Syria would also give Ali control of the lucrative annual Hajj caravan to Mecca and Medina, which commenced in Damascus. No, the Noble Porte would not weaken its authority over Islam by ceding more of its institutions to an Albanian opportunist.

Muhammad Ali's own calculations were not terribly different from the sultan's. Syria and Palestine were also important to him as a buffer against the sultan. And so in October 1831 the Egyptian army, led by Ali's son Ibrahim and following Napoleon's route, began its invasion of Palestine at El Arish, on the southern Sinai desert coast. The army won quick victories at Jaffa and Jerusalem, then routed the Turkish army at Homs in Syria, and later subdued Acre's citadel after bombarding the city with 35,000 cannon shells. The seizure of Acre left Palestine and Syria wide open.

A year later, in December 1832, Ibrahim defeated a Turkish army of 100,000 at Konia across the Taurus mountains, taking prisoner the sultan's chief adviser and de facto head of government, the grand vizier himself. Now the road to Istanbul was undefended. Nothing could stop Ibrahim from toppling the sultanate and replacing Mahmoud II with his own father on the throne—which is probably what he would have done had not his father's caution and foreign intervention stopped him.

While Ibrahim saw things in purely military terms, Ali was shrewder.[3] Ali had learned the hard way that any direct threat to the stability of the sultan's rule over his empire would automatically invite a belligerent response from one or more of the Western nations. He could successfully invade Palestine and Syria because France, an ally, supported him. But any more aggressive move toward Istanbul would invite Western retaliation. Certainly Britain and Russia would see his expansion as a threat to the stability of the Ottoman Empire, and thereby a threat to the delicate power balance among the Western nations themselves. Better than anyone else, Ali understood that the essential question in the minds of Western diplomats—the Eastern Question, as it came to be called—was the future of the Ottoman Empire.[4] And that question could really be reduced to a simple proposition: Who would gain and who would lose by the collapse of the Ottoman Empire? The last thing Ali wanted was to topple the sultan only to become a punching bag for the West.

While Ali was moving into Palestine and Syria, Britain, whose external affairs were in the hands of its resourceful foreign secretary, Lord Palmerston, was so busy with Western problems as momentarily to ignore the cry for help. But Russia did not.

Here was an ironic reversal. For decades Britain had propped up a declining Ottoman Empire to keep both France and Russia from expanding into the Middle East. The Chanuk Treaty of 1806 had been signed to keep Russian and other foreign ships of war out of the strategic Dardanelles and Bosphorus straits, which linked the Black Sea to the Mediterranean. Now, because of Ali's aggressiveness, Russia seized an opportunity to achieve advantage over both Britain and France, and rushed to the rescue of the sultan.

In February 1833, only two months after Ibrahim's stunning victory at Konia, the Russian fleet sailed into the Bosphorus and disembarked troops on the Anatolian shore. Turkey's archenemy for centuries had effectively rescued the sultan. But at a stiff price. In the Treaty of Unkiar Skellesi with Russia, in July 1833, the sultan agreed to close the Dardanelles to all non-Russian warships. For the first time in her history Russia had access to the Mediterranean, where she could compete with the British fleet.

Now Palmerston had to pay attention. With Russia greatly strengthened in the region, the collapse of the Ottoman Empire would put Britain and Russia at sword's point. Rather than encouraging Ali's ambitions, the British foreign secretary thought it better that Britain join Russia in containing the Egyptian threat against the

Ottoman throne in order to maintain the international balance of power. It was the beginning of a new international order aimed, once again, at preserving the Ottoman Empire in order to prevent war among the European nations.

No one understood this better than Ali. He breathed a sigh of relief at the sight of Russian naval ships in the Bosphorus, knowing that the sultan in the pocket of the Europeans was less likely to do him harm. But he refused to break off hostilities for nothing. He preferred total sovereign independence over Egypt but wisely accepted from Mahmoud a hereditary pashalik. Technically Egypt would remain part of the Ottoman Empire, but Ali and his successors were free to govern the country as their own.

Of course Mahmoud had to formally concede to Ali the already conquered provinces of Adana, Tarsus, Syria, and Palestine. But to make sure that these lands did not become a staging ground for future attacks on the sultan's throne, Ali agreed to pay the sultan a "good faith" tax of forty million piastres. The only question was how long Ali would be willing to pay this tribute and continue to remain even technically the sultan's vassal.

NONE COULD HAVE BEEN happier for the advent of Egyptian rule in Palestine than Christians and Jews. Nine years of Egyptian control of Palestine and Syria put an end to three centuries of unfair treatment by the Turks. Ottoman authorities had upheld the Islamic view of Christians and Jews as *dhimmis* (protected ones), who were taxed for their protection but also regarded as inferior to Muslims because they could not bear arms or ride horses. Christians had to wear black, Jews a conical hat; non-Muslims were forbidden the wearing of the Prophet's color of green. In court their testimony could not be heard against a Muslim; but a Muslim's testimony against a *dhimmi* was altogether acceptable. A non-Muslim male might not marry a Muslim woman; but a Muslim male could marry a Christian or Jewish woman, who would then be expected to convert to Islam. Christians and Jews could repair their houses of worship, but they could not build new ones. The most hated symbol of inferiority was the *cizye*, the poll tax levied only on minorities.

The new Egyptian rulers of Palestine acted forcefully to equalize the religious, political, and legal status of the non-Muslim minority. The centuries-old ban against the building of new churches and synagogues was removed. Prohibitions against riding horses, ringing church bells, and carrying the cross in processions were struck down. Christians might wear any color that suited them, and Jews discarded their long hats. When Muslims complained that allowing the *dhimmis* to ride horses put them on a level of equality with Muslims, they were told to ride camels, which were taller than horses.[5]

Sure evidence of the new feeling of religious freedom was the establishment in 1837 by Jews of the first printing press in Palestine. This was followed by presses of the Latin, Armenian, and Greek Orthodox churches.[6]

Palestine's door was opening faster than anyone at the time could have imagined. No one could have been more pleased with this development than Muhammad Ali, who seized every opportunity to fill a treasury chronically drained to pay for the enormous standing army and navy he maintained. To generate income, all of Ali's domain in Egypt, Sudan, Palestine, and Syria was thrown open to foreign investors. It was an unprecedented spur to European involvement in the Middle East.[7]

The new pro-minority policies of the Egyptian rulers, however, insulted Muslims. What particularly enraged them were the decrees that ordered military conscription for all Muslim men and simultaneously allowed Christians and Jews to evade the army by payment of a new exemption tax. Egyptian officials wasted no time in forcing villagers to give up their men to the army. When they refused, old men were seized and threatened with army duty until their places were taken by younger men.

More resentment arose among Muslims when Ibrahim's government introduced a progressive income tax to help pay for heavy military expenses. The rich were thus forced to pay more than the poor—a slap in the face to Palestine's elite. For generations, influential and wealthy Muslims had been able to evade the tax collector. Now everyone paid because the collection of taxes was not in the hands of easily bribed underlings of the regional tax collector but rather the responsibility of Egyptian army officers answerable to their superiors.

Nor did it sit well with ordinary Muslims that the only exceptions to the progressive income tax were the Muslim religious elite and foreigners.[8] In 1834, in protest against forced conscription and heavy taxes, the peasants revolted. Jerusalem came under siege for a short time when rebels stole into the city through water tunnels; but they failed to capture the citadel. The seriousness of the revolt is evidenced by the appearance in the regional capital of Damascus by none less than the pasha himself, Muhammad Ali, who called out his vast army to crush the rebels.

More reforms now followed. In the field of law, the old discrimination against non-Muslims was ended. The testimony of a non-Muslim was now accepted in court, even when it was given against a Muslim. A concerted effort was made to change the nature of the criminal court by appointing judges who were not part of the *ulema,* the religious leadership which had been unfailingly hostile to Christians.

A major change occurred in administration. The office of governor, usually exercised despotically by a pasha, was now checked by the introduction of a second governing body, the collective administration of an appointed council, the *meclis.* The *meclis* was drawn from the Muslim elite but also included influential members of the Christian and Jewish communities.

Seeing so many major changes in so short a time, Muslims grew anxious and rebellious. The *ulema* in the towns spoke resentfully of seeing so many Christian foreigners in their midst. Ibrahim was held in contempt, as in this outburst from a Turkish mosque preacher, who mounted a minaret and shouted:

> Does the Muslim religion exist no longer? Is it dead? Are we not Turks? Let every man who loves the Prophet take up arms against the man without faith . . . Ibrahim Pasha! That drunkard who always drinks spirits and wine, who eats pork and every dirt that comes from the sea, the same as the Christians do, who lives in the convents with the priests and prays with them, but never goes to the mosque.[9]

In one area Muslims, Jews, and Christians alike could credit the Egyptian regime with accomplishment. It was the taming of the Bedouins.[10] By imprisoning Bedouin tribal chiefs and confiscating weapons, horses, and camels, the raiding of Arab villages was severely curtailed. For nine years under the harsh but effective Egyptian regime, an unaccustomed peace prevailed in the Palestinian countryside.

MAHMOUD II and the Western powers had no illusions about Muhammad Ali. Ali rarely paid his tribute to the sultan. With the money he enlarged his army with conscripts from Syria and Palestine. Before invading Syria he had declared the sultan a heretic, persuading Muslim officials in Mecca and Medina to support him in this charge. The implication was obvious. If the masses of imperial subjects could be persuaded to think the sultan was a heretic, he, Ali, who sat righteously over Islam's holy places, had every right to proclaim his own caliphate.

The Sultan Mahmoud II, now old, feeble, and bitter about his rebellious vassal, had wasted no time in retraining his army with the help of Prussian advisers. Mahmoud wanted Ali out of Turkey; he wanted Palestine and Syria back. Most of all he wanted to punish his upstart vassal.

But he could not do so without first obtaining pledges of military support from Britain, Russia, Austria, and Prussia. All the Western powers recognized that if the Ottoman Empire were continually weakened by Egypt, the delicate balance of power in the West would be upset, setting nation against nation. So France, which had earlier encouraged Ali's ambitions, now cautioned him against any move that might provoke a Western reaction.

Meanwhile Britain grew anxious seeing Russia in the Bosphorus and watching Ali build toward a new Islamic empire. It was of concern to Palmerston that Ali already controlled the trade routes to India via the Red Sea and the Indian Ocean. Palmerston considered that if Ali were allowed to stay on indefinitely in Syria and Palestine, eventually Russia would seize an opportunity to form an anti-Ottoman alliance with the Egyptian pasha. The common goal would be the expansion of Russian and Egyptian power in Mesopotamia and the Persian Gulf. And this would mean the blocking of Britain's valuable Mesopotamian land route to her prized colony of India.

The occasion for disciplining Ali was brought on by Ali himself. He had tired of being a vassal and paying a tax for ruling conquered lands. In May 1838, throwing caution to the winds, he announced his intention to declare his complete independence of the sultan. The reaction from Istanbul was slow but predictable. One year later, in April 1839, Mahmoud II, deathly sick and burning with revenge, initiated war to retake his lost territories. But in a major engagement in June 1839, Egyptian forces routed the Ottoman army at Nizip. One week later, on July 1, the sultan died.

Now the Western powers faced a major decision. Russia, knowing that her effort to profit from a weakened Turkey would provoke the West, did an about-face and joined Britain, Austria, and Prussia in forging a military alliance against Ali. France refused to gang up on her Egyptian protégé and stayed out of the Western alliance—thus tacitly supporting Ali.

After Ali refused the request to yield his conquered territories, a powerful allied expedition under the command of Sir Charles Napier was sent to the Syrian-Palestinian coast. Ibrahim's army, unpaid for a year, did not fight well.[11] In a few months it was in retreat from Acre. In September 1841 Mahmoud's young son and successor, Sultan Abdulmejid II, was pleased to receive back from Western hands all the previously conquered provinces. In a gesture of new respect, or out of continued fear for the Egyptian pasha, the sultan reconfirmed Ali's hereditary rule over Egypt.

Britain succeeded in extricating Russia from the Bosphorus in the Straits Convention of 1841, which laid down the principles that no warship would be allowed in the straits in peacetime and that no one nation would be allowed to gain exclusive power over the Ottoman Empire. Thus peace was secured by a careful adjustment of fear and greed.

During the crisis fomented by Ali, Palmerston searched for ways to strengthen Britain's position in the Middle East. Since diplomatic consular offices in the cities of Beirut and Damascus were Britain's eyes in the Arab East, why not widen the scope of vision by having in Jerusalem a consulate which might keep an eye on Russian and French moves? At a propitious moment, when Muhammad Ali was hoping to win the British to his side in the deepening dispute with the sultan, he honored Palmerston's request for permission to open in Jerusalem a vice-consulate, the first of its kind ever in the city.

The British office, opened in November 1838, was to have far-reaching political and commercial consequences, intensifying the competition between nations for influence in Palestine. Within a few years, after the country was securely back in the Ottoman fold, the sultan—for a price—agreed to a host of new foreign consulates there: Prussia in 1842, France and Sardinia in 1843, the United States in 1844, Austria in 1849, Spain in 1854, and Russia in 1858.[12]

The new consulates represented a major advance in the Western penetration of the Arab East. Their declared purpose was to facilitate commercial trade between the Ottoman Empire and the countries represented by the consulates; but the consulates rapidly became centers for the expansion of Western political interests in Palestine. Consuls enjoyed diplomatic immunity and were exempted from Ottoman taxes when importing goods under consular seal. The arrival of the consuls also led to the relaxing of the centuries-old ban against Christians taking up permanent residence in Jerusalem. And this in turn led to the increase of Western land purchases in Jerusalem and throughout Palestine. Before long the Western nations began to look on Palestine and particularly Jerusalem as ripe territory for European living, building, and investment.

The opening of the British vice-consulate particularly had profound religious consequences. A few months after Palmerston had made the decision to do so, Anthony Ashley Cooper (later Lord Shaftesbury), who was his stepson and a devout Christian millenarian, sought to persuade the foreign secretary that government support of the Jewish restoration to Palestine would hasten Christ's Coming as well as serving British interests.

Palmerston, who had little use for religious argument and scarcely any mystical feeling about Palestine, quickly recognized the wisdom of his stepson's advice. With the loyal support of a substantial minority of Jews in Palestine, Britain might compete more favorably in the region with Catholic France and Orthodox Russia. For years, under the trade agreements with the Ottoman government called the Capitulations, France had exercised protection for pilgrims and other Roman Catholics living in the Holy Land, while Russia had done the same for Orthodox pilgrims and the twenty thousand Arab members of the Greek Orthodox church.[13] No doubt both France and Russia used their privileged positions to advance their own national interests in Palestine and elsewhere in the Middle East. Britain, a Protestant nation, had no such privileged position. This might change if Britain would "adopt" the Jewish nation and urge its return to the ancestral homeland. The newly opened vice-consulate might in fact use its offices to facilitate the Jewish restoration. Thus almost eighty years before the Balfour Declaration of 1917 pledging

British government support of a Jewish national home in Palestine, a powerful and fateful British-Jewish connection was formed in the country.[14]

In August 1840 Palmerston wrote to Lord Ponsonby, the British ambassador in Istanbul, stressing that both the sultan and Britain had much to gain economically if the world's wealthiest Jews could be persuaded to support the restoration of their brethren to the ancestral homeland. He instructed his ambassador to convince the sultan to hold out "every encouragement to the Jews of Europe to return to Palestine."[15] Palmerston did not fail to note that 1840 was also the golden year in which Jews expected the return of the Messiah, thus their wish to go to Palestine, as he put it, "has become more keen."

Accordingly, the newly appointed British vice-consul to Jerusalem, W. T. Young, was officially instructed "that it will be part of your duty . . . to afford protection to the Jews generally and you will take an early opportunity of reporting . . . upon the present state of the Jewish population in Palestine." At the time there were scarcely more than nine thousand Jews in Palestine, four thousand of them living in Jerusalem.[16]

Vice-Consul Young had no doubt that whatever the political and commercial aspects of his duties, the heart of his mission was religious. On entering Jerusalem he was greeted warmly by rabbinical representatives of both the Sephardic and Ashkenazic communities. Within a few months of taking up his duties, he wrote to one of his superiors in London: "There are two parties here, who will doubtless have some voice in the future disposition of affairs. The one is the Jew—unto whom God originally gave this land for a possession, and the other the Protestant Christian, his legitimate offspring."[17]

What was meant by protecting the Jews? The answer was legal rights. A consul had the right to extend his own nation's legal rights to those who lacked citizen status in Ottoman Palestine. Before the advent of the consulates, a non-Muslim could not give evidence in court against a Muslim, a situation which guaranteed victory for any Muslim bringing suit against a non-Muslim. But under the consular system, if any non-Muslim, including a Jew, who was not an Ottoman citizen appeared in court, his foreign consul could appear alongside him and plead his case with reasonable hope of a fair hearing from the Muslim judge.

This privilege could not of course be extended to Christians and Jews who were legally Ottoman subjects. Their legal rights were set forth under the conditions of the millet or "nations" system in which the minority peoples of the Ottoman Empire were locally governed by their own ethno-national leaders. The leader of the minority Greek community was the Greek Orthodox patriarch residing in Jerusalem. The leaders of the small Armenian, Coptic, and Abyssinian communities were also the religious patriarchs of their respective churches. The head of the small Sephardic Jewish community, the Hakham Bashi or "Wise Elder," was a recognized Ottoman official. These leaders exercised legal control over their peoples within the wider framework of Muslim state law.

A British vice-consulate in Jerusalem was a major reversal in centuries of Islamic religious policy which dictated that Europeans might visit the Holy City but not permanently live there. The local Turkish-appointed governor of the Jerusalem district welcomed the first vice-consul Young. But the city's Muslim religious leadership could see the Britisher's presence only as another sign of self-serving accommodation of foreign infidels. That perception was validated when it was learned that, apart from the stated duty of facilitating trade between Britain and the Levant, Young was also to "afford protection" to Palestine's Jews. The question in Muslim minds was, Why would Britain, the world's most powerful empire, send her diplomat to Palestine to succor the friendless Jews—if not to use the Jews to advance British interests in Palestine? And did that not then mean an eventual British takeover of Palestine? For the time being, these questions went unanswered.

THE SULTAN'S THRONE had been preserved when the Western nations drove Ibrahim's army out Syria and Palestine. But in their nine years of rule the Egyptians had infected Syria and Palestine with the idea of legal and social equality, an idea which the Ottoman government was reluctantly compelled to respect. Even before the military action against Ibrahim's regime, the West compelled the sultan to honor the principle of human equality. The price for Western military support against Ibrahim took the form of an imperial decree (Gulhane) issued in November 1839, promising equality for all non-Muslim subjects of the empire. Thus the West received assurance that with the resumption of Ottoman rule in Palestine and Syria,

Christians and Jews would be treated no less fairly than they had been treated under the Egyptians.

The crucial passage of Gulhane read: "The Muslims and non-Muslims and other peoples who are among the subjects of our imperial sultanate, shall be the object of our imperial favors without exception."[18] The language, tactful but ambiguous, promising equality, seemed formally to change the status of Christian and Jews. But the daily lives of non-Muslims were not much changed. Significantly, the government did not abolish the hated poll tax levied on non-Muslims, a symbol of their inferiority. That would happen only with a decree of 1856, issued in the wake of the Crimean War.

The initial Turkish attempt at reform was feeble because of a lack of military power to back up the language of reform. Where the Egyptian rulers had continuously employed in Syria and Palestine an army estimated at seventy thousand, the Turks by contrast rarely put in the field more than a tenth to a quarter of that force. The consequences were predictable. Bedouins returned to raiding villages; clan chieftains resumed their old practices of extortion; peace and security gave way to terror and despair.[19]

The decree of 1839 promised a new era of reform, or Tanzimat (Turkish for "reorganization"), throughout the empire. Tanzimat had been championed by the sultan's able, Western-minded grand vizier, Resid Pasha, who had to battle entrenched religious conservatives in the government to win the sultan's support. It was not only to win Western military backing against the Egyptians that Resid pressed for Tanzimat. He had his own vision of a modern Turkey. With Tanzimat he was showing that however much Turkey shared the bond of Islam with the Arab subjects of the empire, the future of Turkey politically and economically lay with the West.

None understood this motive better than Palestine's Muslims, whose resentment of Istanbul was demonstrated by their consistent refusal to accept reform. To them the Tanzimat was a betrayal of Islam. Only physical force had made them comply with the earlier Egyptian decrees, and only force again would make them conform to the Tanzimat.

The Turks had planned to impose a centralized state authority on Palestine but made contradictory decisions that undermined their plans. Inexplicably, the old system of pashaliks, which had been the source of despotism and chaos in the time of al-Jazzar, was restored.

Yet the new pashas lacked authority and force to carry out the Tanzimat reforms. As noted earlier, the pashas were further weakened by the councils, the *meclis,* which had begun to assert their governing authority in every town of Palestine. Istanbul listened to the pashas but heeded the *meclis,* which meant greater power for those Muslim urban notables who sat in the *meclis.*

The abolition of the Egyptian law on conscription was welcomed by Muslim families, but it meant that scores of Muslim youth were now free to be hired as mercenaries in a number of private armies that made their appearance. Increasingly, these armies and not the regular Ottoman troops provided protection. And protection was needed. The old factionalism reappeared with the resumption of family clan feuds in the main cities of Hebron, Nablus, Gaza, and Jerusalem. The roads again were unsafe, and it required bribes to highwaymen to assure the safe passage of the Hajj caravan from Damascus to Mecca and of Christian pilgrims traveling from Jaffa to Jerusalem.

The Turkish decree of 1839 promised political equality for all non-Muslims of the realm, but in Palestine the actual practice rendered the promise empty. This was seen in the *meclis,* which because of Tanzimat had to include a few token Christian and Jewish members. But the dominance of Muslim members rendered the non-Muslim voice mute. One contemporary observer describes the intimidating atmosphere of the *meclis.* The non-Muslim members, he notes,

> rarely attend and when they are called, they are seated on the extreme end of the mat but not on the Divan. . . . Their Mussulman colleagues make them light their pipes . . . they take no part in the deliberations and are treated with utter disregard, never venturing to express dissent in any decision even though it be calculated to injure their brother Christians . . . sometimes . . . placing their seals falsely to Mazbattas [reports] merely from fear of displeasing the Mussulman members.[20]

The Ottoman mismanagement of Palestine following the regime of Ali and Ibrahim could also be seen in the refusal to address problems of infrastructure. Roads, bridges, and inns—all vital to the economy—were neglected in favor of forts, barracks, and the pasha's palace. Hospitals were built because the Ottoman government feared disease, and it knew that without hospitals foreigners were not likely to invest in the country or encourage pilgrimages.

Contributing in unanticipated ways to the decline of the internal economy were the government's actions to encourage foreign trade. Money was spent to improve port facilities, particularly at Haifa and Jaffa. And because of foreign trade the port city of Haifa became prosperous, experiencing a sharp increase of population from twelve thousand in 1840 to fifty thousand in the late 1850s. The granting of trade privileges to foreign investors had begun with concessions, the Capitulations, as they were called, granted in the sixteenth century by Suleiman the Magnificent to the French king Francis I. By the middle of the nineteenth century virtually every trading country had a substantial set of agreements that made trade with the Middle East lucrative. Palestine exported cotton and wool to Europe at preferred rates and received finished goods at cheap prices. The exchange was profitable to many Christian families that concentrated on foreign trade. But as the country was flooded with large quantities of well-made, cheaply purchased foreign goods, the products of local industry and crafts went without buyers. The local clothing industry was devastated as people switched to Western-style clothes, which were now imported.

Dramatizing the decline in the textile trade was the dwindling number of looms as measured by Damascus, which saw the number fall from 34,000 in the first half of the nineteenth century to 4,000 in the late 1850s.[21] As more foreign goods were purchased and fewer local goods were marketed abroad, the country saw a drain of gold needed to cover purchases.

The peasants now suffered most. The Bedouins might come and go, but there were always taxes, which in the past had fallen so hard on the Palestinian peasantry that agriculture was ruined and villages abandoned. The Egyptians too had imposed heavy taxes but had arranged an efficient system of collection. The Ottomans wished to continue the same system but failed to do so; their promise to abolish tax farming and replace it with direct taxation was not kept. Gradually the hated bribe-taking tax collector reappeared.

The changing economic conditions in Palestine benefited a few Christian trading families, some Jews in moneylending, and a handful of wealthy urban Muslim families who monopolized agriculture, particularly in the export of wheat and citrus. And there were fortunates among those who lived in the interior towns. One was the town of Nablus, surrounded by fertile fields and known internationally for its production of soap. Nazareth, Bethlehem, and Jerusalem, relying mainly on the sale of locally made religious articles, were actually helped by foreign trade, which also stimulated pilgrimages. But most of Palestine's people, and especially the peasants, were headed for eventual impoverishment. Their future could be glimpsed in one sad fact: a country that had exported grain for centuries now had to import it in order to guard against famine.

The presence of the foreign trader indicated the spread of foreign political influence, beginning with the foreign consuls. While the consuls ostensibly represented the economic interests of Western nations, much of their time was spent advancing Western political objectives in Palestine and Syria. The Ottoman government came to regret the granting to the consuls rights of protection over their nationals in the region. For the consuls soon took on airs of Christian-style pashas, constantly interceding for their respective flocks: Britain and Germany for Protestants and Jews; France, Austria, and Italy for Catholics; Russia for the Greek and Arab Orthodox.

A declining economy, deepening poverty, the enlarging presence and influence of foreigners, the increasing wealth of Christians—all these developments provoked Muslim resentment to the point of violent reaction. Muslims had come to believe that a conspiracy of European and local Christians aimed to steal the country from Islam. Weight was given to these suspicions by the occasional Christian notable who openly expressed his wish that Europe would invade Palestine in order to restore the country to the faith of the church.

The first violent anti-Christian demonstration occurred in 1850 in the city of Aleppo. Later hostility intensified with the publication of the sultan's Humayun decree of 1856, emphatically reasserting equal rights for all non-Muslim subjects of the realm. That decree, coming in the wake of the Crimean War of 1853–1856, and like the earlier decree of 1839, was the Turkish acknowledgment of Western help for supporting the sultanate against its Russian enemy.

Muslim reaction to the 1856 decree was fierce, summed up in this sentiment voiced at the time: "Today we have lost our sacred national rights which our ancestors gained with their blood; while the nation used to be the ruling nation, it is now bereft of this sacred right. This is a day of tears and mourning."[22]

What most provoked Muslim hostility was the abolition of the poll tax traditionally levied on Christians and Jews, and the consistent refusal of Christians to pay the military exemption tax, the *bedel,* which in Muslim eyes was a flaunting of their exemption from conscription. Further sources of insult: the sight of wealthy Christians building lavish homes, the opening of taverns for the sale of wine and spirits, the ringing of church bells, and processions in which the cross was publicly displayed. Muslims resented the sight of Christians on horseback, brandishing weapons newly allowed to them under the Humayun decree. Nor did Muslims like to see Christians engaging in public displays of dancing or the raising of foreign flags at consular offices. The appearance of the French tricolor in Jerusalem and the Union Jack in Nablus actually provoked riots.

The refusal of Christians to pay the *bedel* turned Muslims against Christians, leading to mass slaughter in 1860 in Damascus. This event marked a major turning point in Palestine's human relations, showing that the Western penetration of the Middle East could proceed only so far before producing violent reaction.

CHAPTER FOUR

Ascending to the Land of Israel

The truth is that living in Eretz Yisrael is very good
for the elderly but not for the young.
—Yakir, Nephew of the Baal Shem Tov, 1760

A Jew in Jerusalem is not much estimated
above a dog.
—William Young,
England's Vice-Consul in Jerusalem, 1839

Piety, poverty, and persecution were the major forces that caused eastern European Jews in the late eighteenth century to leave their countries for Palestine. The Kingdom of Poland experienced an economic crisis with destructive consequences for the country's large Jewish population. Government officials and Roman Catholic bishops blamed Jews for the economic decline and for corrupting the Christian peasant society. Holding monopolies on the production and sale of beer, wine, and spirits, Jews were blamed for peasant drunkenness. Jewish moneylenders were accused of exploiting the poor. The medieval blood-libel charge was repeated, and Jews were tortured and executed after accusations of child kidnaping, sorcery, satanism, and desecration of the Eucharist were brought against them. Mobs assaulted Jewish villages and town ghettos. The worst outrage occurred in 1768 when Cossacks and armed peasants rampaged through the Ukraine and Silesia, killing Jews, burning homes, and looting synagogues. The response of Jewish community leaders was the habitual one of seeking to moderate persecution by agreeing to pay the extortions of Catholic bishops and government officials.

But Christian persecutions do not alone explain the Jewish exodus from Poland. We should add the element of piety. In the mid-1770s small groups of devout Orthodox Jews began immigrating from Poland to the northern Galilean towns of Tiberias and Safed. They heeded a call that became more insistent with the years. Rabbi Jacob Emden put it this way: "Every person . . . must abidingly and firmly resolve in his heart to ascend to the Land of Israel to live in it, at all events, when he shall have acquired the expenses and some position to afford him a living . . . so that he may settle the land, which is desolate without its sons."[1]

Palestine, or the Land of Israel as Jews customarily called it, had never been really "desolate without its sons." From the time of the Hadrianic expulsion of the Jews from Judea in the second century C.E., Jews had stubbornly refused to quit the Land of Israel. They continued to live in Jerusalem, defying an official ban on their residence there. Galilean Jews, who had not participated in Bar Kochba's rebellion against the Romans (132–135 C.E.), evaded Hadrian's decree of expulsion and continued to live in the land for generations. Beginning in the sixteenth century, thousands of Spanish Jews, Sephardim, heeding the Catholic church's official decree of expulsion, immigrated eastward, many of them finding their way to Palestine, a country ruled by a fairly tolerant Ottoman Turkish government. The new immigrants settled in the Galilee and made a new Jewish religious capital of the mountain town of Safed. It was the beginning of a slow steady march of Western Jews to the ancestral homeland.

The march was quickened in the seventeenth century by the mass movements inspired by Sabbatai Zvi and other self-styled messiahs preaching the "End of Days." It took only a few days in the Land of Israel for even the most devout of the messianists to realize that the land was impoverished, inhospitable, ruled over by despots. Yet the Jewish march to the Land of Israel continued despite false messiahs and harsh governors.

In the winter of 1777 a group of three hundred Hasidic Jews ("pious ones") from the Polish-speaking provinces of Podolia and Volhynia in White Russia, moved by religious feeling for the land, immigrated to Palestine to await the coming Day of Redemption. They were adhering to the Talmudic injunction to leave the Diaspora and "ascend" (*aliya*) to the Land of Israel. By settling in Israel, raising their families there, and building synagogues and schools, by studying, praying, and delighting in the grace of the Lord with song and dance, the Hasidim believed they would hurry the footsteps of the coming Messiah.

The Hasidim adhered to the Jewish revivalist movement inspired by the Baal Shem Tov in mid-eighteenth-century Poland. The Baal Shem Tov (Master of the Good Name) inspired an emotion-filled Judaism which appealed to ordinary people not learned in Torah and Talmud, as were the religious scholars. The Baal Shem Tov stressed the simplicity of faith in a God who could be encountered not only in prayer and fasting but also in the experiences of eating, drinking, and dancing. In formulating a mode of Judaic practice that stressed immediate, subjective experience, the Baal Shem Tov challenged the generations-old communal office of the rabbi in guiding every aspect of the daily lives of Jews by interpreting and administering the ritual law. In place of rabbinic authority, Hasidim recognized the inspired spiritual genius of the Tzaddik, the "righteous one."

And so in 1777 the spiritual ardents set out on a journey to the Land of Israel that would last six months. They traveled by animal-drawn carriages and carts to the port city of Odessa on the Black Sea. From there they were carried by a large sea barge to Istanbul, where they met with the local Sephardic Jewish officials. The Turkish Jews looked down on such a ragtag group but, given the sacredness of their journey, secured for them the necessary documents for immigration to Turkish-governed Palestine.

The Hasidim journeyed down the Turkish coast to Izmir, and after several storms and days of seasickness arrived in the Bay of Haifa, where they endured the ordeal of a hazardous approach by rowboats from the anchored barge to the sandy beach. With the first steps in the Covenant Land, the Hasidim burst forth in song; they danced, wept, prayed, and kissed the earth and one another.

After resting a few days, the group climbed onto donkeys to begin the journey to the Galilean hill town of Safed. They would have preferred to go to Jerusalem, but they feared that the Turkish authorities would extract from them thousands of piastres for a tax debt left by the last eastern European Ashkenazi group to settle in Jerusalem at the beginning of the eighteenth century. After

Jerusalem, no city held greater sanctity than Safed. It was the place where Cabalistic mysticism had developed and where so many Jewish sages and saints had laid their bones. The mountain air of Safed was clean and pure; the food was cheap, delicious, and plentiful. The leaders of the Sephardic *kollel* (community) met the Hasidim and showed them houses left empty by Jews who had perished in an earthquake.

The Sephardim found the ways of the Hasidim strange. Making no allowance for the hot summer climate, the Hasidim persisted in wearing the heavy black gabardine coats and fur-trimmed hats for which they were known in Poland. Unlike the Sephardim, they knew no Arabic and refused to learn any. Nor did they know the Spanish Ladino dialect which the Sephardim used among themselves. As for Hebrew (technically a common language), the Ashkenazic pronunciation was so guttural, so hard on the ears that the Sephardim could not bear the sound.

From the time the Hasidim arrived in Safed, the Sephardim, knowing there was no money to build new synagogues, invited the Hasidim to their own synagogues and allowed them to hold their own services there. The sight and sounds of the Hasidim at prayer dramatized the differences between the two peoples. At one point "the Sephardim had generously agreed to partition their own synagogue into two sections, with a thin wall dividing the two congregations. To their surprise and horror, the Sephardic prayers were drowned out by the cacophonous outpourings of Hasidic devotional passion."[2]

Istanbul Jewish officials, who had sent emissaries to raise money from Sephardic communities throughout the Mediterranean basin, could now canvass eastern Europe for funds to support the Hasidim as well as the Sephardim. And money was needed more than ever. For the Hasidim, continuing the tradition of their community in Poland, declined to work in Palestine. Theirs was a life of prayer and study. In Poland their devotions were subsidized by charity and by wives who opened shops to support their husbands and children. But in Palestine all the shops were run by Arabs or by Sephardim who were in business with Arabs.

At the beginning of the nineteenth century, Hasidism's archrival, the Perushim, also began immigrating to Palestine. These Jews, also an Ashkenazic community, filled the Talmudic seminaries of Poland and Russia, and took their inspiration from the Gaon of Vilna. A pietist and Orthodox Jewish rabbinical movement, the Perushim, or "separatists," believed that the Law meant separation from the secular world. In the eyes of the Perushim, the Hasidic movement, which stressed emotional prayer and embraced the charismatic personality of the Tzaddik, was an illegitimate cult. The Gaon of Vilna deplored Hasidism for preferring religious ecstasy to Talmudic study. The lowest point of relations between the Hasidim and Perushim had occurred in 1772, during the Passover festival, when the Gaon of Vilna excoriated the Hasidim, excommunicating them from the House of Israel. They should be "ostracized, cast out, and isolated," he said, and "no good Jew should have anything to do with them."[3] The condemnation poisoned relations between the two religious communities in Palestine through the nineteenth century down to the present day.

But the Perushim were driven to Palestine by the same forces of anti-Jewish oppression in Poland and White Russia that had earlier caused the exodus of the Hasidim. Tsar Alexander I created a huge Jewish ghetto in 1804 when he issued the proclamation that confined Jews to the Pale of Settlement, a narrow, infertile piece of western Russia. And Napoleon's threatened invasion of White Russia in 1806 created such turmoil that the Gaon of Vilna was moved to remind his followers that now, more than ever before, a Jew's presence in the Land of Israel would hasten the Redemption and liberate all of world Jewry from wicked gentile rulers. The Gaon's words could not hide the Perushim's jealously that the Hasidim were already in the Land of Israel, spreading their gospel of the Tzaddik and practicing their cult of spontaneous prayer.

The Sephardim in Safed received the Perushim with the same generosity they had earlier shown to the Hasidim, but with different consequences. It was not long before the Sephardim recognized that the Perushim were smarter and more disciplined, but less warm and flexible, than the Hasidim. The Sephardim could also see that the Perushim had no inclination to respect the seniority of the Sephardim in the land, to allow the Sephardim to represent them to the Turkish government, and to live from the moneys made available to them by Sephardic leaders in Palestine and Istanbul.

The distinction among the three groups of Jews could be seen by where they lived in the mountain town of Safed: Hasidim at the upper level, Perushim at the lower level, with Sephardim in rows of tiny stone houses between them, mediating the endless quarrels between the two communities of Ashkenazim, united only in their common use of the Yiddish language.

Only natural disaster would bring Palestine's Jews together. It occurred on Sunday, January 1, 1837, when the Galilee suffered a devastating earthquake. The earth exploded, consuming houses, people, and whole villages. Tiberias and Safed were destroyed. The American missionary William M. Thomson, who went to Safed to offer his help, observed that "It is not in the power of language to overstate such a ruin.... Safed was but is not ... [a] most hideous spectacle.... Nothing met the eye but a vast chaos of stone and earth, timber and boards ... mingled in horrible confusion."[4] Jewish houses built on the side of Safed's mountain lay in the path of the destruction; Muslim houses, built on level ground below, suffered less. All of Safed's fourteen synagogues were destroyed; half of Safed's four thousand Jews were killed.

The earthquake convinced six hundred Perushim to leave Safed for Jerusalem, where they collided with both the Sephardim and the Hasidim, also driven to the city. Beginning with dress. The distinctive black coats and hats of the Ashkenazim (Hasidim and Perushim together) the Sephardim saw as unsuitable to Jerusalem's oppressive summer heat and ridiculous in appearance. In the eyes of the Ashkenazim, the Sephardim were Jews in Arab disguise. Sephardic men wore long flowing robes and turbans on their heads that made them indistinguishable from Muslims. The Sephardim would not defer to the superior religious wisdom of the Ashkenazim, for the Sephardim also had their share of religious scholars, whose studies were supported by the community treasury.

Unlike the Ashkenazim, the Sephardim were willing to work. More than half of Jerusalem's Sephardim were employed in a variety of crafts and trades as silver- and goldsmiths, tanners, dyers, glaziers, shoemakers, and weavers. So heavily were the Sephardim involved in the merchant life of Jerusalem's central market that Muslim shoppers had to observe the Jewish Saturday Sabbath because so many shops were closed.

The Sephardim and Ashkenazim of Jerusalem had little in common beyond a common fear of Turkish and Arab tax officers and an urgent need for the charity money raised abroad to sustain the entire Jewish community of Palestine. The competitive search for charity money, and the endless wrangling over how that money should be distributed, increased the divisions among all three groups.

The thought of the hardships to be endured in Palestine without money tempered the desire of potential Ashkenazic immigrants, who otherwise extolled the Land of Israel and emphasized the *mitzva*, or "good deed," performed by anyone willing to undertake the arduous journey. At times it seemed that only the elderly were encouraged to make *aliya* to the sacred land. The nephew of the Baal Shem Tov declared: "The truth is that living in Eretz Israel is very good for the elderly but not for the young. . . . When you reach seventy and have enough money then you may joyously come here. . . ."[5] Even Hasidic leaders such as the Maggid of Mezrich looked suspiciously on the argument that immigration to Palestine was the ultimate goal of Jewish life. "To service God in exile," he once said, "was therefore more within the grasp of the devout than to serve Him in Palestine."

Still, for the sake of charity money many Perushim immigrated to Palestine—so many that by the twentieth century they outnumbered both Sephardim and Hasidim combined. This money, known in Hebrew as *haluka* ("distribution"), was the life's blood of the community. *Haluka* made possible the growth of the Jewish community of Palestine from 5,000 in 1839 to 10,000 in 1856, and then to 25,000 in 1880.[6]

But *haluka* also mired Jews in poverty, indolence, ignorance, and despotism. The rabbinical leaders of the Ashkenazic community who presided over the *haluka* enjoyed powers of life and death over all members. In time, Jerusalem's Jews would come to fear their rabbis almost as much Turkish governors and Arab tax collectors.

The *haluka* distribution tended to underscore the social differences among the Jews, favoring the religious scholar above the workingman. In the Sephardic community little or no *haluka* was given to those who worked; charity was bestowed only on the poor and the full-time religious scholar. A sizable percentage of *haluka* was set aside for payment of the community tax, most notably the poll tax. The Ashkenazim varied the *haluka* slightly. Every member of the community received charity, scholars or not; but those who were not scholars were required to put in at least three hours of religious study daily in order to be eligible for charity.[7]

The practice of *haluka* and the recognition that Jews abroad were willing to send money to their fellow Jews in Palestine emboldened Turkish tax authorities to inflate their tax assessments of Jews, and arbitrarily to add new assessments to a lengthy list of customary taxes. In addition to the head tax levied on all *dhimmis* in Muslim society, Jews were taxed for entering the country or for traveling from one place to another. Always there were taxes for setting foot in Jerusalem, for praying at the Western Wall, or for burying one's dead in the Jewish cemetery on the Mount of Olives. Muslim villagers in Silwan in the Kidron Valley were paid to avoid desecrating Jewish grave sites in the neighborhood. There were taxes for repairing a synagogue, for purchasing sacramental wine, for obtaining clean water. As the interest on unpaid Jewish taxes mounted, tax money went to paying off these charges, leaving the principal hardly touched.

Tax demands were often arbitrary. The annual tax was set at 2,000 piastres, a sum that might rise to 50,000 or 75,000, depending on money needed by the provincial pasha to pay his own debts or make a remittance to Istanbul. Jews could be taxed with impunity because, unlike Muslims, neither the sultan nor the provincial pasha feared a Jewish tax rebellion. Taxes kept the Jewish community of Palestine destitute. In 1816 the Jews of Tiberias had to mortgage their synagogue to pay off their tax debt.

Extorting money from Jews reached new levels of refinement. The villagers of Silwan in the Kidron Valley made a practice of dumping unsold produce on the doorsteps of Jewish homes, then returning the next day to demand payment for their goods. Jews paid, out of fear that the police would be called to collect their tax debt. A British traveler noted that "the extortions and oppressions were so numerous that it was said of the Jews that they had to pay for the very air they breathed."[8] Another traveler observed that "when a Jew walked among [the Muslims] in the market, one would throw a stone at him in order to kill him, another would pull his beard and a third his ear lock, yet another spit in his face." In 1839 the newly arrived British vice-consul wrote, "What the Jew has to endure, at all hands, is not [to] be told."[9]

When the Muslims were not imposing taxes, the Jews were taxing themselves. The Ashkenazim resented the Sephardim for exploiting their seniority in the Holy Land by forcing the Ashkenazim to pay a tax both for meat provided by Sephardim slaughterers and for burying the Ashkenazi dead in burial grounds controlled by the Sephardim. Eventually the Ashkenazim gained their own meat slaughterers and cemeteries, but until they did so they were at the mercy of Sephardic taxes.

Hasidim and Perushim had come to the Holy Land to pray in wait for the Messiah. Ashkenazi boys went to religious study from about the age of ten; girls prepared for puberty, marriage, and the immediate bearing of children. The historian Sherman Lieber tells us that "Many girls were matched and mated at the age of 12 to 14; unmarried girls of 16 were labeled spinsters."[10] These early marriages ruined the health of the girls, who by the time they reached their twenties had borne four or five children, with more expected. Yet they were not meek women, silent in the presence of men, unwilling to take issue with a male's opinion. An English physician remarked, "The Jewesses in Jerusalem speak in a decided and firm tone, unlike the hesitating and timid voice of the Arab and Turkish females; and claim the privilege of differing from their husbands, and maintaining their own opinion."[11]

Like their Muslim and Christian counterparts, Jewish women went to market fully covered, but without a veil. A Jewess covered her head with a cloth, wore long sleeves and a shawl, and left her jewelry at home. So concerned were Ashkenazi men that their women not distract them from their prayer and study, that a set of prohibitions prescribed where and at what times a woman might appear outside her house. Women under sixty were not allowed to appear in a gentile's house at all, nor in another Jewish home unaccompanied by her husband, nor at the bakery without escort, nor in the evening hours on the street.

In Jerusalem, Jews were the object of cruel contempt from Muslims and even more so from Arab Christians and their clergymen. For centuries under Muslim rule, Jews were prohibited from setting foot on the Temple Mount, and if they were seen in the vicinity of the Church of the Holy Sepulchre they risked being stoned or beaten to death. On the streets of any town in Palestine, a Jew was in danger of being robbed or simply accosted for being a Jew.[12] It was not uncommon to hear of Jews kidnaped and held for ransom, as was Rabbi Mendel of Shklov, an Ashkenazi community leader who, after settling in Palestine in 1808, was ransomed for six thousand piastres.

No story more poignantly dramatizes the harshness of life for Jews in Jerusalem than that of the Bergman family. Eliezer Bergman, a Bavarian Jew of thirty-five years of age, with his wife, five children, and widowed mother, arrived in Palestine in January 1835, during the regime of Ibrahim Pasha. Bergman was a promising religious scholar who did not disdain common labor. He believed that working Israel's land would hasten the Redemption. For travel funds he turned to Jewish officials in Amsterdam, who were responsible for arranging Jewish immigration to Palestine. They refused him help on the argument that only those exclusively dedicated to a life of prayer and scriptural study deserved charity money. Any Jew, like Bergman, willing to work should stay in the Diaspora, make money, and contribute toward the sustenance of Palestine's religious scholars. Bergman received the money he needed from his father-in-law.

The Bergmans traveled from Germany to Venice, and from there by sailboat to Beirut. In Beirut they met other Jews bound for the Land of Israel, and proceeded to Istanbul, where they boarded a ship bound for Jaffa. Arriving in Jaffa, they lost their money and belongings after the ship was driven by storm onto the rocks. Not undeterred, they made their way to Jerusalem, where they settled. They found the land "large and very good," and Jerusalem "very pretty."[13] Fruit and bread were available in quantity. Celia, Eliezer's wife, wrote about an exotic food—tomatoes, unknown in Bavaria: "They are used here as in Italy, as a salad, in soups, and as cooked vegetables. They can be prepared six different ways—and they are so tasty.... They are very healthy and are prescribed by doctors even for sick people. They are grown here, like potatoes with us [in Bavaria], but they are more expensive."[14]

Wanting first to try his luck as a farmer, Eliezer requested funds to purchase fields and vineyards and was refused by both community leaders and by his father-in-law. He settled for selling buttons and mirrors with stock purchased from a loan made to him by the Perushi community of Jerusalem. Not forgetting his father-in-law and the family he left behind in Bavaria, he sent a barrel of holy soil to them. He tutored adults in the Hebrew Scriptures. It was a surprise for him to learn that a number of Sephardim and even a few Ashkenazim were ignorant of Hebrew.

Celia ran her household with the help of her mother-in-law and did not employ a domestic "because they already marry at the age of 14. . . ."[15]

When he wasn't selling buttons and studying Torah, Eliezer was writing to Jews back in Bavaria to join him, advising them how to travel and what to expect when they arrived in the blessed land. He pointedly suggested that they bring an Arabic grammar but reassured them that in Jerusalem they could speak Hebrew or any of the major European languages. Celia simply wrote, bring *"Gesundheit and Geld,"* health and money.

Eliezer had interesting things to say about the all-consuming matter of the *haluka*. Jews who depended on *haluka* "live in terrible distress and poverty," he wrote, but he did not think that only the wealthy should therefore think of immigrating. For he believed that "the God of our Fathers will help" new settlers. Celia, however, warned that God could not always help.

> It is not an easy thing to live here. Therefore I do not advise a person [to come here] who is not strong enough to stand all this: one must suffer greatly. But of course that depends on how one stands the test. And after all has passed, the heart is lighter. It was especially hard for me because of the baby who made things difficult. May God grant her a long life.[16]

And the Bergmans did suffer. Celia's baby Sara died in May 1836, a few weeks after the death of her older sister, six-year-old Leah. Two years later, on consecutive days, the two Bergman sons died, leaving one child who would later die of the cholera epidemic that ravaged Jerusalem in the late 1830s. During a trip overseas in 1844, Eliezer received news that his wife had been murdered by Christians while walking in the alleyways near the Church of the Holy Sepulchre. And in 1852, while on a fund-raising mission, Eliezer himself died of typhus and was buried in Berlin.

Lamenting the woes of Palestine's Jews, one rabbi appealed directly for a British messiah: "Oh, when will the King of England come and deliver us."[17] The king of England did not come, but he did send his missionaries to convert the Jews. And he sent one of his noblest and richest Jewish subjects, Sir Moses Montefiore, a six-foot three-inch giant of energy, wealth, and goodwill.

Moses Montefiore was a ritually observant, progressive-minded, English-Jewish blue blood, who was married to a Rothschild daughter. He made so much money in investments that he quit the brokerage business in 1824 at age forty to devote himself to the cause of Jewish philanthropy. The goal he set for himself was nothing less than the rescue of Palestine's Jews from their impoverishment, a task which proved more difficult than he realized.

Montefiore made seven trips to Palestine, the first in 1827, the last in 1874 at the age of ninety. In that period of nearly fifty years the Jewish community of Palestine grew greatly, particularly in Jerusalem where a Jewish majority over Christians and Muslims was achieved by 1870. In those years Palestine emerged from the medieval world.[18] Palestinians began to wear Western clothes. Western Christian investors and philanthropists established banks, hospitals, and schools. New churches were built and old ones restored. Montefiore saw what the Christians were doing for their communities and vowed to do the same for his own brethren. From his first visit to Palestine, he fell in love with the country and embraced its problems.

To comprehend the scope of the Jewish economic problem, Montefiore commissioned a census, paying a Spanish dollar to every Jewish adult and a half-dollar to every Jewish child under thirteen willing to be counted.[19] Jerusalem's Ashkenazi rabbis reacted furiously to this census as a sinful violation of the divine prohibition that God had uttered against King David, who had also undertaken to count the House of Israel.

But Montefiore persisted. From his census he discovered a Jewish poverty so great that fathers sold their children to monasteries rather than see them die of hunger. If poverty and hunger were to be ended, projects had to be devised to get Jews off *haluka* and make them economically self-sufficient. Here Montefiore ran straight into the wall that Jerusalem's rabbis had erected between Jews and the outer world. For the rabbis understood that any gains in Jewish self-sufficiency would bring a lessened dependency on *haluka* and thereby a decline in the powers of the rabbis administering the funds.

Again Montefiore persisted. Apart from many gifts of money, he endeavored in his five decades' involvement with Palestine to fund the work projects desperately needed. Jewish economic revival had to begin with agriculture. Palestine's Jews, like their ancient Israelite ancestors, had to return to the land. So Montefiore bought fertile land in Safed and Jaffa, paid for seed and for Jews to farm the land, whose produce he then bought and sold in order to return the money to its producers.

More works followed.[20] In order to draw Jews away from the medicine dispensed by Christian missionaries, in 1838 he opened the first Jewish medical clinic in Jerusalem. To move Jews away from the overcrowded and oppressed Jewish quarter, he built outside Jerusalem's walls a long stone house of worker apartments, Misheknot Sha'nanim (Dwellings of Tranquility), for local craftsmen. Other projects were less successful. Planned trade schools for young men and women failed because of rabbinical opposition, as did the construction of a windmill intended for a flour mill in Jerusalem.

Montefiore's philanthropic efforts were largely a failure, as were later agricultural projects funded by Baron Edmond de Rothschild. Few Jews were willing to risk rabbinical censure and the possibility of community ostracism, including the loss of *haluka,* by participating in the projects of a man who brought with him ideas from a Western secular culture. Yet Montefiore's great achievement was to have planted the seeds of Jewish self-sufficiency in Palestine. In his own paternalistic way he was a precursor to the Zionist ideologues and pioneers who followed him to Palestine a quarter-century after his last visit in 1875.

Through most of the nineteenth century, the Jews of Palestine lived from *haluka* and huddled together in tiny communities in Jerusalem, Safed, Hebron, and Tiberias. They suffered what they had to suffer from the Muslim masters of the land, and from year to year prayerfully awaited the Messianic Redemption. Their lot was significantly improved when the Ottoman government began to institute legal reforms following the Crimean War of 1853–1856. But it was not until the last quarter of the nineteenth century that these pious traditionalists were decisively challenged when a new kind of Jew made his appearance in Palestine—a Zionist Jew with a significantly different idea of who he was and what it meant to live and work in the ancestral land.

PART TWO

The Holy Land Reclaimed

CHAPTER FIVE

Millenarian Missionaries

> I will give unto thee and unto thy seed after thee the
> land of thy sojournings, all the land of Canaan for
> an everlasting possession.
> —Genesis 17:8
>
> If the grant of the Almighty maker and governor of
> the universe can constitute a legal title to an
> everlasting possession, the claim of the Jews to the
> land of Palestine will always be reasonable.
> —Charles Jerram, English millenarian, 1796

The Western penetration of Palestine from the early nineteenth century through the period of Muhammad Ali's rule was spurred by an extraordinary burst of Christian religious energy in Britain, known as millenarianism. This was the belief that only after the Jews returned to their ancestral homeland would Jesus return to earth to inaugurate the thousand-year reign of God over the world.

We have already seen how Lord Shaftesbury's efforts in the late 1830s to influence Lord Palmerston with millenarian thinking played a role in shaping British policy toward Palestine and the Middle East. Millenarians not only preached the gospel of the Jews' restoration, they journeyed to Palestine to work for it. Their preaching, soul saving, and philanthropy confirmed British leaders in their belief that Palestine belonged to the Christian West and that the Jews were Britain's best friend in Palestine.

In 1799, the year of Bonaparte's invasion of Palestine, the

Church Mission Society was established in Britain. Ten years later arose the Society for the Propagation of Christianity among the Jews, or the London Jews Society, as it was called. The founding of these two organizations in the wake of Napoleon's defeat in the East united evangelical Christianity with imperialistic expansion—two of the most powerful forces in Britain at the turn of the century. Together they spread a brand of Christian colonialism that had not been seen in Palestine since the Crusades.

Palestine was not just another foreign colony to Britain's empire builders. Palestine was the Holy Land. In the warm memory of Sunday School Bible days, the Holy Land was the Englishman's spiritual motherland, as much *his land* as the land of Muslims, Jews, Greeks, and Syrians who actually lived there. Christian religious sentiment could not help but be part of every political decision regarding Palestine taken by the British government. By first planting himself in the country and later by taking possession of it, the Britisher, churchman and politician, layman and aristocrat, believed he was adding not just another foreign colony to a distant empire but in some profoundly spiritual way "returning home." And none desired more fervently to return home than the millenarians, those scores of Englishmen who anticipated the imminent return of Christ on earth and who saw the return of the Jews to Palestine as the necessary prelude to the millennium.

In the years following the French Revolution of 1789, and as the turn of the century neared, millenarian beliefs gained currency among the British Christian public. Foremost was the belief in the prophecies of the Book of Daniel and the Apocalypse of Saint John in the New Testament—that earthquakes, fires, floods, and wars would be "signs" that the world had entered the Endtime before Christ's Second Coming. The bloody upheaval of the French Revolution was interpreted to be one of those signs.

Millenarians, who were in the forefront of the religious revival under way in Britain in the mid-eighteenth century, had deep roots going back to the sixteenth-century Puritan revolution. By the late eighteenth century the millenarians counted in their number such distinguished thinkers as the chemist Joseph Priestley and the mathematician Isaac Newton. Millenarians scorned church authority and tradition. The bedrock of their beliefs was the acceptance of the Bible as the literal Word of God. Nowhere had the Bible spoken more clearly, millenarians said, than in the Hebrew prophetic vision. They interpreted Daniel's reference to the Fourth Beast to be ancient pagan Rome, whose wicked powers had been inherited by the Holy Roman Empire, at the heart of which stood the medieval Catholic church.

In the late 1790s millenarians preached that the evil Catholic empire had begun to collapse. The fall of the French Catholic monarchy in the revolution, the subsequent military defeat of the Papal States, and the exile in 1797 of Pope Pius VI himself—these events were taken by the millenarians as sure evidence of the fulfill- ment of the scriptural prophesy that the centuries-old reign of the evil empire had come to a halt. The Endtime was at hand. And when Bonaparte invaded Egypt in 1798, marched into Palestine a year later, and threatened the very existence of the Ottoman Empire, mil- lenarians (who linked the sultan to the pope as the anti-Christ) were convinced that these events were scripturally foretold as the cata- clysmic signs of the Endtime. Bonaparte was taken to be an instru- ment of divine will, just as the Persian King Cyprus had been heralded by the prophet Ezekiel as God's instrument. As one should not oppose the divine will, so the millenarians preached that the British government should not oppose Bonaparte, nor should it align itself with the satanic Turkish sultan. In the days following Bona- parte's return to France from Egypt, when the English expected a cross-channel invasion by the French, men assigned to military de- fenses in an English channel town reportedly refused to work, be- lieving that Napoleon's invasion was divinely ordained.

Among the most influential English millenarians was Joseph Bicheno. In 1792 he wrote a book whose long and vivid title was in- tended as a warning bell: *The Signs of the Times, or the Overthrow of the Papal Tyranny in France, the Prelude of Destruction to Popery and Despotism, but of Peace to Mankind.* Bicheno argued that the Hebrew prophets who proclaimed the Messianic Redemption spoke of God's ending of Israel's exile. To Bicheno and his avid readers the implica- tion was obvious: since the world had now reached the Endtime, Jewish "wandering" too would end. God's chosen would be restored to the Covenant Land.

The medieval Catholic church, following the theology of Saint Augustine, had taught that the Jews were exiled from their home- land and forever damned for rejecting Christ. Bicheno reversed that argument, arguing that the law, the land, and the promise of messianic Redemption were first given to Jews. He believed with the Hebrew prophets that Israel's exile and dispersion were instructive punishments meant to bring about repentance and obedience. But that punishment was now ending. Citing Saint Paul's injunction that eventually "all Israel will be saved" (Romans 11:26), Bicheno held that the restoration of the Jews to their ancestral homeland and their conversion to Christian faith was a part of the Endtime, a prelude to the Second Coming. So confident was Bicheno of this eschatological vision that he published a timetable. The Jewish restoration would begin in 1819; forty-five years later in 1864, after all the world's Jews had returned to the Holy Land, Christ would return to earth.[1]

Millenarians disagreed among themselves as to whether the Jews' restoration or conversion came first; but there was no disagreement about the crucial role God had assigned to the Jews in the cosmic drama of Redemption. For Bicheno this meant that Britain must submit to the divine will and bend every effort to end the exile of the Jews and bring about their return to the homeland. This idea of the Jewish restoration found favor among the English masses; it even entered the circles of the established Anglican church and influenced many clergymen. The Jewish restoration became a fertile idea which blended with Britain's imperial ambitions.

By the third decade of the nineteenth century, both the Church Missionary Society and the London Jews Society had begun to send their missionaries to Palestine with the specific charge to convert the Jews to Christianity and do everything possible to aid and comfort them in the Last Days prior to the Second Coming of Christ. The earliest of the English missionaries was Joseph Wolff, the converted son of a Bavarian rabbi, who reached Jaffa in late December 1821.[2] Energetic, irascible, and a dogmatic messianist, Wolff wasted no time in making contact with leaders of Jerusalem's Jewish community, which numbered 2,800 persons (half of Palestine's Jewish population) in a city of 10,000 Muslims and 4,500 Christians. He befriended the Jewish merchant Joseph Amzalag, who opened doors for him, and Amzalag looked to Wolff to be his window to the world. For in Amzalag's eyes Wolff and the missionaries who followed him, for all their zealotry about the Last Judgment and Christ's Second Coming, had important connections to the British Empire. They could intercede with Muslim authorities in behalf of

Jews, and with their European contacts they could provide valuable information about economic and political developments. They could also post letters that evaded the Jews' own mail censor.

From the beginning, the obstacles Wolff encountered in Jerusalem were formidable. He could not have arrived at a worse time. The Greek rebellion against Turkey had begun, and Muslims suspected all Christians of revolutionary tendencies. An Ottoman law prohibited Christians from living in Jerusalem. Exceptions were made only for heads of minority communities or keepers of holy places.[3] To the chagrin of local Latin and Greek church leaders, Wolff was made an exception because he was a representative of Britain, the powerful Western nation that had helped the sultan evict the infidel Bonaparte from the holy soil of Islam. Further, Protestantism was not a recognized religious minority, had no status in the Ottoman category of non-Muslim minorities, and therefore was not despised by Muslim religious authorities.

Wolff took up residence in the Jewish quarter, struck up conversations with any Jew who would talk to him, and, with the help of Amzalag, got himself invited to Jewish homes, not a few of them the homes of rabbis. The rabbis were drawn to him, as he to them, by that odd logic which says that anyone who could be so woefully wrong about so fundamental a matter as the Messianic Redemption is worth talking to.

Wolff struggled to learn Hebrew in order to argue with rabbis about Jesus Christ, often until early morning. Rabbis who learned that he was a converted Jew believed it to be their duty to convert him back to the faith of Israel. One of the favorite topics of their discussion was the date of the Redemption, and how to interpret current signs of that event.

When he was not studying Hebrew or cultivating relations with the rabbis, Wolff was busy in Jerusalem's old city alleys, handing out copies of the New Testament in Hebrew to Jews who would burn them, wrap their food in them, or sell them to the Muslims, who were happy to find scarce paper. Those few Jews who showed an interest in the Christian Scriptures ran the severe risk of being publicly flogged by community elders or ostracized altogether by the Jewish community. Some Jews simply tore out the New Testament pages of Wolff's Bible and happily kept the Old Testament parts.

One outspoken Jew, fed up with Wolff's complaints about closed-minded Jews, faulted his naiveté about the local Christians of Jerusalem.

> You wish to convert us to Christianity. Look to Mount Calvary, where Jesus of Nazareth was crucified, of whom you say that he came to establish peace on earth. Look to Calvary; there his follow-ers reside—Armenians, Copts, Greeks, Abyssinians, and Latins; all bear the name of Christians, and Christians are shedding the blood of Christians on the same spot where Jesus of Nazareth died.[4]

If Wolff found Jerusalem's Jews closed-minded, they found him obsessed. It seemed to them that this Christian missionary, who went to great lengths to proclaim his love of the Jewish people and their place in divine providence, was especially offensive in expounding his views of the rabbinical wisdom represented by the Talmud. Wolff refused to study the Talmud, discuss its contents, or have anything to do with Jewish ritual derived from it. He once embarrassed his Jew-ish host by refusing to wash his hands before the blessing for the evening meal because he viewed it as a Talmudic ritual.[5] To Wolff, as to all the Christian missionaries who would follow him, the Talmud was an illicit rabbinic commentary on the Torah, wrongly interrupt-ing the continuity between the true promises of God made known in the Torah and the real fulfillment of those promises revealed in the New Testament.

Missionaries who followed Wolff noted the vulnerability of Jews to the exploitations and bullying of Muslims. W. B. Lewis, who in 1823 was sent by the London Jews Society to establish a permanent Protestant mission in Jerusalem, observed firsthand the despicable treatment of Jews at the hands of the ruling Muslim majority.[6] Be-yond the crippling taxes which kept Jews as well as Christians in a permanent state of poverty, Jews were harassed daily. In the streets they feared for their very lives.

Commiserating with the pitiful conditions of Jewish life in Palestine was not enough for Lewis; he wanted to change those con-ditions. He was one of the first to recognize that while Palestine's Latin Christians were protected by Catholic France, and the Greek and Arab Orthodox shielded by Russia, the Jews had no European nation they could look to for support against the exploitiveness of Ottoman rule. In Lewis's mind, only Protestant Britain could provide Jews the support they needed.

In 1825 the London Jews Society sent George Dalton, a medical missionary to the Jews and the only physician in Palestine in his time. Jews, defying the rabbinical prohibition against cooperating with missionaries, sought his services. The need for medicine overcame their fear of exclusion from the Jewish community.

Dalton found Palestine a disease-ridden country. Jews in particular faced major health problems. The Jewish quarter of Jerusalem was a breeder of disease, its houses confining, suffocating, and unhealthy. Missionary John Nicolayson, who joined Dalton in 1825, reported that "one great cause of the shocking diseases and accumulated wretchedness among Jews here, is the manner in which they are compelled to crowd and herd together; three or four families in one little dark, damp and dirty room."[7]

Nicolayson, who succeeded Wolff as Britain's missionary to the Jews, was no less indefatigable in preaching the gospel of Christ's Second Coming. But the Jews ignored him as they had Wolff. In Tiberias, Nicolayson once tried to converse with some Hasidim, but they loudly sang melodies whenever he steered the conversation to religion.[8] Nicolayson often teamed with the American missionary William Thomson, who, in contrast to the more genteel Nicolayson, was more outspoken in condemning Jewish stubbornness in refusing conversion. About the Jews, Thomson confessed: "I have no heart to enter into their history, or dwell on their absurd superstitions, their intense fanaticism, or their social and domestic institutions and manners, comprising an incredible and grotesque mélange of filth and finery, Pharisaic self-righteousness and Sadducean licentiousness."[9]

Thomson led the American missionary venture in Palestine. Americans did not share the British belief in the central role to be played by Jews in the restoration and the Second Coming. To them the Jews showed no sign of recognizing and receiving Christ, and were plainly doomed; no missionary work could turn them around. The Americans spent a few years in Palestine before leaving that area to the British and moving on to Beirut, where they directed their efforts toward Muslims and the Arab members of the Greek Orthodox church.

The Jewish Messiah did not appear in 1840, as predicted, nor did world Jewry answer the British call for a return to the Holy Land. The conditions of Jewish life in Europe were not so deplorable as to make journeying to an impoverished, diseased Muslim country desirable. For most Jews, the Psalmist's refrain "If I forget you, O Jerusalem . . ." was honored in prayer alone.

Despite the rejection of the message of Christ brought to them, Palestine's Jews felt that Wolff, Lewis, Dalton, and Nicolayson were working for their benefit. At no time was this feeling more dramatically reinforced than in 1840, in the terrible time of the Damascus Blood Libel charge. A Syrian Jew was accused of kidnaping a Christian in order to use his blood to bake unleavened Passover matzos. The accusation—one with ancient origins—touched off mob actions against Jews throughout the Middle East. Upon hearing of the events, Nicolayson acted heroically. He sent a fellow missionary to Damascus to investigate the charge, then published articles and wrote letters to various Muslim authorities in Damascus and Istanbul calling the accusation false and urging protection of the Jews in Palestine.

Despite his zeal, Nicolayson proved no more successful in converting Jews than Wolff. In April 1839, after three and a half years of instruction, Nicolayson administered the holy sacrament to the four members of the Simeon Rosenthal family, said to be the first Jewish family to convert to the church since earliest Christian times.[10] Apart from this single accomplishment, the Christian mission to the Jews in Palestine was a failure. Out of dire need Jews might accept medicine, money, even a job, but not the Christian religion. The missionary preaching of Christ to Jews had only the effect of forcing Ashkenazim and Sephardim, who otherwise detested each other, into a common front.[11]

THE APPOINTMENT of a permanent British vice-consul to Jerusalem was the first objective of Lord Shaftesbury and his fellow millenarians in the London Jews Society; the second was to build a Protestant church in Jerusalem. Nicolayson raised money and purchased a site inside Jaffa Gate, on the edge of the Armenian quarter, where in 1839 construction began of a Gothic building that would be consecrated a few years later as Christ Church. To head this church the British Parliament in 1841, with the strong approval of Queen Victoria (who was responding to the entreaties of Prussia's devout

King Frederick William IV), enacted a law to establish a joint Anglican-Lutheran bishopric for Jerusalem.

What joy for the millenarians! First a British consulate which would actively encourage the restoration of the Jews to the Holy Land; then the construction of Christ Church in Jerusalem; and now the establishment of a Protestant bishopric for the city. The Messiah, they rejoiced, could not be far behind.

The millenarians had had an impact on the staid Church of England. The Archbishop of Canterbury and other Anglican clergy felt that only with a church in the Holy City could the Church of England demonstrate to the English missionaries that their clergy did not lag behind them in love for Christ's homeland. The building of a church was a symbol of the seriousness of Britain's missionary goal. As Vice-Consul Young put it, "The Protestant communion is the only Christian church in the world that is yet without a temple on Mount Zion to her Master."[12]

Palmerston had prevailed on the sultan to grant permission for the building of Christ Church despite the old Islamic policy that allowed only the repair of old churches, not the building of new ones. Muslims in Jerusalem were now shocked to see rising, within Jaffa Gate and a stone's throw from the city's prison, an imposing new Protestant church. Christ Church was consecrated in January 1849 at a ceremony boycotted by all the local Christian churchmen. Latins, Greeks, and Armenians, who had their own churches in Jerusalem, saw the Gothic structure as a grandiose Protestant and Western intrusion into a Holy Land that they considered their own possession. Arab Christians refused to attend services at the church because the Bible was read in Hebrew. Jews declined to attend for fear of being punished by their rabbis.

Michael Solomon Alexander, a converted Jew who had taught Hebrew at King's College in London, was the first Anglo-Prussian bishop appointed to Jerusalem. He was, in the historian A. L. Tibawi's nicely turned phrase, the "Hebrew Christian who was to lead fallen Israel to Christian truth."[13] But it was Alexander himself who would fall from an overdose of bad luck. He refused to travel to Palestine on the British ship assigned to him because of its name, *Infernal,* and reluctantly agreed to leave on a second ship, *Destruction.* During his brief stay in the country, Alexander had no success in converting Jews. Jerusalem's rabbis, quickly responding to the dan-

ger they saw in the arrival of the bishop, issued a writ of excommunication against any Jew who went near Alexander or accepted gifts of
food, money, or medicine. Alexander died prematurely in 1845, short
of four years after taking up his post.

Considerably more success with Jews was enjoyed by James
Finn, Britain's second appointed consul (now a full consul) to
Jerusalem and perhaps the most fascinating of the Christians to settle
in Palestine. Finn, who had previously served in China and had
written books about the Jews of China, had become an expert in Jewish history and the Hebrew language. With his irrepressible wife
Elizabeth, in his long tenure as consul (1845–1863) he became a
zealous champion of the Jewish people and of their conversion to
Christ. If the nineteenth century was the "great century of Christian
missions," James Finn was the great man of his century in Palestine.

Finn arrived in Palestine in the spring of 1845. A photograph
shows him erect, with a slightly pompous lean of his back, dressed in
full consular uniform, hat, gloves and sword, mutton-chop whiskers,
curly hair, sensuous lower lip. Here was a man who truly believed
that God had gifted Britain with empire in order to spread the word
of Christ's gospel.

Finn worked indefatigably. He rose at dawn to an hour or two
of language study, concentrating on Hebrew, Arabic, and Turkish,
all of which he taught himself. After morning prayer services in the
consulate and later at Christ Church, he would turn to consular duties. When he was not on consular business he arranged for lectures
at the Jerusalem Literary Society, which he founded in the hope of
advancing the scholarly study of Palestine and the authentication of
the Bible.

Finn's consular duties often became indistinguishable from his
mission to the Jews. He found jobs for Jews and interceded with
Jerusalem's pasha to protect them from excessive taxes, unfair arrest,
or harassment by Muslims or Christians. He would ride out to the
sheiks, the tribal strongmen who controlled the roads, and through
bribery or persuasion arrange for safe passage of pilgrims coming
from England and continental Europe. He purchased land around
Jerusalem at a time when such purchases were officially prohibited
to foreigners. Like Moses Montefiore, he was well ahead of the times
in believing that farming the land was the only way for Jews to break
their economic dependency on Jerusalem's rabbinate. Finn's was a

Christian-inspired form of Zionism, stressing Jewish agricultural labor. There was no denying the sincerity of his attitude, which could take a romantic turn. Observing Jews as they worked in Abraham's vineyard, one of his land purchases near Jerusalem's Damascus Gate, he wrote that Jews were "carrying their baskets and tools on their shoulders; a ragged troop, very ragged but very happy, singing a chorus in Hebrew, 'We are laborers in the field of Abraham, our father.' "[14]

Finn's religious zeal was a match for his literary energy. He kept an extensive diary throughout the nearly two decades of his consulate, a diary later published as *Stirring Times* (1878), which provides a vivid account of Jerusalem and Palestine at midcentury. But Finn's extraordinary career ended in disgrace. His interminable meddling in the affairs of the Ottoman government finally embarrassed his superiors in London, and his quarrels with Bishop Samuel Gobat, Alexander's successor, damaged his relationship with the church. His philanthropy in behalf of poor Jews bankrupted him. After being ordered to resign, he left Jerusalem in 1865 owing a substantial sum to Jewish moneylenders, who petitioned the British government for payment.

Samuel Gobat became the new bishop of Jerusalem in 1845, after Alexander's death. Since the Archbishop of Canterbury had appointed Alexander, it was Prussia's turn to appoint the new bishop. Gobat, a French-speaking Swiss pastor ordained in both the Lutheran and Anglican churches, was fully a match for James Finn in missionary zeal and total dedication to his ideas. It was destined that these two men should dislike each other and work for the other's downfall.

The manifest failure of Bishop Alexander's mission to the Jews explains Bishop Gobat's decision to ignore them and instead to concentrate all his efforts on converting to Protestantism the Arab members of the Greek Orthodox church. "I knew that it was not the object of those who had appointed and sent me to Jerusalem that I should restrict myself to the work of an ordinary local pastor or missionary to the Jews," he once said. "I was a debtor not only to the Jews, but also to the ignorant Greek, Romanists, Armenians, Turks."[15]

Gobat's global vision was not popular in Britain, where religious leaders from the Archbishop of Canterbury to officials of the

London Jews Society regarded the mission to the Jews as the essential obligation of the Protestant bishopric in Palestine. Nor were government leaders pleased to learn that the Prussian appointment would upset the delicate balance between the churches in Jerusalem, putting at risk Britain's relationship with Orthodox Russia and with the Christian subjects of the sultan. But Gobat had his supporters among the members of the Church Missionary Society, who were disappointed that more than a decade of active preaching and service to the Jewish community had produced no more than thirty Jewish converts. A fortune in pound sterling had been spent in winning these precious souls to Christ. Gobat saw a more fertile field for Protestant converts among the Arab Orthodox, who were often alienated from the Greek bishops of the ancient Byzantine church in Palestine.

Gobat was like Finn in many respects, particularly in his obsessive study of foreign languages. In his autobiography he remarks on his rigorous routine: "I repaired to my room, shut the door, and wrote upon it, 'I will not open thee until I can read Ethiopic.' I had calculated that it would take me the whole day; but, behold at the end of the two hours, I could read pretty fluently."[16] Where Finn was naive and noble, Gobat was shrewd and calculating. He knew that the true candidate for conversion was not the adult but the child, and that a reliable way to reach the child was through education. First offer education, then preach Christ and the Protestant religion. Gobat lost no time in establishing a new set of Bible-reading schools in Jerusalem, Nablus, Nazareth, Jaffa, and Bethlehem, and in small towns in Transjordan. Inducements to students included free board and clothing, medicine, loans of money, and food. Gobat had no trouble recruiting teachers when he offered to pay decent and regular salaries.

Responding to these benefits, Muslim parents and their children were drawn to the schools, which instantly provoked the hostility of Muslim religious authorities. The opposition to Gobat in Nablus brought together Muslim clerics and Greek priests, who sought to discredit him. Gobat's reply was openly to castigate the "godless Greeks," as he called them. As for the Muslims, he agreed (a rare occurrence) with James Finn who had once said that "Mohammedan religion and Turkish misgovernment have degraded

Palestine to its present state." To both Gobat and Finn, the Muslims were victims of a false prophet.

It would not take long for Gobat's aggressive proselytizing of Arab Orthodox and Catholic youth to produce a reaction. In April 1851, in the tiny Transjordanian town of Salt, local Greek priests ran the teacher from Gobat's school out of town. It was a genuine loss, for the teacher offered, along with Bible, useful instruction in mathematics and languages. In a second incident in Nazareth, a Catholic mob attacked another Gobat school of the Church Missionary Society by smashing furniture and stoning the missionary teachers.[17]

Yet violence only seemed to strengthen Gobat in his convictions that for the sake of their souls Arab Christians had to be liberated through Protestantism from the superstitions of the Greek and Roman churches. The bishop's attitude caused consternation among his superiors in London and Berlin, who worried about their relations with the Vatican and the Greek patriarchate of Jerusalem. For the Anglican and Lutheran churches had established their combined bishopric in Palestine not only to win over the Jews but to promote unity among the churches of the Holy Land. In the thirty years of his residency in Jerusalem, Gobat had turned his back on both goals.

THROUGHOUT THE nineteenth century, millenarian Christians came to restore Palestine to the glory of Christ not known since the medieval Crusades. Behind them and others lay the politicians of Britain, Prussia, France, Russia, and Austria—all of them determined to gain influence in Palestine at a time when everyone knew that an international scramble for property and power would accompany the collapse of the Ottoman Empire. For that reason it was vitally important for the West to prop up the Noble Porte, particularly if tsarist Russia might benefit from a collapse. The test of that policy came with the outbreak of the Crimean War.

CHAPTER SIX

Building the New Jerusalem

> I certainly share the wish . . . to elevate Jerusalem to
> the status of a Christian Kingdom.
> —Kaiser Frederick William IV, 1840
>
> After God, [the consuls] are the most important
> persons in the Holy Land.
> —A German consul in the 1850s
>
> I shall never concede to these crazy Christians any
> road improvement in Palestine or they would then
> transform Jerusalem into a Christian madhouse.
> —Ottoman Vizier Fuad Pasha, 1850
>
> The Muslims and Jews do not hate each other . . . but
> to the Christians the Muslims bear hate.

The defeat of Ibrahim's army in 1841 returned the provinces of Syria and Palestine to the sultan. For the moment the confrontation feared by Europe, Turkey, and Russia was averted. But it was only a question of time before a new crisis provoked war. That crisis would occur with continued Russian aggression against Turkey, a development which a few years later brought about the Crimean War of 1853–1856 and plunged the West even more deeply into the life of Palestine.

To understand these developments we must look back on Russia's struggle against the Ottoman Empire and her deepening involvement in the Holy Land. Since the reign of Peter the Great (1689–1724), Russian policy had been to undermine the Ottoman Empire in order to introduce a Russian-led Eastern Orthodox church as the dominant religious force in the Middle East. Russian Slavophiles believed that the mission of Holy Russia was to save their Slav brethren from the Muslim infidel, beginning with the liberation of Palestine.[1]

In the 1774 Treaty of Kutchuk Kainardji, Orthodox Christian Russia had won from the sultan the right to protect the lives and properties of all Orthodox Christians in the Ottoman Empire. In that treaty Russia had also gained the former Ottoman provinces of Crimea, Wallachia, Moldavia, Bessarabia, and Georgia. Thereby the stage was set for Russian promotion of religious and nationalistic independence among all Ottoman Orthodox subjects, wherever they lived in the empire.

Yet little was done to extend Russian Orthodox influence in the Holy Land until the appearance of a British consul in Jerusalem in 1838. The establishment a few years later of the Anglo-Prussian bishopric provoked the Russians, especially when under Samuel Gobat the bishopric began proselytizing among Arab Orthodox Christians. Another source of concern to Russia was the rising numbers of Arab Orthodox who had already converted to the Catholic church. Many Arab Orthodox in Palestine, as in Lebanon and Syria, had joined the French-supported Uniate church, which worshiped according to the Byzantine rite but which, in protest against Greek hegemony over the Orthodox church, had aligned with Rome and recognized the pope's primacy.[2]

The Russian response in 1843 was to send out Archimandrite Porfiry Ouspensky on a ten months' expedition to investigate the situation of the Arab members of the Orthodox church in Palestine. The church was headed by ethnic Greek bishops who were perpetually in conflict with the predominantly Arab laity. Porfiry's task was to look for ways to reconcile Arabs and Greeks, and establish a Russian religious presence that would counter Protestant, Catholic, and Uniate influence.

It was not an easy task. The Arabs complained to Porfiry of poverty and hunger. They felt humiliated that their own Arab Orthodox priests were unschooled and that the Greeks would ordain only married Arab clergy so as to prevent any Arab becoming eligible for advancement to the rank of bishop. They further grumbled that money sent annually from Russia for the repair of churches fell into Greek pockets. "The only career [of every Greek priest]," it was said, "is to obtain more money to be able to intrigue . . . to become patriarch."[3] "Our millet is backward compared with others," Arabs lamented. "We have no ecclesiastical schools, no scientific library, even no properly organized preparatory schools. . . . We have to send our children to Western schools."[4]

Taking Arab complaints to the Greek patriarch and bishops, Porfiry heard in response well-rehearsed denials. The Greeks protested that they had spent all available funds as bribes to keep the Arab Orthodox from converting to other churches. Arabs were themselves to blame if schools were lacking and their churches in disrepair. Porfiry was reminded that the Greek bishops were the legal head of the Orthodox church in Palestine and guardians of the holy places. Weighed against those enormous responsibilities, the education and welfare of the Arab Orthodox community had to be secondary concerns.

To the argument that the Arab laity had a right to greater responsibility for the guardianship of the holy places, the Greeks replied that their guardianship was guaranteed by the decree of Selim I, conqueror of Jerusalem, to Patriarch Germanos—a decree which also excluded Arabs from the church's governing Brotherhood of the Holy Sepulchre.

It did not escape Porfiry's notice that in Greek eyes the Arab Orthodox, despite their devout faith, were merely "Arabs" and therefore indistinguishable from Muslims. And, like Muslims (Greeks were quick to point out), the Arab Orthodox practiced veiling, kept harems, and engaged in blood revenge.[5]

Nothing better conveys Greek contempt toward the Arabs than this exchange which took place between Ouspensky and Greek Patriarch Cyril:

> CYRIL: The Arabs are rascals. . . . They hate and defame us. You have no affection for us and defend them.
>
> OUSPENSKY: God knows the extent of my love towards you, but I pity the Arabs and I am prepared to defend them before anyone.
>
> CYRIL: They have no faith; they are barbarous, villains.

OUSPENSKY: You must teach them faith for you have fostered their unbelief.

CYRIL: They will not listen to us.

OUSPENSKY: This is not surprising, for you do not love but despise them. They are a martyr people. They are persecuted by the Muslims yet receive no protection from you. They even have nowhere to pray. The village churches are in a miserable condition.

CYRIL: We do not accept Arab priests among us so as not to lower our episcopal dignity.... Nor do we understand their language.

OUSPENSKY: Why not learn Arabic, or if you are too old, why not have an interpreter forward their requests?

CYRIL: We cannot introduce new customs.

OUSPENSKY: So you cling to your old habits. There will be no school for the sons of Arab priests; Arab widows and orphans will receive no shelter in convents; no Arab will be a bishop or head a monastery.[6]

Greek indifference to the Arab Orthodox had clearly cost the church members. There had been a precipitous decline of Arab Orthodox in Palestine, from ninety thousand in 1800 to only twenty thousand forty years later. Orthodox were scattered in seventeen villages and towns throughout the country. Meanwhile Catholic numbers, chiefly due to Arab Orthodox converts, had tripled.[7]

The Greek bishops' indifference to the Arab members of the Orthodox church illustrated the defensiveness of a church hierarchy obsessed with its status and survival. The Greek bishops could not pay attention to the Arab Orthodox because their minds were on the Turks who governed the empire. However much they feared the Turks as their masters and despised them as Muslims, the Greeks, in order to ensure their own powers and privileges, sought to please the Turks, pay them exorbitant taxes, support them diplomatically in times of war, and act as the most loyal of the sultan's numerous non-Muslim minorities.

To appreciate the Greek dependency on Turkish rule, one must recall the fall of Constantinople (Istanbul) in 1453. In that year Sultan Mehmet the Conqueror had conferred on the Greek ecumenical patriarch the civil as well as religious headship of the Orthodox Christian millet (or nation), which included Greeks, Bulgarians, Serbians, and Arabs. By virtue of his office the ecumenical patriarch of Constantinople also assumed greater control over the Orthodox churches in Alexandria, Antioch, and Jerusalem. Headed by Constantinople's patriarch, the Orthodox millet became a semi-autonomous community within the framework of the Ottoman Islamic imperial state. That autonomy was expressed in religious and administrative functions. The Orthodox were free to worship according to their own traditions, and the various Orthodox patriarchates could establish religious courts to exercise ritual law affecting the family status of their members. Orthodox priests presided over marriages, divorces, deaths, and wills. The religious leaders of the Orthodox millet were assigned responsibility for the collection of taxes levied by both the state and the millet. Ottoman support for the millet system was the chief reason the Greek-led Orthodox church was able to survive as an entity throughout centuries of Turkish Muslim domination. None knew this better than the Greeks, who did nothing to endanger the system.

The Turks, confident of Greek loyalty, had confirmed the Greeks in their role as keeper of the Church of the Holy Sepulchre and custodian of the holy places. The Greek attitude was that any deviation from their prime duty of preserving Orthodox control of Jesus' Tomb and numerous other holy places harmed the Orthodox church in the Holy Land and further jeopardized Orthodox-Ottoman relationships in Istanbul. So to preserve their own ethnic hegemony over the church, the Greeks were prepared to risk losing Arab Orthodox to the Uniate, Latin, and Protestant churches.

The ties between Greeks and Turks began to loosen only with the rise of Greek nationalism at the beginning of the nineteenth century. The bond broke with the outbreak of the Greek war for independence in 1821. After the war, once a large number of Greeks were outside the Ottoman Empire, the Arab members of the Orthodox church in Syria, Lebanon, and Palestine began to lose the feeling of corporate identity with the Greek clerical hierarchy. The Greek clerics, in turn, had even less reason to show support of any kind for the Arab members of the Orthodox church.

In supporting the Arab Orthodox against their Greek bishops, the Russians sought to create a breach within the Orthodox church that could be exploited. Russian resentment of the Greeks developed after the Russian church had become independent upon the fall of Constantinople to the Turks in 1453. From that time the Russian church began to exercise influence over all the Orthodox churches in the Ottoman Empire. The Russians had a sense of divine mission to rescue the Orthodox faith from Turkish domination, for Constantinople, the "second Rome," citadel of orthodoxy, was in Muslim hands. Byzantium was no longer. Russia had now become the principal Orthodox religious power in the world. The Patriarchate of Moscow (created in 1589) was looked upon as the "third Rome." Yet the Greeks, envious of Russian power, had relegated Moscow to the fifth of the patriarchates, after Constantinople, Alexandria, Antioch, and Jerusalem. In retaliation, Peter the Great restricted the gifts of money that the tsars had formerly sent to the Greek Orthodox and other Eastern churches.

Thus the Russians were eager to foment anti-Turkish separatist movements wherever they occurred among Orthodox communities within the Ottoman Empire. They did so by supporting the drive for independence of the Bulgarian church from the Ecumenical Patriarchate of Constantinople. They did so again by supporting the Arab Orthodox in their revolt against the Greek church in Jerusalem. It was a split that would widen with the years and shape Arab nationalistic consciousness.[8] Arab Orthodox, who saw themselves as victims of both Turks and Greeks, would in later years unite with Muslims against both Zionists and the British government.

THE OUTBREAK of the Crimean War in 1853 resulted from another of Russia's many efforts to weaken Turkey and strengthen her own position in Palestine. Behind the war lay the ongoing rivalry among the Western nations to gain advantage in the Middle East. The spark igniting the conflict was the theft of Bethlehem's nativity star. Franciscan monks accused the Greek Orthodox of uprooting the star from the marble floor in the Nativity Church's grotto and then hiding it. Greek Orthodox monks controlled the grotto, and Franciscans had possession of the star, whose light, according to the New Testament Gospels, pointed the Wise Men to the birth of the Christ child. A similar charge by the Franciscans against the Greeks had been made a century earlier, in 1747.

This new Franciscan accusation against the Greeks raised a storm because Russian church and government officials chose to be provoked by it. Not surprisingly. For in the Russian mind any Catholic gain in the Holy Land was viewed as a setback to the tsar's policy for eastward expansion. Russian apprehensions mounted when France placed herself on the side of the Franciscans. France, which had extracted from the sultan a concession to exercise her own protectorship over all Catholic institutions in Palestine, was not about to take second place to Russia in the contest for control of the Holy Land. And Britain, always fearful of Russian penetration of the Ottoman East, added another war cloud by pledging her support to France.

All the parties understood that the real issue was not the stolen star but control of the holy places and in time of the Holy Land itself. And they also sensed that the issue of the Holy Land was inseparable from the uncertain future of the sultan's throne and the enlarging appetite of Western nations for property and power in the Middle East.

Only a few months after its theft, the star was miraculously returned to Bethlehem's Grotto on Christmas Eve, 1852. No matter. Russia was determined to grab what she could from the Ottoman Empire. One year after the star's return, the Crimean War began. It was Russia's ninth war against Turkey in two hundred years. This time Russia, fighting without allies, was defeated by Turkey, who received aid from France and Britain. The decisive battle was the Anglo-French victory against the Russian naval base at Sevastopol on the Crimean Sea. The war, fought mainly in the Black and Baltic seas, was brought to a close in 1856 with the Treaty of Paris.

Russia's loss in the Crimean War only whetted her appetite for Palestine. In the sixty years afterward, the tsar made a major financial and cultural investment in the Holy Land. Three thousand Russian pilgrims annually journeyed to Jerusalem right up to the time of the Bolshevik Revolution of 1917, when the new Soviet leaders turned their backs on the country. Many Russians came intending to stay and die in Christ's homeland. Packed in ships built for one-fifth their number, they endured bad food, disease, and foul weather over the arduous voyage which took them through the Black Sea and down the Syrian-Palestinian coast.

Disembarking at Jaffa port (many of them barefoot), they began the long climb of several days through the Judean hills to Jerusalem. One of their number was a monk named Grigory Rasputin, later to be the mystic counselor to the tsar. It was said that hundreds of pilgrims had once carried a church bell of several tons by hand from Jaffa to Jerusalem.

The zenith of Russian pilgrimage occurred in 1900 when eleven thousand arrived in Palestine. The pilgrims' proudest possession on their return voyage was the tiny lamp carrying a flame drawn from the Holy Fire ritual enacted on Easter eve. The flame would be used to light the local church lamp back home. Protestants, shocked at the sight of so many superstitious peasants leaving Jaffa port for the return to Russia, flaming lantern in hand, spoke of them as "holy pagans."[9]

The Greeks, too, had no wish to see so many Russian pilgrims entering the country annually, anxious that they were spear points of Russian imperial expansion. If the monks who accompanied the pilgrims remained in the country, one day they might replace the Greeks as custodians of the churches of the Nativity and the Holy Sepulchre.

But the pilgrims, although poor by European standards, brought money which directly benefited the Greeks. So the Greek Orthodox patriarchate of Jerusalem offered housing, food, guides, and special prayers to heal the sick and dying left back home. Money to support the pilgrimages came from the common pilgrim fund created from one day's pay annually of every Russian soldier and seaman.[10]

Following the Crimean War, the opening of the Russian consulate in Jerusalem in 1858 inaugurated a campaign for land purchase and the spread of Orthodox religion. Russian building projects proceeded at a phenomenal rate. On the old parade ground north of Jaffa Gate, the sultan, after signing the peace treaty in 1856, sold to Tsar Nicholas II thirty-two acres of prime land, on which rose an enormous Russian compound of churches, a hospital, and pilgrim dormitories. On the Mount of Olives was built a magnificent church in the onion-domed Muscovite style, together with the Church of Ascension, with its tower defining the skyline. The large Church of Alexander Nevsky was constructed within the walls of Jerusalem. For the benefit of the country's Arab Orthodox, Russian churches, schools, hospices and hospitals, and orphanages were built throughout the country. Russia bought so much land that in a short twenty-one years, from 1856 to 1877, it became the greatest non-Muslim property holder in the Middle East.[11]

BRITISH AND RUSSIAN EXPANSION into Palestine challenged France. For more than three centuries France had been the dominant Western Christian power in the Arab East. She had gained superior privileges in the Levant from the Capitulations of 1535 granted by Sultan Suleiman to King Louis IV. Originally these Capitulations (from the Latin *capitulae*, or "chapters," in the treaty) granted France trade and tax concessions in the Ottoman provinces of the Middle East. But as the Ottoman government came increasingly to rely on France and other Western nations to help preserve her empire, those privileges were extended to include immunities for non-Muslims from military conscription, freedom from Ottoman law and courts, and the right to buy and build on land, even in the city of Jerusalem.

At the forefront of Catholic activity were the Franciscans, largely Italian and Spanish monks, who arrived in the Holy Land in the early fourteenth century, a hundred years after the visit of Saint Francis. Urged by France to throw themselves into the struggle to control Christian holy places, the Franciscans in 1740 won an important Turkish decree which granted the Catholics pre-eminent rights of worship (and themselves as custodians) in the Holy Sepulchre and Nativity churches, over their Greek Orthodox rivals. But after the revolution of 1789, the spread of anticlericalism in republican France led to a loss of interest in Palestine and the holy places. When France declined to join the Greeks in pay-ing for the repair of the roof of the Church of the Holy Sepulchre, damaged by fire in 1808, Catholics lost their worship advantages in the church. After the repairs were completed, Catholics complained that the Greeks had made unlawful changes in the church, including hiding the tombs of the Latin Crusader kings Godfrey and Baldwin.[12] It was just one of a thousand complaints between Greeks and Catholics throughout the nineteenth century.

French indifference to the holy places was to change at midcentury, especially after 1838 when France watched Britain establish its vice-consulate in Jerusalem, then later collaborate with the Prussians in establishing a joint Protestant bishopric. The final humiliation was the construction of the new Anglican Gothic church, the first new church of modern times to be constructed within Jerusalem's walls. Now France sent missionaries and money to enlarge its stake in Palestine, beginning in 1843 with the appointment of her own consul to Jerusalem.

The vigorous new Catholic expansion into Palestine was carried out by a French secularist republic, a republic intent on spreading the French language and culture, safeguarding Arab Catholics from Protestant missionaries, and competing for raw goods and trade that Britain threatened to dominate. To counter the establishment of the Anglo-Prussian bishopric, and to compete with the large and influential Greek Orthodox patriarchate, France urged the Vatican to revive the Latin patriarchate of Jerusalem, an office dormant since the last Crusaders were evicted from the Holy Land in the thirteenth century.

Joseph Valerga, the new Latin patriarch who arrived in Jerusalem in 1847, wasted no time in gaining the support of the Franciscans to present a united front against all non-Catholic Christians, Muslims, and Jews. He did so with the encouragement of Louis Napoleon, who, to gain the political support of French Catholic conservatives, had decided to reassert France's claim on Palestine's holy places.[13]

With France's encouragement, the Franciscans expanded their system of schools, hospitals, orphanages, and pilgrim hospices. Setting up the largest and best printing press in the country gave them a major advantage over the Greek Orthodox church. Offering money, medicine, and modern education, the Franciscans lured many Arab Orthodox to the Catholic church. By the late nineteenth century they established forty centers in towns and villages across the country. According to the historian Alex Carmel, "The number of Arab Catholics in Palestine enjoying French protection grew from about 4,000 in 1840 to 12,000 at the time of the Congress of Berlin" in 1878.[14]

French-funded Catholic building activity was extraordinary. Jerusalem's Church of Saint Anne, the finest Crusader-built church in the Middle East, was reconstructed. The new and massive Notre-Dame de France hospice instantly became a showpiece in Jerusalem; it was located next to the French hospital of Saint Louis, one of the largest hospitals in Palestine at that time.[15] Because the Greeks controlled most of the Church of the Nativity in Bethlehem, money was raised from Catholics in the Austro-Hungarian Empire for the construction in 1882 of Saint Catherine's Church adjacent to the Nativity.

Just as France sought to advance her own interests in the Holy Land, so the new climate of religious and political toleration decreed by the Ottoman government encouraged other Catholic Christians to send missions there. As they did so, France found that in her bid to dominate Christian life in Palestine she was competing not only with Greek Orthodox and Protestants but with Catholic Germany, Austria, Italy, and Spain—each deciding to open its consulate in Jerusalem and establish its own churches, charities, hospitals, and schools.

As competition among Catholics, Anglican Protestants, and Russian and Greek Orthodox proceeded on one level, inter-Catholic rivalry among French, Germans, Austrians, and Italians occurred on another. Before long it seemed that every European Catholic religious order wished to establish itself in Jerusalem. Following in the footsteps of the Franciscans came many monastic "families," including the Sisters of Nazareth, the Sisters of Saint Joseph, the Fathers and Sisters of Zion, the White Fathers, and the Christian Brothers.

National rivalries often obstructed the collective Catholic effort to win Palestine. The Franciscans were proud of being Catholic "seniors" in the Holy Land. After being evicted from their monastery on Mount Zion in the fourteenth century, the Franciscans were not happy that the German Catholic church had built the lovely church of Dormition Abbey on Mount Zion, on the highly sacred spot where tradition placed the "eternal sleep" of the Virgin Mary. Nor did they welcome the arrival of Patriarch Valerga, who represented the Vatican. Not surprisingly, German and Austrian Catholics were put off by French efforts to ensure that all Catholic activities in the Holy Land were under their control. German Catholics and Protestants alike protested the French practice of flying their flag over German Catholic institutions. In 1855 the heir to the Hapsburg throne canceled his visit to the Stella Maris Monastery because the Carmelite nuns refused to remove the French flag from its roof.[16]

FOLLOWING THE Crimean War, no Western nation did more to modernize Palestine than the Germans, who were trusted by the Turks where the French, British, and Russians were not. The Berlin-Istanbul axis was forged out of the mutual affection of Kaiser

William II and Sultan Abdulhamid II, who granted to the kaiser a concession to build a railway linking Berlin and Baghdad. When the French government learned of this strategically important development, it became furious at what it saw as a German expansion into French spheres of influence in Syria, Lebanon, and Palestine. The Germans, sensitive to their European allies and competitors, agreed to limit the scope of their railway, whereupon the French obtained a concession to build a railway between Jaffa and Jerusalem.

Germany's modernization of Palestine began with the arrival of the small, hardworking community of Protestant Templars. The Templars of Swabia, Germany, a unique group of millenarian Christians, began immigrating to the Holy Land in the 1860s. Their aim was to gain control of the land that God had once promised to the Jewish people, but which because of the Jews "apostasy" was now given over to them, the new and righteous "people of God," settling in the Holy Land to await the messianic Deliverance.[17]

By 1875 only some 750 Templars had immigrated to Palestine to await the Deliverance. Others would join them to form a set of communities in Haifa, Jaffa, and Jerusalem which had a profound influence on the country's economy in the decades preceding World War I. Alex Carmel writes that the Templars "reached a level of development unparalleled in Palestine in planning, beauty, and organization, they had no equal in the country."[18]

The Templars excelled in viticulture and were the first to utilize motors for irrigation and steam-powered flour mills. They made numerous innovations in agriculture; built the country's first machine factory in Jaffa; introduced the first wheeled cart; organized regular carriage passenger service from Jaffa to Jerusalem; and laid the first roads of iron and sand for wheeled carriages. They also established the first European-style hotels. The site of a Templar settlement was familiar to everyone: neat rows of square stone cottages, exactly duplicating the cozy domiciles they had left in Swabia.

The energy, skill, and manifest success of the Templars seemed only to arouse the jealousy of Palestine's Muslims. The first Templar settlements were located on cheaply purchased, uncultivated land, without Arab tenants. But Muslims watched the value of this land grow with its productivity under the superb farming skills of the newcomers. Carmel writes, "Against the background of the already prevalent xenophobia, it was impossible to root out the feeling of the local population that the Germans had come to evict them and suck their blood."[19]

The Muslims were also hostile to the Templars as Christian foreigners, who, like Jewish immigrant settlers arriving in the late 1870s, seemed haughty and aloof. They suspected both Templars and Jews as being agents of a European conspiracy to steal Palestine from Islam and subjugate the Muslims. The well-organized and prosperous Templar farms seemed to mock the poverty and misery of neighboring Arab villages.

The Templars returned the Arabs' hostility in kind. A German writer of the times declared that "our honest, direct and slightly rough Swabian settler will never feel sympathy towards the Arabs."[20] Another German characterized the Arab as "the naturally impudent and arrogant son of the Orient, whose main characteristic is thievery and beggary and who bows his head only before power and money."[21]

The Templars strove for and achieved a remarkable self-sufficiency in Palestine; but they were vulnerable to international politics and often had to turn to the German government for protection. The struggle of Balkan Christians in the war of 1875–1878 to free themselves from the sultan was seen by Palestine's Muslims as an assault on Islam. Now all Christians were suspect in Muslims' eyes. On more than one occasion, Muslim threats against the Templars forced Germany to send gunboats to the Palestinian coast. The sight of German warships, long guns in ready, was usually enough to intimidate local Turkish authorities into arresting Muslim mob leaders and offering protection to the Templars and other Christian communities.[22] The Prussian government came to the aid of the Templars for reasons of country, not theology, for as millenarian sectarians the Templars stood against the established beliefs of the Protestant Evangelical church of Prussia.

The Templars' attitude toward the Jews was a complicated one. The Jew was central to the Templar theology as an "apostate," one who had forfeited the land by rejecting Jesus as the Christ. Because of their faith in Christ, the Templars had become "God's people," the "new Israel," who rightfully could claim the land that God had originally promised to the Jews.

Yet theology was set aside when the Templars had to deal with the practical realities of living in a country more than 90 percent Muslim. Templars actually welcomed the large stream of new Jewish settlers who began arriving in the 1870s and 1880s. As the years passed, a quiet bond of solidarity formed as Templars saw that the Jews also worked hard and skillfully to make barren land productive—and that their successes had also made them a target of Muslim scorn. The Templars' attitude changed when heightened Jewish immigration at the turn of the century led to competition between Templars and Jews in agriculture, trade, and commerce. The sharp increase of Jewish immigration before World War I (85,000 Jews versus 2,100 Templars) only worsened the relationship.

Matching the Templars in vision and industry was the German Protestant pietist Christian Friedrich Spittler, who made a lasting contribution to the life of Palestine without ever leaving his native Switzerland. Spittler dedicated his life to the revitalization of the Holy Land and its people. He played a major role in inspiring, funding, and sending to Palestine Johann Ludwig Schneller, who was to establish the immense Syrian Orphanage, and Conrad Schick, who was to design many of Jerusalem's best houses and buildings, including the Mea Shearim quarter.

The Syrian Orphanage was built in 1860 to receive young Syrian boys orphaned by the massacre of Christians in Syria and Lebanon. At the orphanage they were housed, schooled, and taught trades. Later, in the 1890s, refugee children from the Armenian massacre were brought to the Syrian Orphanage, which also established special facilities for the housing and education of blind children.

Soon the clean, well-run, and well-funded German schools, hospices, hospitals, and orphanages began to attract Arabs, who were now prepared to leave the Russian Orthodox, Catholic, and Anglican churches to identify themselves with the new and powerful German Protestant Christian presence in the Holy Land. The joint Anglo-Prussian bishopric, begun in 1854, was dissolved in 1886 as competition gradually replaced cooperation between the two countries. After the dissolution, German Protestants wasted no time in buying a large piece of property in old Jerusalem's Muristan quarter, adjacent to the Church of the Holy Sepulchre, where a magnificent new church, *Erloserung,* "The Redeemer," was built and dedicated in 1898 by Kaiser William II. The building of the Redeemer was followed by the construction in 1910 of the massive Augusta Victoria hospice on Mount Scopus, the largest and most impressive building in Palestine of that era.

German church construction was part of Europe's economic and strategic penetration of the Middle East. But it should not be forgotten that in Germany, no less than in Russia, Britain, and France, there was great popular Christian support for travel to and building in the Holy Land. Most of the cost of the Augusta Victoria was paid for by the raising of two million marks, a kingly sum, from ordinary German Protestant churchgoers.

THE CRIMEAN WAR impoverished Palestine. Food, fuel, and police protection were scarce as regular Turkish soldiers were removed to the war. The country relied on Arab boys conscripted as irregular soldiers, who wasted no time in extorting money and food from the people they were ordered to protect. Bedouin raiding returned. The historian Arnold Blumberg tells us that "The dreaded Taamri Bedouin, whose range normally lay between the shores of the Dead Sea and the outskirts of Bethlehem, sent armed men to the walls of Jerusalem . . . and the great clan of Abu Ghosh, which held the mountain passes between Jaffa and Jerusalem, struck an alliance with kindred clans to seize the village of Ein Kerem, west of Jerusalem. . . ."[23]

Despite impoverishment, it seemed that a brighter day had dawned for Christians, who could now say that Turkey had been saved from defeat by European Christian powers. For the moment Muslims looked with less hostility on Christians, particularly in Jerusalem. Whereas in 1843 Muslims had torn down the French flag when it was unfurled in Jerusalem, in 1856 the flag was flown to a cheering crowd celebrating the end of the Crimean War.

The old anti-Christian governor of Jerusalem was replaced by Kamal Pasha, a young aristocratic Turk in his early twenties, who left no doubt of his love of Europeans. He opened Jerusalem to them as never before and set precedent by allowing all the consulates to fly their national flags. He attended services at Christ Church and sent a model of the Church of the Holy Sepulchre as a gift to Queen Victoria. He offended Muslims by opening the mosques of Jerusalem's Haram esh-Sharif to Christian and Jewish visitors. Not the least of those offended were the Sudanese Takruri tribesmen, who by tradition were trained to guard against foreign intrusion into the Islamic sanctuary. Kamal allowed religious processions, which included the public display of a crucifix in the streets of Jerusalem. In all these actions Kamal acted in accord in the spirit of Hatti-i Humayun, the new imperial decree of 1856, issued after the Crimean War, which reinforced the legal equality extended to non-Muslims.

In the euphoria of winning the Crimean War for Turkey, and in the wake of the Humayun decree, Christians began to flex their muscles. Evidence of Christian economic and religious power was now everywhere in Palestine.[24] New consulates exploited their legal and taxing privileges by extending them to Arab Christians and foreign nationals. If anti-Christian troubles arose, European warships were sent to the coast of Palestine to threaten bombardment.

Muslims were offended by the Humayun decree. Despite Christian support for the sultan in the Crimean War, the new decree planted anew the seeds for future anti-Christian violence. Christians were relatively safe in Jerusalem and in the coastal cities protected by the Turkish government, which was eager to stay in the good graces of the European powers. But Christians knew enough not to wander into the heart of Muslim rural life in the central hill country, from Hebron in the south to Nablus and Jenin in the north. There the popular view was that the sultan had sold out to the Europeans. He had first agreed to the Capitulations, then to the decrees of Gulhane (1839) and Humayun (1856) because he needed European military support against his enemies; and now he had acquiesced to the power of the consulates because he was in need of foreign money. Out of political weakness and his own moral corruption, he had betrayed Islam. The Muslims of Syria and Palestine would not join him in that betrayal. For although they feared the soldiers of the sultan, they feared Allah more.

What particularly angered Muslims was the sight of Christians flaunting their privileges and their new sense of equality. The ringing of church bells, the public processions displaying the cross, the opening of wine shops, the flags, the mounting evidence of Christian wealth, the proliferation of Christians in the Ottoman bureaucracy— all these developments convinced Muslims that the Turkish reform decrees made Christians superior to Muslims.

Several incidents of anti-Christian violence following the Humayun decree pointed to a deep undercurrent of Muslim hostility against Christians and all the new foreigners who had begun to exercise influence in the country.[25] In early April 1856, Bishop Samuel Gobat, joyous over the issuance of the Humayun decree, ordered the ringing of the church bells in the Anglican chapel of Nablus. It was a foolish act, because Nablus historically was a religiously conservative Muslim town. Muslim sensibilities thus were already boiling when a day later, to celebrate the birth of the French crown prince, flags were flown in town by English and Prussian consular agents. In Muslim eyes, the sight of the flags meant that Europeans were asserting, more than simply their religion, a sense of triumph over Palestine and its Muslim inhabitants.

On April 3 the noon prayers in the central mosque were interrupted as worshipers, responding to the preachers' exhortations, left the mosque for what was intended to be a peaceful demonstration. Then something truly unforeseen and tragic happened. A Muslim beggar was accidentally shot to death by an English missionary, the Reverend Lyde of Cambridge University. Lyde proved to be deranged, but Muslim rage could not be overcome. The incident touched off an anti-Christian riot in Nablus, led by the local Muslim religious leadership. A bloody massacre was averted only by the intervention of the local governor and his troops.[26]

Significantly, Jews were not harmed during the incident. It seemed to Muslims that the new legal status of the Christian religion was less important than how that status was expressed. Jews, who remained outwardly subservient to Muslims, avoided becoming a target of Muslim resentment.

While tensions between Muslims and Christians led to isolated incidents of violence in Palestine, it was a different story in Damascus, a city known for Muslim extremism and out of reach of European gunboats. In mid-July 1860 Christians in the thousands were massacred, women raped, children abducted, consular offices ransacked, and churches and convents burned.[27] Jews, who were "said to have given refreshment to the rioters," were left untouched.[28]

Behind the Damascus riot lay the deadly combination of Christian arrogance and Muslim resentment that appears throughout Palestine's modern history. To the high displeasure of Muslims, Maronite Christians in Damascus had installed a great bell in their church. Christians had opened wine shops in the central market, and Christian women had openly sported green dresses. Muslim resentments deepened at the sight of Arab Christians growing rich from their trade with foreigners and enjoying the material benefits of government employment.[29]

What especially angered the Muslims was the reluctance of Christians to pay the military exemption tax. After the Humayun decree many Damascus Christians stopped paying the tax because it was high and violated the principle of equality set forth in the decree. In Muslim eyes, these Christian actions were tantamount to insurrection and thus offered a convenient reason for Muslims to punish the entire Christian community.

The incident that triggered the Damascus massacre was the arrest of a group of Christian boys who had painted crosses on pavements in the Muslim quarter. In retaliation an angry Muslim mob turned on the local Christians. Soldiers sent to arrest the rioters joined them in plunder and rape. Local religious leaders, Damascus's mufti, and some of the religious judges and members of the local council, helped to foment the riot. The government in Istanbul also bore some of the blame for the Damascus massacre. In promulgating so weighty a decree as Humayun, it failed to provide the kind of military protection that would have prevented or contained the predictable Muslim reactions in the Arab provinces.

The Damascus riot was a portent for Palestine. If Muslims would not accept Christians as equals, in time and under different circumstances they would not accept Jews. And since they saw European Christians as foreigners, and Arab Christians as agents of foreigners, so they would see Zionists as foreigners and local Jews as agents of foreign powers. For in Muslim eyes, Palestine and Syria were Islamic sacred land, which could not be shared with Christians and Jews claiming equality. Seventy years after the massacre of Christians in Damascus, Muslims would massacre Jews in Hebron, Tiberias, Safed, and Jerusalem.

One of the major consequences of the Damascus massacre of 1860 was the exodus of Christians from Syria and Palestine to Lebanon, Egypt, Turkey, and countries in Europe. The response of the Christian West to the Damascus massacre was to accelerate missionary activity, including the building of more schools. "From these schools," the historian Moshe Ma'oz writes, "there emerged the first modern Arabic writers and journalists, all Christians; around them literary societies were formed, an Arabic theatre was set up, and printing presses were established, most of them in Beirut—the center of the new cultural revival."[30] The dominant themes of this Arabic cultural revival were language, secularism, and patriotism. Here was the budding of new secular values which would in time become the basis for a new Syrian-Palestinian political nationalism. Christian Arabs embraced this secular rationale because they had found the religious conflict to be so explosive and divisive. Ma'oz writes,

> These ideas of patriotism and secularism . . . were not acceptable to the Muslim population of Syria, which regarded them as subversive to the character of their society and state. In the eyes of the Muslims, the Ottoman Empire was primarily a religious state in which they alone formed the political community; any change in this basis would mean not only the end of their dominant position in the state, but also the collapse of the Empire.[31]

This Muslim attitude was to change after World War I, when Syria and Palestine ceased to be Ottoman imperial provinces and came under the control of Britain, the greatest of the West's Christian powers. When that happened, Palestine's Arab Christians pressing for a new secular nationalism, and Muslims agitating for removal of the foreigners, joined in a struggle against what they perceived to be a common enemy.

The cost of the Crimean War bankrupted the Ottoman government in Istanbul. But after the war Palestine experienced an economic boom because of Western investors and entrepreneurs. An emerging economic elite of Arab Christians, Greeks, Armenians, and Jews benefited from trade and moneylending. The growth of the export market for wheat, citrus, and other foodstuffs increased the value of agricultural land, bringing land speculation by a rising class of Muslim town notables, the *ayan*. The end result was the enrichment of Christians and a handful of Muslim families, and the increasing impoverishment of the peasantry.[32]

The reforms of 1839 and 1856 helped encourage Western investment in Palestine, and the arrival of new immigrants, first German Templars and later Jews from eastern Europe, also contributed to the country's economic improvement. But the key to Palestine's new prosperity was the linkage of its economy to the world, and especially to the economies of Europe.[33] The export trade made booming ports of Jaffa and Haifa, each of which saw dramatic increases in their population. Jaffa by 1915 grew to become Palestine's main port and second city (after Jerusalem), with a population of fifty thousand. Eventually Jaffa would be surpassed in population by Haifa, which could boast of a larger natural deep-water port. Shipped out of that port on newly built steamships went casks of olive oil, crates of sesame and grapes, bales of cotton. Annual crops of oranges, grapefruit, and lemons were bought by the English; Egyptians purchased Nablus's prized olive-oil soap; thousands of crosses and crèches of olive wood and mother-of-pearl produced in Bethlehem and Jerusalem were boxed for shipment to European Christian homes eager to have a piece of the Holy Land. Leading all exports was grain, mainly durum wheat bought by Italians for macaroni, and barley coveted by the English for the making of whiskey and beer.

Palestine's economic prosperity in the wake of the Crimean War led to major improvements in infrastructure. German and French engineers built railways that crisscrossed the country, linking major towns. Roads were paved; passenger carriages came into service; a telegraph system linking Palestine to Europe was established; European banks opened branches. Church communities established schools throughout the country. By 1914 some nineteen hospitals were operating in Jaffa, Haifa, and Jerusalem. In 1869, the year of the opening of the Suez Canal, the country's first post office appeared, along with modern Western-style hotels in Jaffa and Jerusalem to accommodate an increasing number of businessmen, tourists, and pilgrims. Ten thousand to twenty thousand visiting pilgrims each year had become a lucrative source of income, particularly for Jerusalem. The frantic building of this "New Jerusalem" by a foreign Christian group meant handsome profits for the city and for neighboring Bethlehem, the source of building materials. The economic historian Alexander Scholch writes that "long lines of camels approaching Jerusalem from Bethlehem with heavy loads of lime and stones, grain and wood were a daily spectacle."[34]

In the 1870s and 1880s, in order to make Palestine a safer place for European Christian trade and investment, the Noble Porte improved roads, placed more soldiers in the field, increased security, and brought an end to Bedouin banditry and the despotic rule of village sheiks.[35]

Improved sanitation, more hospitals, and the availability of medicine led to a substantial increase in Palestine's population. A population of 300,000 in 1800 had grown to 350,000 by 1850. Overcoming the cholera epidemic of 1865–1866, the population by 1900 was slightly less than 700,000, one-third of which were in 13 towns, and two-thirds in some 650 villages.[36] Muslims constituted 85 percent of the population, Christians 11 percent, and Jews 4 percent. New settlers included Christians from Europe and Arabs from neighboring lands attracted to Palestine for jobs; many of them were Jews who fled pogroms in Russia and Rumania for Palestine beginning in the early 1880s.[37]

Evidencing Palestine's new prosperity were fancy new imports of sugar, coffee, tobacco, Western clothes, Swiss clocks, German tools, English coal, and timber brought from Lebanon's forests for the making of heavy furniture. The Turks were in a quandary about this increased trade with the West. Wanting the tax money that trade brought, they made a modest effort to improve Palestine's ports. But they worried that better ports would open Palestine and Syria to Western power and lead to the loss of these countries. And they had reason to worry. In the wake of the West's successful defense of Istanbul in the Crimean War, Europe's political and religious leaders talked increasingly of establishing a Western protectorate over Palestine, for after all it was the Christians' own Holy Land. At the close of the nineteenth century the typical Ottoman Turkish attitude, as expressed by a nameless official was: "We want no discoveries; we want no attention paid to Palestine; we want no roads. Leave the place alone. If it becomes rich, we shall lose it; if it remains poor, it will continue in our hands."

CHAPTER SEVEN

Dream and Reality

Palestine is no more of this workday world. It is
sacred to poetry and tradition—it is dream-land.
—Mark Twain, 1867

Palestine is a country to see once, not revisit. The
scenery is not often picturesque or even pretty. There
is much greater need of cultivation than in Greece
and much less chance of making it pay. For the
surface is in many places all rocks and stones.
—Lord George Curzon, 1882–1883

How any man can be disappointed with the Holy
Land I cannot understand. Some of the Palestinian
tourists have been chiefly impressed by the fleas, the
filth, and the beggars. To me, the scenery, if it had no
sacred associations, would be appealingly majestic.
There is nothing in America or Europe that surpasses
it for a mingling of beauty and grandeur.
—T. De Witt Talmage, Presbyterian minister, 1897

When Britain upended Bonaparte's Eastern adventure and later
at Crimea beat back Russia's bid to absorb Syria and Palestine,
British hearts were filled with pride in nation and religion. The
words "Holy Land" had a fresh meaning. No one stated that meaning more plainly than William Thomson, the Archbishop of York, in
1865 at the inaugural meeting of the Palestine Exploration Fund in
London:

This country of Palestine belongs to you and me, it is essentially ours. . . . It is the land towards which we turn as the fountain of our hopes; it is the land to which we may look with as true a patriotism as we do this dear old England of ours, which we love so much.[1]

Thomson's sense of possessing the Holy Land was shared by thousands of American Protestants, who began visiting "their Holy Land" after the Crimean War. What mattered to British and American Protestants was no particular sacred site, rather it was "the Jesus of the land," the historical Jesus who stood behind the church and who was the inspiring source of the Bible. One could spiritually encounter that Jesus in the Holy Land and nowhere else.[2]

This encounter with Jesus was above all not one of reason but of faith. For Protestants knew that the birthplace of Jesus, his crucifixion, and a hundred other sacred sites had been called into question by archaeologists and Scripture scholars. Just as unfortunate, the traditional sacred sites were the property of venal monks, whose rituals, mixing mysticism and materialism, were nauseating to Protestants.

No, Protestants sought a different way of validating their faith. It could not be a holy place in the Holy Land that proved the truth of the Christian religion. It had to be the land itself, that land which God himself had chosen to reveal his miracles. As Archbishop Thomson said, ". . . it is the land towards which we turn as the foundation of our hope." In the Protestant mind, seeing the Holy Land, walking it, painting it, photographing it, writing about it in diaries and for the public press—these were nothing less than sacramental acts. Visiting the Holy Land made possible a sacred communion with the real Jesus, the one to whom the original disciples bore witness before the existence of Bible and church.[3]

Like Volney and Chateaubriand before them, Protestant pilgrims were prepared to make a theological judgment about the corruption of the land under Muslim rule. Typical was the attitude of John Kelman, who traveled to Palestine at the turn of the century and wrote a widely read travel book, *The Holy Land* (1904), contrasting the blessed Christian village of Bethlehem with the accursed Muslim town of Hebron, which was as "stagnant as a deserted pond . . . moribund with vengeance. The sullenness of people you meet on the road give a token of its spirit before you enter. . . . Women draw aside their veils to curse us as we pass."[4]

In the mid-nineteenth century, travel books were published by the score in England and America. In 1869 Thomas Cook began inexpensive, second-class package tours from Southampton and New York to Egypt and Palestine. The tours proved so popular that the Prince of Wales and later Kaiser William would travel to the Holy Land under Cook's arrangements. By 1882 some five thousand "Cookies," as the local people called them, had visited the Holy Land.⁵

Many travelers were paid commissions to bring back reports or write a book or draw a picture of the Holy Land. Their works were bought by an avid public that eagerly consumed personal accounts of the Holy Land, where dream outweighed reality. But one writer-traveler, without losing a sense of the dream, kept her eyes open to the reality of Palestine. This was the young Englishwoman Mary Eliza Rogers, whose travel journal offers a vivid portrait of the country following the Crimean War. In sharp contrast to Rogers's experience of Palestine were the reactions of a young American, Samuel Clemens, whose satiric travel articles on Palestine would speed the career of the writer we know as Mark Twain. Both authors give us an intimate portrait of Palestine at midcentury.

Rogers departed for Palestine on June 14, 1855, on a boat in the Thames River, London. She returned to England several years later after traversing most of the country on foot or by horse, and after poking her head into every town, village, and Bedouin tent she came by. She traveled wide-eyed, open-minded, and with an innocent heart. She was neither a genteel visitor nor a debunker. She stayed in the country long enough to become friends with Christians, Muslims, and Jews, with the highborn and the simple. She learned Arabic and mastered the principles of Islam and Judaism. She expressed her own Protestant faith in universalistic terms, stressing tolerance and moral justice. She noted all that was backward, ignorant, and ugly about Palestine. She delighted in sites of beauty. She had as clear a sense of both the blessing and curse that attached to Palestine as anyone who ever visited and wrote about the country.

How very different were the reactions to Palestine of Mark Twain. In the summer of 1867, at the age of twenty-eight, Twain was a member of the first organized group of Americans to undertake a packaged tour of the Middle East. He matched Rogers in appetite for adventure and in skills as an observer; but his conclusions were his own. He wrote of Palestine for *Alta California,* a San Francisco newspaper that paid his travel expenses. The articles were later republished in a book, *Innocents Abroad,* that brought him fame and fortune.

If Rogers was generous in her approach to the peoples and places she encountered, Twain, despite the title of his book, was sourtempered and cynical. Employing the techniques of invidious comparison, comic distortion, burlesque parody, and the timely wisecrack, he derided Arabs, Turks, Jews, women, children, camels, horses, the desert, and the Bedouin desert dweller. He was least generous with the physical landscape, which he found dreary and desolate, a "blistering, naked, treeless land," and a total disillusionment from the image of grandeur instilled in him by hours of Bible reading.

Yet, in spite of his cynicism, he was accurate in describing how the Western misperception of Palestine sprang from the tendency to see a foreign land through the familiar lenses of one's own religious culture. Twain wrote:

> I am sure, from the tenor of books I have read, that many who visited this land in years gone by, were Presbyterians, and came seeking evidences in support of their particular creed; they found a Presbyterian Palestine, and they had already made up their minds to find no other. . . . Others were Baptists, seeking Baptist evidences and a Baptist Palestine. Others were Catholics, Methodists, Episcopalians, seeking evidences indorsing their several creeds. . . . Honest as these men's intentions may have been, they were full of partialities and prejudices, they entered the country with their verdicts already prepared, and they could no more write dispassionately and impartially about it than they could about their own wives and children.[6]

Mary Eliza Rogers seems to evade Twain's strictures about the foreigner's perception of this country. One reads her *Domestic Life in Palestine* with the feeling that its author was one of those who entered Palestine not with "verdicts already prepared" but with a fresh spirit for observation and friendship. Hers was an experience of Palestine that was both dream and reality.

Rogers's delight at arriving at Jaffa is mixed with a sense of real danger. The large harbor is all reefs, sandbars, and great jutting rocks that make it necessary for ships to drop anchor offshore. Rogers, like thousands before her, was obliged to come to port in a small rented boat tossed about by sea swells. "As we approached the belt of rocks, I felt that it was impossible to escape being dashed to pieces, and while steering through the narrow pass I was silent with fear. . . ."[7]

On her first day in Jaffa she notes that no woman is to be found in the bazaar and is surprised to learn that in the Middle East men do the shopping. In succeeding months she will learn that the world of Arab women is in kitchens, salons, and gathering together in internal courtyards. It is a warm world of children, cooking, and endless preparations for festive days.

Invited to the home of an Arab Christian woman, her eye fixes on a picturesque salon.

> A number of gentlemen were in the body of the room. They, as well as the ladies, were smoking narghiles. Strong coffee, without milk, and in tiny cups without handles . . . were handed round; after partaking of which, it is customary to incline the head slightly, raising the hand to the forehead, and thus to salute the host or hostess, who, in turn does the same to the guests.[8]

Charmed by the warmth and generosity of her Arab acquaintances, Rogers goes native. She dons Arab dresses and learns to smoke a narghile.

Leaving Jaffa after a few days, she begins a journey inland on horseback. After passing the town of Ramle, she reaches the Judean hills, then begins the ascent to Jerusalem. Amid the rocks she sees a country rich with flowers and fruit. It seems that plenty has replaced poverty in the country. High in the sky are eagles, vultures, and kites. The air is alive with songbirds. Her eyes become a camera, recording the wonder.

> I watched numbers of green lizards and strange reptiles, running rapidly in and out of the cracks, and under and over the rocks, pausing sometimes, opening their eyes of fire to the sun, and nodding their large heads quaintly. Wild ducks were flapping their wings above our heads. Camels every now and then passed in strings of three or four together. As we passed, some of the peasants wore scarcely any clothing; flocks of goats and cattle were

browsing on the scanty burnt-up pasture, and the shepherd boys
were piping on rude instruments made of cane or reed.[9]

As she climbs the hills of Judea, her sense of spiritual communion with the land deepens.

> Here there is a well of sweet and excellent water, and round it
> olives, figs, locust-trees, and evergreen oaks grow; a party of
> Bedouins were watering their camels at the stone trough con-
> nected with the well; under the pleasant tree-shadows we rested;
> and on a bank of wild thyme and sweet marjoram we spread our
> simple provisions—a basket of summer fruit, a few thin cakes of
> flour, and some new wine.[10]

Later that day she reaches the village of Abu Ghosh, a fiefdom
named after the legendary bandit chieftain. It is a short ride to
Jerusalem. Here the dream gives way to grotesque reality:

> We . . . went to the ruins of the Church of the Knights of St.
> John . . . passed under a wide low Norman arch, rich with zigzag
> and dog-tooth moldings, marble columns, and carved capitals; we
> climbed over a dustheap, where vegetables and dead bodies of dogs
> and cats were rotting, where flies and fleas were regaling them-
> selves, and half-naked, wretched-looking children were playing
> and munching melon parings; we crossed a courtyard, full of
> abominations, assailed by barking and snarling dogs, but tempted
> on by the strange beauty of this neglected relic of ancient chivalry.[11]

Jerusalem's promenade was an old Turkish parade ground,
where Rogers saw all the colors and shapes of Palestine's humanity.
Men's garments ranged from the "somber robes of monks" to the
loud, embroidered jackets of Turkish officers. Jews were noticeable
by their high-pointed hats and Muslims by their turbans and bright
sashes; Arab Christians could be spotted by their red tarbooshes.
Women kept to themselves in groups separate from men and were
"shrouded in sheets," often followed by their black slaves who went
barefoot.

One could also find the undressed in Jerusalem. On a market
street within the walled town, Rogers encounters a "tall gaunt Jew,"
a self-styled prophet, wearing "a ragged strip of sackcloth round his
loins" and carrying a long staff in one hand and a large stone in the

other. "The city shall be made desolate, fire shall consume it, because of its wickedness," he cries out in Arabic. He was thought to be "mad." Rogers elaborates: "Orientals invariably treat with kindness and consideration those who are thus afflicted, believing them to be under the especial protection of God. . . . In the East a 'madman' and a 'prophet' are almost synonymous terms."[12]

Costumes and cosmetics made Arab women exotic to Rogers. In one of Jerusalem's bazaars she is fascinated (even a touch envious) of the brightly dressed young peasant girls selling vegetables.

> They did not wear the white shroud of the townspeople; their dresses were chiefly in indigo-dyed linen, and made like long shirts, girdled with red shawls or sashes; their heads were covered with colored handkerchiefs or shawls, or white towels, so arranged as to partially conceal their faces which were very dark and tattooed with blue stars and dots on the forehead and round the lips; their eyes looked larger and darker on account of the kohl on the eyelids, and the black pigment on the eyebrows. They wore colored glass bracelets, silver anklets, and some of them had necklaces of coins and silver rings.[13]

The Arab woman's obsession with her body's appearance could be carried to an extreme. Rogers takes a dim view of the crude practice of hair removal from the face. This involved the use of adhesive plasters of sweet gum, applied to the face and then torn off, bringing with it "all the soft down or hair." The result left the skin quite bare, "with an unnaturally bright and polished appearance, much admired by Orientals." Caustically Rogers adds:

> When women have once submitted to this process, they look frightful, if from time to time they do not regret it; for the hair never grows so soft and fine again. Perhaps this is one of the reasons why aged Arab women, who have quite given up all these arts of adornments, look so haggard and witch-like.[14]

The Greek Catholic church threatens excommunication of women who use "kohl, and henna, and rouge." But Rogers knows that Arab Christian women will continue these practices as long as they believe it "adds to their beauty, and to their powers of attraction." For "their respect for custom is stronger even than their fear of the Church, and if the priests persisted in carrying out their threats of excommunication for such offenses, their congregations would soon be scattered. . . ."[15]

On one occasion Rogers meets with a Greek Catholic priest who opens her eyes to the subtle connection between a woman's dress and Middle Eastern economics. He tells her that in 1859 a shipment of black silk mittens was sold in Haifa by a peddler from Beirut. Within days many of the women throughout Palestine were sporting new black silk mittens in church—to the consternation of the priest who denounced them from the pulpit. The priest also cautioned against "exposing any part of their ornamental head-dress in church."

After asking the priest for an explanation of his attitude toward the mittens, Rogers describes his reply.

> He said he considered it very important to check, if possible, the inroad of Frank [or Western] taste among the Arab women; for, if they were to adopt the Frank dress, which requires many changes of apparel, and alters its fashions frequently, a trousseau would be so expensive that young men would not be able to marry, and early unions, which are so desirable in the East, would be prevented. The costly articles of a genuine Arab wardrobe last a lifetime, and are heirlooms, whereas the gala dresses of a Frank wardrobe must be renewed every year. The priest spoke feelingly, for he was an Arab, a husband, and the father of a large family of girls.[16]

Another aspect of women's life that drew Rogers's attention was the low esteem in which women were held by men, irrespective of their religion. The exclusion of women from social gatherings particularly bothered her. One day she confronts several Muslim men invited to a social evening at her home in Haifa.

> Is there any law (which you regard as sacred and binding) that forbids you to see and converse with women out of your own individual families? If there is such a law, I will not cause you to disobey it, but will help you to keep it, by hiding myself from you.[17]

The men replied that not religion but custom alone kept women secluded in harems and apart from male company. But there was also women's obtuseness to consider:

"If we gave [women] their liberty, they would not know how to use it. Their heads are made of wood. They are not like you. When you speak, we no longer remember that you are a girl: we think we are listening to a sheik. To live in knowledge and wisdom are necessary. Our wives and daughters have neither wisdom nor knowledge. Give them wisdom and we will give them liberty."[18]

Rogers found all the peoples of Palestine naturally religious. She found this quality in the simplest gestures.

If a piece of bread fall to the ground, an Arab will gather it up with his right hand, kiss it, touch his forehead with it, and place it in a recess or on a wall, where the fowls of the air may find it, for they say: "We must not tread under foot the gift of God." I have seen this reverence exhibited constantly, by all classes of people, by masters, servants, and even by little children, Moslems and Christians.[19]

Rogers was no pietist. She criticized the formalism of Muslim religious practices, contrasting them with the simplicity of Anglican worship. "Moslems, both men and women, have the name of 'Allah' on their lips; but they do not appear to realize the presence and power of God, or be conscious of spiritual communion with Him."[20]

She is troubled that Muslims do not share a Protestant's sense of spirituality, where "talking with God" is a common expression. Here she exposes her naiveté, born of Western religious bias. It does not occur to her that when religion fills the entire daily life of every Muslim, Jew, and Christian of the East, a Protestant spirituality, the need of "talking with God," is alien and unnecessary. The same bias shows in her otherwise perceptive observations about Muslim prayer.

The Muslim ejaculations [or prayer] before and after eating, and during the performance of ablutions, though beautiful and appropriate, are now merely exclamations of self-congratulation, without reference to any superior or unseen power. And the regular daily prayers so scrupulously said by men, though generally neglected by women, are reduced to ceremonial forms; while the words uttered are, in many instances, sublime and magnificent.[21]

If Rogers was critical of Muslim formalism, she condemned the Eastern Christian ritual of the Holy Fire. According to Eastern Orthodox tradition, fire miraculously appears over the tomb of Christ on Saturday of Easter Week, a day before Resurrection Sunday. The faithful take the fire to be God-given proof of Jesus' coming back to life.

The Church of the Holy Sepulchre, crowded through the Easter Week, is jammed with pilgrims on Saturday. Everyone is eager to witness the miracle of the fire. Pilgrims from Greece, Armenia, and Russia are everywhere in the church. Many have saved money all their lives to pay for this once-in-a-lifetime pilgrimage. The spectacle of the fire on Saturday afternoon and the midnight Resurrection service on Easter are the crowning dramas in this annual reenactment of Christ's death and rebirth in Jerusalem.

The church built over Christ's tomb is a dangerous place at this time. Ecstatic pilgrims have sometimes trampled each other to death at the sight of the sacred flame.[22] Rogers, aware of the danger, writes: "The pilgrims were running and leaping in all directions, uttering wild cries, and a monotonous sort of chant. The noise was almost bewildering." It must have been repulsive but also fascinating for this English lady, accustomed to the decorum of Anglican worship, to watch those leaping bodies.

At the next moment, as if on cue, the formal part of the ceremony begins.

> The wild mob had been driven back to make room for the entrance of an orderly procession formed of bishops and priests in gorgeous robes. They ... chanted with solemnity and great emotion in a beautiful litany, while they walked three times slowly round the sepulchre.[23]

At this moment a priest comes forth. He has paid a large sum of money for the right to receive the fire from an opening in the marble enclosure covering the tomb. For this honor he will be called the "bishop of the holy fire." People cluster around him. In an effort to gain a clearer view of the flame which will appear when he withdraws his head and arm from the opening, the pilgrims begin to pummel him. Suddenly there is a hush in the church.

> Every one in the area had either a torch or a taper ready to be lighted. A pause of eager expectancy—a silence almost as exciting as the noise, was succeeded by a startling and tremendous shout,

which shook the building to its foundation. A voice from within the Sepulchre had proclaimed that the miraculous fire was kindled! The bishop now drew forth his head from the hole, and held up a mass of fire, amid cries of thanksgiving and rejoicing from the multitude.[24]

Not everyone rejoices. Fighting starts among Armenians and Greeks, each trying to extinguish the other's torch. The "bishop of the holy fire" has distributed the fire unequally, giving to one group before the other.

As the fighting continues, flaming torches are tossed about recklessly, followed by clubs and sticks. Turkish soldiers are summoned. In the melee Kamal Pasha, the governor of Jerusalem, is jostled about, "losing some of his decorations in the scuffle." Women run for safety. The church itself comes under attack when pictures of saints and martyrs are "destroyed by sharp-pointed sticks being thrust into them."[25]

The fighting lasts a quarter of an hour. When it is over the authorities, led by the pasha, take counsel. It is "decided that the Greek and Armenian services should for the future be held at different hours, so that such disgraceful and dangerous collisions in the church might be avoided."[26]

And what of the Holy Fire? Some of the educated Greek priests admit that it is a "pious fraud," Rogers informs us. But no one thinks of ending it. Why disturb the "faith of the mass of the people, who were thoroughly impressed by the belief that God Himself descends, and with His glorious presence kindles the fire over the tomb, every year on Holy Saturday"?[27] The ritual of the Holy Fire continues in Jerusalem to the present day.

As the Holy Fire was a religious event for the Easter pilgrims, so the pilgrims were an economic boon to Jerusalem. Rogers understood that both must continue: "Priests, shopkeepers, relic manufacturers, householders, owners of camels, horses, and other beasts of burden, would all more or less feel it, if the annual pilgrimages were to cease; and as the Holy Fire is the chief attraction, the temptation to encourage the delusion is very great."[28]

NO ONE OF THE TIME would have sympathized more with Rogers's repugnance at the spectacle of the Holy Fire than Mark

Twain, for whom the reality of Palestine seemed to overwhelm any appreciation of the dream.

Twain's travel letters from Europe and the Middle East to *Alta California* expressed his disdain for pious effusions about Palestine.[29] This was not the land of "milk and honey" he had read about in the books of Lamartine, Chateaubriand, Kinglake, and William C. Prime. He could not share their lyrically expressed sentiments about the country. In extolling Palestine's past glory, they had closed their eyes to the evidence of dirt and desolation everywhere. Without sentimentality (but not without a certain haughty disdain), Twain reports on the real Palestine. Here is his description of entering the Arab Christian village named after Mary Magdalene, where he and his travel companions had to pay out "bucksheesh."

> As we rode into Magdala not a soul was visible. But the ring of the horses' hoofs roused the stupid population, and they all came trooping out—old men and old women, boys and girls, the blind, the crazy, and the crippled, all in ragged, soiled, and scanty raiment, and all abject beggars by nature, instinct, and education. How the vermin-tortured vagabonds did swarm! How they showed their scars and sores, and piteously pointed to their maimed and crooked limbs, and begged with their pleading eyes for charity! ... As we paid the bucksheesh out to sore-eyed children and brown, buxom girls with repulsively tattooed lips and chins, we filed through the town.[30]

From Magdala, Twain rode on horseback to the town of Tiberias where he found "particularly uncomely Jews, Arabs, and negroes." He tells us that "squalor and poverty are the pride of Tiberias." His scorn, touched with traditional Christian contempt, falls heavily on the small community of Hasidic Jews in town.

> They say that the long-nosed, lanky, dyspeptic-looking body-snatchers, with the indescribable hats on, and a long curl dangling down in front of each ear, are the old, familiar, self-righteous Pharisees we read of in the Scriptures. Verily, they look it. Judging merely by their general style, and without other evidence, one might easily suspect that self-righteousness was their specialty.[31]

At other times Palestine brings out the American chauvinist in Twain, as when he described Lake Tiberias (the Sea of Galilee) as smaller and not as blue as California's Lake Tahoe. "... When we come to speak of beauty, this sea [Galilee] is no more to be compared to Tahoe than a meridian of longitude to a rainbow."

With one stroke of his pen, Twain punctures the Christian's emotional image of Jesus walking on the Sea of Galilee. "Silence and solitude brood over Tahoe; and silence and solitude brood also over this lake of [Galilee]. But the solitude of one is cheerful and fascinating as the solitude of the other is dismal and repellant."[32]

Twain abhorred engravings of Palestine—like those of David Roberts—depicting the timeless beauty of its landscape, the exotic charm of its people, pictures that gave a romantic sense of the country. To counter such images Twain writes an unsparingly harsh description of Arab girls at a desert well, the Virgin's Fountain, in Nazareth:

> This "Fountain of the Virgin" is the one which tradition says Mary used to get water from, twenty times a day, when she was a girl, and bear it away in a jar upon her head. The water streams through faucets in the face of a wall of ancient masonry which stands removed from the houses of the village. The young girls of Nazareth still collect about it by the dozen and keep up a riotous laughter and sky-larking. The Nazarene girls are homely. Some of them have large, lustrous eyes, but none of them have pretty faces. These girls wear a single garment, usually, and it is loose, shapeless, of undecided color; it is generally out of repair, too. They wear, from crown to jaw, curious strings of old coins, after the manner of the belles of Tiberias, and brass jewelry upon their wrists and in their ears. They wear no shoes and stockings. They are the most human girls we have found in the country yet, and the best natured. But there is no question that these picturesque maidens sadly lack comeliness.[33]

Twain was particularly irked by the effusions of the scholarly American traveler and his contemporary William C. Prime, as when Prime extols his first days in Jerusalem:

> To rise in the morning early, and go along the Way of Grief to the gate of St. Stephen, and out on the brow of Moriah, there to see the sun rise over Olivet; to go down and wash your eyes, heavy with sleep, in the soft waters of Siloam, that they might never ache

again; to climb the sides of Mt. Zion, and come in by the Zion gate, and so up the streets of the city to the Holy Sepulchre to visit Calvary and the Tomb; to press our knee on the cold rock where the first footsteps of the risen Saviour were pressed; and then, as the twilight came on, and the moonlight fell softly in the valley, to go down to Gethsemane and to pray! Think of days thus spent![34]

To distance himself from Prime, Twain is determined to be even more the caustic observer. He finds Jerusalem on first sight to be "mournful and dreary and lifeless." Like Mary Eliza Rogers before him, he recognizes grotesque absurdities all about town. Life here is a burlesque of beggars and bearded holy men, of countless cats and exposed carcasses of rotting meat. The rounded domes of the houses within Jerusalem give the appearance of a city as "knobby with countless little domes as a prison door is with boltheads." Houses are crowded together within the city walls, and the streets are so narrow and crooked that viewed from a height they seem to disappear. The houses themselves, each with a "cage of wooden lattice-work projecting in front of every window," give the impression of chicken coops.

Twain succeeded (where ten years earlier another American writer-traveler named Herman Melville had failed) in gaining entry to the Dome of the Rock shrine. He found the place dull and lifeless. The pool of Bethesda proved to be a cesspool. And the pool of Hezekiah, where Bathsheba had bathed when David spied her, he declared a "frog-pond." If that was not enough for his readers, Twain roundly condemned Judas "for hanging himself on a hill outside the city instead of inside its walls, for it meant one more stiff climb for the visitors."[35]

But it seems Jerusalem, though "mournful and dreary," eventually works its wonder on Twain, puncturing his cynicism. He does not run from but rather lingers in the Church of the Holy Sepulchre, and is fascinated by the many holy sites and the devout who stream to them. He writes: "When one stands where the Savior was crucified, he finds it all he can do to keep strictly before his mind that Christ was not crucified in a Catholic church."[36] The manifest evidence of faith gnaws at the cynic. With a touch of awe for religious faith, he exclaims: "Oh, for the ignorance & and the confidingness of ignorance that could enable a man to kneel at the Sepulchre & look at the rift in the rock, & the socket of the cross & the tomb of Adam & feel & know & never question that they were genuine."[37]

Upon entering the small marble enclosure built over the tomb of Jesus, Twain mentions the "tawdry gee-gaws" heaped on the sepulchre. Yet he is moved by an image of the Crucifixion. For standing there at the sight, one "fully believes that he is looking upon the very spot where the Savior gave up his life."[38]

Twain is impressed by the sheer diversity of Jerusalem's peoples: "Moslems, Jews, Greeks, Latins, Armenians, Syrians, Copts, Abyssinians, Greek Catholics, and a handful of Protestants." Fourteen thousand souls living amid "rags, wretchedness, poverty and dirt." These conditions, Twain comments, are surer evidence of Muslim rule "than the crescent flag itself."

Nothing nauseates Twain more than the sight of the sick and deformed crowding Jerusalem's shrines.

> To see the numbers of maimed, malformed and diseased humanity that throng the holy places and obstruct the gates, one might suppose that the ancient days had come again, and that the angel of the Lord was expected to descend at any moment to stir the waters of Bethesda. Jerusalem is mournful, and dreary, and lifeless. I would not desire to live here.[39]

With all his disdain, Twain worried about whether *Innocents Abroad* might offend his readers. The Holy Land seems to have affected him in ways he did not fully understand. One must suppose he never outgrew the Bible lessons taught to him in Sunday school in Hannibal, Missouri. When he left Palestine he brought gifts to his mother and sister—a Bible bound in balsam, olive wood prayer beads, and a vial of water from the Jordan River.[40] They were just the sort of sacred souvenirs that pilgrims, whom he took pleasure in deriding, had always brought home.

Palestine did not make a believer out of Twain. He was honestly a skeptic and, like Mary Eliza Rogers, an incisive critic of religious tawdriness. Yet in spite of himself he experienced the power of the Holy Land to evoke a sense of wonder about the life of Jesus in that otherwise dirty and desolate country. The dream could outweigh the reality, even for him. In a letter he wrote to his friend and mentor, Mrs. Mary Fairbanks of Cleveland, Ohio, he described his feelings about the Nativity Grotto in Bethlehem:

And now that the greasy monks, & the noisy mob, & the leprous beggars are gone, & all the harsh, cold hardness of *real* stone & unsentimental glare of sunlight are banished from the vision, don't you realize again, as in other years, that Jesus was born there, & that the angels *did* sing in the still air above, & that the wondering shepherds *did* hold their breath & listen as the mysterious music floated by? *I* do. It is more real than ever. And I am glad, a hundred times glad, that I saw Bethlehem, though at the time it seemed that that sight had swept away forever, every pleasant fancy & every cherished memory that ever the city of Nativity had stored away in my mind & heart.[41]

". . . That Jesus was born there." In one telltale phrase Twain admits to the spiritual power of the Holy Land, the same power that captivated Mary Eliza Rogers. Like thousands of English and American Protestants, Twain became the tourist-pilgrim who found the Bible stories "vivified and verified" in Palestine.[42] He was not the cynic when he wrote, "I am glad, a hundred times glad, that I saw Bethlehem. . . ."

CHAPTER EIGHT

Palestinians and Zionists: New Identities for an Ancient Land

> You and your kinsmen should realize that you are
> Turks and that there is absolutely no such thing as an
> Arab people or an Arab homeland.
> —Turkish lecturer to cadets at the military academy
> in Istanbul
>
> Land is the most necessary thing for our establishing
> roots in Palestine. Since there are hardly any more
> arable unsettled lands in Palestine, we are bound in
> each case of the purchase of the land and its
> settlement to remove the peasants who cultivated
> the land so far, both owners of the land and tenants.
> —Arthur Ruppin, Jewish Agency official

The economic boom in Palestine that followed the Crimean War was fueled by the lucrative grain export market. The life of the Arab peasant was momentarily improved by the new prosperity. British Consul James Finn reported that the peasantry, notwithstanding the losses sustained by extortion of their own sheiks and of the tax farmers, had accumulated an unprecedented degree of wealth—"but they bury their coin in holes, they purchase arms, and they decorate their women."[1]

Surprisingly few Arabs made money in the late nineteenth century. For while two-thirds of the Arab Muslim population depended on agriculture, in the midst of general prosperity more than 25 percent of them earned no more than subsistence income.[2] Those who fared well did so despite exploitation by land speculators, who made fortunes from the Arab peasant's alienation from the soil. Kenneth Stein describes the dismal trap into which the peasant inevitably fell:

> The Palestine fellah had a lifelong personal and ancestral attachment to his land and was philosophically opposed to selling it. But oppressive taxes, enormous debt, inefficient land usage, and climatic vicissitudes were the burdensome pressures which forced the fellah to relinquish his independence as an owner.[3]

Need and greed were behind land exploitation. In chronic need of money, peasants sold their land in the late nineteenth century to village sheiks and mukhtars, moneylenders, bankers, land agents, and town notables, and finally to the new Jewish immigrant colonizers who began arriving in the 1880s and 1890s. By the early twentieth century, a peasantry once living and working on land it considered its own had increasingly become a class of tenant sharecroppers—a class that in time would be further reduced to the level of paid farm laborers.

The roots of the peasant's alienation from the land lay in the important Ottoman Land Law of 1858, enacted after the Crimean War. The law affected nearly all of the land farmed by peasants, for legally all of Palestine's land, save for small privately owned household plots, was *miri,* or crown land, leased to the peasantry, which had the right of usufruct. In actual practice, however, the peasants' generations-old cultivation of land bestowed virtual ownership, which even allowed the bequeathing or selling of a lease to the land to others.[4]

The Land Law was a rude breaking of the traditional connection between the peasant, his use of the land, and his sense of ownership. The ostensible purpose of the law was to put an end to the passing of land into private hands and to increase land tax revenue. This was to be done by requiring the peasantry to register their use of land, which then made it possible for the government to tax peasants more effectively and to control the buying and selling of land leases.

But the Land Law had the opposite effect of what it intended. Most peasants resisted registering their use of land for fear of having their names appear on land rolls and thus exposing them to taxes and military conscription. Rather than register land in their own names, peasants registered land in the names of town notables and other moneylenders who were able to pay the taxes, keep the peasants' names off tax rolls, avoid their conscription, and generally act as intermediary between them and the feared government. Thus rather than slow the passing of land into private hands, the Land Law accelerated it.

The failure of the Ottoman Land Law to stop land alienation is evidenced by the fact that at the beginning of the twentieth century peasants owned only 20 percent of the land in Galilee and 50 percent in Judea; all other land was in the hands of Arab absentee owners, town notables, Christians, and Jews.[5] By 1923, 75 percent of land owned collectively by villages had passed into private hands, mostly town notables, so that with increased population more peasants were living on less peasant-owned land.[6]

The alienation of peasant land was further hastened when tax assessments and approvals of land ownership were put in the hands of local town councils (*majlis idara*), dominated by the wealthy urban elite who had the most to gain from approving land transfers.[7] While the *majlis* was supposed to be a representative body, in fact Muslim peasants, Arab Christians, and Jews were woefully underrepresented on the councils.[8] It was not unusual for a prominent urban family to own from seven thousand to fifteen thousand acres.

Unregistered lands were reclaimed by Ottoman authorities, who auctioned them off at rock-bottom prices to the urban notables. One of the most notorious instances of this practice occurred with the auctioning of a huge estate in the area north of the plain of Esdraelon. Here were some seventy square miles of land, which included twenty villages and four thousand people. Two-thirds of the purchase price of this estate went to the Turkish intermediary who arranged the sale, and only one-third to the Ottoman government, the seller. The purchaser of the estate was a family of Arab Orthodox Christians, the Sursuq brothers of Beirut, shrewd bankers who purchased the land for the paltry sum of $20,000 and immediately gained an annual income of $12,000 from the land's produce. They watched the value of the land appreciate, and then in late 1910 sold it at great profit to Jewish land purchasers.[9]

The alienation of the Arab peasant from the land had far-reaching consequences. A whole class of Arab town notables became wealthy from the sale of land chiefly to European Christians after 1860, and immensely wealthier when after 1880 the Jewish demand for land led to inflated prices. And by virtue of owning land, the urban notables were able to control the flow of grain to the towns. It was not uncommon for notables to manipulate the price of grain by withholding supply, forcing up the price during the scarcity, then selling it at enormous profit.[10]

Once the urban notables began selling land to Christians and Jews, the Arab peasant, who was usually poor, also became landless. The historian Kenneth Stein sums up the situation of Palestine's peasants by speaking of "an overwhelmingly illiterate and unsophisticated peasantry that had no interest in political involvement, was not cognizant of its legal rights, and did not have promise of financial betterment."[11] Having little stake in the land, the peasant had no reluctance in leaving it. Thus the increase in agricultural productivity in citrus created a need for farm labor and led to a shift of Arab population from the central hill country to the coastal plain. Hillside villages were left behind while a new Arab proletariat came into being in the coastal towns.

The rise of a new urban elite further stratified Palestine's Arab society. A handful of wealthy and powerful landowning families dominated; at the bottom were a mass of impoverished, illiterate, and politically impotent peasants. The midcentury Ottoman effort to break the hold of village sheiks and mountain lords on Palestine's society had largely succeeded; but by end of the century the failure of the government to handle the land problem had produced a new dominant class of urban notables in place of the despotic sheiks. This urban class grew more powerful in the twentieth century as it gained government appointment to numerous religious, political, and administrative municipal and district offices. In virtually every Palestinian town, from Acre to Gaza on the coast, and inland from Jenin to Jerusalem and Jericho, a handful of families controlled the affairs of the country. The peasantry had, as Stein says, "no voice in the management of their own affairs in Palestine during the late Ottoman period."[12]

FOR CENTURIES the Arab provinces of the Ottoman Empire remained loyal to the sultan because of the common bond of Islam. That tie had begun to loosen in the eighteenth century when Arabs felt that the sultan was weakening before the growing power of the Christian West. Russia had inflicted military defeats and won a major diplomatic victory in representing all Orthodox Christians in the realm. Napoleon's occupation of Egypt showed that the sultan could not safeguard his empire and could preserve his only throne by negotiating defense treaties with Britain and other European powers.

More humiliations followed. The Greek War of Independence, 1821–1828, resulted in the breakaway of a major Ottoman province. The insurrection of Egypt's Pasha Muhammad Ali in the 1830s threatened to topple the sultan's throne, and the dependency of the Noble Porte on the West increased as a consequence. The opening of foreign consulates in major cities extended Europe's power into the heart of the empire. Responding to European pressure, the Ottoman government in the late 1830s embarked on a major campaign to overhaul and modernize the administration of the empire. The resulting Tanzimat Reform Laws proved a two-edged sword. In granting equal legal rights to non-Muslim subjects, the government gained the support of Western nations but lost favor among Muslim clerics and intellectuals. Evidence that the Ottoman Empire had fallen behind Western Christian nations in scientific knowledge, financial power, and military might deepened the sense of humiliation.

After the Crimean War it was clear that the Ottoman Empire could no longer stand on its own feet. Arab voices were raised deploring the malaise into which the empire had fallen and suggesting remedies for the restoration of Ottoman health. A renewed Arab national and cultural self-consciousness took shape, with enormous political consequences.[13]

The first of those voices was that of Jamal al-Din al-Afghani, who in the 1870s in Egypt preached a powerful gospel which condemned the Western values poisoning the Ottoman state. Afghani called for a revitalization of the empire by a return to primitive Islam and the Arabic Koran. But this was no mere religious fundamentalism. Afghani was prepared to accept whatever the West had to offer the East in scientific knowledge and technical invention; he insisted, however, that the Ottoman Empire could not regain its glory without returning culturally, morally, and spiritually, to its "Eastern" or Arab roots.

Afghani's cry for Islamic renewal inspired other voices: Muhammad Abdu (1849–1905), Tahir al-Zairi (1851–1920), and, at the turn of the century, Rashid Rida in Damascus and Rahman al-Kawakibi in Cairo. After Afghani, the anti-Western theme was more stridently expressed, as when Abdu "warned against sending Moslems to the schools of the missionaries, who were 'foreign devils.' . . ." Unlike his mentor Afghani, Abdu had no respect for Western learning. Muslims, he believed, should rely only on the soundness of religious faith: ". . . It is sufficient for us to return to what we have abandoned and to purify what we have corrupted. This consists of our religious and humanistic books, which contain more than enough of what we seek. . . ."[14]

To Rashid Rida, Islam and Arabism were one: "To be filled with passion for the history of the Arabs, to strive to revive their glory, is the same as working for Islamic union, which in the past was achieved only through the Arabs and which will not be regained in this century except through them."[15]

Kawakibi argued that Muslims need not envy Western knowledge or seek to imitate it. For devotion to Islam inspired scientific inquiry leading to knowledge and truth. "The one who follows true pure Islam . . . increases his faith whenever he increases his science or exercises thought, for . . . he will not find in [true Islam] anything which reason rejects or scientific investigation refutes."[16]

Afghani and those who followed in his footsteps were content to be reformers of the Ottoman state, not revolutionaries. They wanted greater rights for the sultan's Arab subjects within the Ottoman system, not political independence from it. In preaching the gospel of the pure Arabic roots of Islam, they hoped to return Ottomanism to the creative sources of its own being.

Yet this message of a pure Arabic Islam, stressing as it did the Koran and Arabic literary and religious studies, isolated the idea of Arabism and gave it priority over Ottomanism. In that respect, without perhaps aiming to, Afghani and other reformers were promoting an image of Arab national independence and superiority. As the historian C. Ernest Dawn has so acutely observed, "The Ottomanists attempted to make a single nationality of the diverse ethnic elements which peopled the Ottoman Empire. The Arabists raised a single people, the Arabs, to a position of pre-eminence."[17] In thus stressing the dominance of Arabism in Islam, the Arabs and their religion, language, and culture—indeed, Arabism itself as a political value—were put in tension with Ottomanism. But that tension did not erupt into political action until after the dethronement in 1908 of the sultan by the Young Turks who, organized as the Committee on Union and Progress, undertook a new central government in Istanbul.

Not only Muslims such as Afghani and his followers championed the Arabic national idea. That idea also found warm support among Arab Christian intellectuals, beginning with Ibrahim al-Yazigi and Adib Ishaq in Beirut in the late 1870s, who extolled the glories of Arabic people and culture. These men were even prepared to accept the religion of Islam as the finest expression of Arabism. One Syrian Christian summed up the attitude: "Let every one of us say I am Arab . . . and if being Arab is only possible through being Muslim, then let him say I am an Arab and Muslim. . . ."[18] Needless to say, many Arab Christians could only identify with Arabism if it was expressed in a secular manner, emphasizing Arabic language and literature rather than Islam and the Koran.[19] The voices of those who took this view were heard after the Young Turks came to power.

The cataclysmic event of modern Turkish history that ended the despotism of Abdulhamid II introduced a new and seemingly progressive government under the aegis of the Committee on Union and Progress and a new constitution for the empire. Press censorship was ended, leading to the founding of scores of newspapers, many of them in Arabic. The sultan's vast network of spies and sycophants was dismantled.

The response to these changes on the part of Arab intellectuals, both Muslim and Christian, was instant. New social and literary clubs were opened in Istanbul, Beirut, Damascus, and Basra. Picking up where earlier Arab reformers had left off, much of the talk at these clubs was about the glorious achievements of the Arabs, and about acquiring more rights for Arabs under the new Turkish government.[20] Arabs who attended these club meetings did not hide their desire to one day soon achieve independence. What form that independence might take and what territories it would cover remained vague. But certainly it meant independence from the Turkish central governing authority. This new "Arab Awakening" culminated in the convening of the Arab Congress in Paris in January 1913, where the main agenda item was Arab rights in the Turkish Empire. But the hidden agenda of Arab independence won the day.

Just before the Arab Congress, two new, revolutionary-minded Arab secret societies had been formed. The first was the Young Arab Society (al-Fatah), founded in Paris in 1911; two years later in Istanbul, a newly formed group of Arab military officers called themselves the Covenant Society (al-Ard). The members of these societies numbered fewer than two hundred young men, well educated, from families that represented the higher economic and cultural strata of Arab society throughout greater Syria.[21] Meanwhile the masses of Arab Muslim peasants throughout the empire knew nothing of political independence and continued to view their Arab identities within the indissoluble bonds of Islam and Ottomanism.[22]

The revolution carried out by the Committee on Union and Progress gave Arab intellectuals a false sense of hope about their future in the empire. It did not take long for the Turkish revolutionaries who deposed the sultan to reassert Istanbul's hegemony in the form of centralized Turkish control over the empire's Arabic provinces. A new ideology deemphasized the common Islamic bond of the empire stressed by Ottoman rulers in favor of pan-Turanism, a new nationalistic expression of the superiority of Turkish language and culture.

Once again, under the new regime, Arabs began to feel second class. The first ominous warning that the Committee on Union and Progress would be no less despotic than its predecessor was the banning of all non-Turkish ethnic societies, which drove Arab intellectuals underground.[23] What followed were imprisonments of Arabs suspected of revolutionary conspiracies.

Arabs were further alienated by the imposition of the Turkish language in Arab schools at every level. Watching the ideology of pan-Turanism take hold in the empire confirmed Arab intellectuals in their view that Arab independence could not be won without rebellion. From underground meetings of Fatah and Ard, Arabs eventually planned an armed rebellion against Turkish rule in greater Syria.[24]

ARAB RESENTMENT of Ottoman authority was exacerbated when Arab Muslims and Christians saw that the government allowed mass Jewish immigration to Palestine beginning in the last decades of the nineteenth century. The marked increased in the numbers of Jews entering the country, and the news of their land purchases, circulated from one Arab town to another, reviving fears that Westerners—this time Jews—were embarked on a campaign to steal the country from its rightful owners.[25]

To understand the social and ideological forces behind the Jewish immigration to Palestine, we must start with the liberal reign of the Russian tsar Alexander II (1855–1881), which ended in his assassination. What followed was the reactionary government of Alexander III, who enacted the May Laws of 1882 under which Jews could not live without special permission beyond a designated strip of western Russia called the Pale of Settlement.[26] Barred from purchasing land and from traveling anywhere in Russia without official permission, Jews were confined to this one enormous rural ghetto.

The May Laws crushed any Jewish hope for emancipation in Russia and eastern Europe. Pogrom followed pogrom in Russia, Poland, and Rumania, with the result that masses of Jews migrated to the West, most of them headed for America, whose doors were then open to east European immigrants. Between 1880 and 1900 more than a million Jews reached the United States. A fraction of that number, most of them with strong religious and nationalist feelings about Eretz Yisrael, immigrated to Palestine. In some instances tsarist officials, glad to be rid of a nuisance minority, allowed Jews to travel from Odessa on Christian pilgrim ships bound for the Holy Land.[27]

In reaction to the deplorable situation facing Jews in Russia and eastern Europe, a movement arose for national revival called, in Hebrew, Hovevei Zion (Lovers of Zion). Hovevei Zion called for the restoration of Jews to their ancestral homeland. Jewish societies devoted to the idea sprang up in the major cities of eastern Europe, particularly in Russia. In June 1882 a group of fourteen Russian Hovevei Zion, including one woman, reached Jaffa port and made its way to a Jewish training farm called Mikveh Israel, founded in 1870 by the French philanthropic society Alliance Israelite Universelle.[28] They were the first of a new *yishuv* (settlement) that would in time transform the country.

This first wave of immigration, lasting from 1882 to 1903, represented a different human element than the Sephardi and Ashkenazi traditionalists (the Old Yishuv) who had lived in Palestine for generations or had settled there in the nineteenth century for religious reasons. While some of the New Yishuv were practicing Orthodox Jews, none were messianic fundamentalists. They did not expect divine intervention to solve Jewish problems, and they emphasized economic self-sufficiency. If they believed in a messianic redemption at all, it was with the understanding that the Messiah's coming would be hastened by Jewish labor and practical good works. They did not expect to be supported by *haluka* charity money raised abroad. They wanted to work, build, and till the soil in order (according to a slogan of the time) "to bring forth bread out of the earth."

The first agricultural settlements these new pioneers established on the coast foundered because, with all their desire and energy, they lacked farming skills.[29] One of their many mistakes was to limit themselves to raising vegetables and other field crops for their own consumption, rather than the cash crops (wheat, almonds, olives, citrus) that would have brought profit and growth. The original settlements, no more than a half-dozen, were rescued from financial ruin by the wealthy French philanthropist Baron Edmond de Rothschild, who, like Montefiore before him, had taken an interest in reviving Jewish life in Palestine. But with this difference: Rothschild, unlike Montefiore, was determined to sponsor agricultural projects that would show a profit. Rothschild's agents took possession of the new farms in 1883 and for the next sixteen years turned them to the growing of vines for wine production. In the process they made of the pioneers a group of paid plantation workers, living from the baron's paternalism. This first experiment in Jewish economic self-sufficiency in the ancestral land ended when Jews refused to accept the status of paid workers on a rich man's farm.

Although the pioneering zeal of the first Lovers of Zion waned, they planted the first seeds of Jewish national renewal in Palestine. They were followed by mass immigrations organized and financed by the Zionist movement, brought into being by the ideas and work of Theodor Herzl.

At Basle in 1897 Herzl officially founded the World Zionist Organization, which declared that the aim of Zionism was the creation for the Jewish people of a "home in Palestine secured by public law." Herzl left no doubt as to what "home" meant. After the Basle meeting he recorded in his diary: "Were I to sum up the Basle Congress in a word . . . it would be this: at Basle I founded the Jewish state."[30]

Herzl and his colleagues at Basle understood Zionism and a future Jewish state to be a solution to the problem of perpetual insecurity for Jews in a non-Jewish world. Their solution was to achieve political independence for Jews in a specific territory. Some, including Herzl, said the territory might be anywhere. The prevailing majority argued that the territory, for historic and religious reasons, could only be Palestine, Eretz Yisrael, the ancestral homeland.

But Herzl and Zionism alone could not have brought about the mass immigration of Jews to Palestine that began at the onset of the twentieth century. Russian pogroms too played a role. In 1903 a bloody pogrom which broke out in Kishniev led to a major exodus of Jews from Russia, many of them bound for Palestine. That immigration, known as the Second Aliya, lasted from 1903 to the outbreak of world war in 1914, and brought to Palestine more than thirty thousand industrious, educated, and skilled Jews who had definite views about Jewish labor, nationalism, and relations with the Arabs.[31]

Where the First Aliya lacked technical agricultural competence and relied on cheap Arab labor to help farm the land, the Jews of the Second Aliya, stressing their new Zionist-socialist slogans ("conquest of the land," "Jewish labor"), spurned Arab workers and insisted that Jews must provide for themselves.[32] Out of that sharpened sense of Jewish autonomy came institutions of self-government, the Kibbutz Movement, the labor federation known as the Histadrut, and the military defense force called the Haganah.

When the Zionist movement was founded in 1897 there were already 50,000 Jews in Palestine and 18 modern settlements of Hovevei Zion.[33] By 1914, on the eve of World War I, there were 40 to 50 Jewish agricultural settlements, and the total number of Jews was estimated at 80,000 to 90,000, or about 14 percent of a Palestinian population of between 600,000 and 700,000, overwhelmingly Muslim.

The Orthodox Jewish pietists of the Old Yishuv, living on *haluka,* predominated in Palestine until after World War I, when Zionist-sponsored immigration created a majority of the New

Yishuv. Whenever they arrived, Jewish immigrants were not met with an easy life in Palestine. Between 1881 and 1914 as many as 50,000, one of two, left Palestine for the West. Despite these departures, Jewish population increase had a dramatic effect on Jerusalem. In the last quarter of the nineteenth century, Jews achieved a majority there, in 1914 numbering 45,000 in a city of 80,000.[34]

From its inception the Zionist movement in Palestine exacerbated relations among Jews in the country. Traditional tensions between Ashkenazim and Sephardim, and between Hasidim and Perushim continued. But now there was a new layer of contention. Orthodox pietists opposed the often outspoken secular nationalist ideology of Hovevei Zion. In 1888–1889 the pietists tried unsuccessfully to force the Zionist agricultural pioneers to observe the biblical edict of Shemmitah, which allows the earth to lie fallow every seventh, sabbatical year. The pioneers resisted religious pressure, knowing that observance of Shemmitah meant the ruin of their farms.[35]

The gulf between religious and secular Jews widened further when Eliezer Ben-Yehuda, the architect of the modern Hebrew language, criticized traditional Ashkenazi-Sephardi factionalism for undermining Jewish national unity. The pietists struck back by slandering Ben-Yehuda as a revolutionary and in 1894 arranging his imprisonment by Turkish authorities. Ben-Yehuda took sweet revenge by using his time in prison to begin writing the first comprehensive dictionary of the modern Hebrew language, one of the major achievements of the Zionist movement.[36]

The main Zionist-sponsored settlement of the land occurred on the coastline and in the lower Galilee, not in Zion itself or in Jerusalem, a stronghold of pious orthodoxy. The factional strife between Orthodox Jewry and secular Zionists continued through the twentieth century and abated only when both sides faced a common Arab threat.

The success of Jewish immigration to Palestine from the 1880s to World War I is all the more remarkable because it occurred in the face of official Ottoman opposition. In 1882, following pogroms, and with the first signs of spontaneous mass immigration of Jews out of Russia and eastern Europe, Ottoman authorities decreed that Jews were welcome to move to any part of the empire *except* Palestine. At a time when the Noble Porte faced separatist movements among Bulgarians, Rumanians, Serbs, and others in the Balkans, and was sensitive to Arab nationalist feeling, the last thing the empire wanted was a sizable new Jewish element stirring up trouble in Arab Palestine. Having fought four wars with Russia in the nineteenth century alone, the Ottoman government (ignoring Russian anti-Semitism) was suspicious of Hovevei Zion as a type of Russian revolutionary organization. Why, thought Istanbul, encourage another nationalist-separatist element to take root in an Arab-Muslim land?

Turkey in the time of Sultan Abdulhamid II and later under the regime of the Young Turks (1908–1914) feared that if Palestine's doors were opened, anti-Jewish hostility in Russia and eastern Europe would force vast numbers of Jews through those doors. Most of the world's estimated twelve million Jews lived under the influence of the Russian tsar. The thought that a large percentage of world Jewry might seek to immigrate to Palestine caused consternation among the sultan's advisers.[37]

No one better recognized the situation than Sultan Abdulhamid. After first refusing to see Herzl in 1896, he granted an audience to the Zionist leader, who made an astounding offer. In exchange for Jewish money to pay off the Ottoman world debt (a vain promise which Herzl could not keep), might the sultan grant a charter to the Jews to establish Jewish autonomy in Palestine?[38] The sultan, who badly needed funds, was not about to risk more instability in his already tottering empire. He saw clearly that he had much more to fear from an Arab anti-Jewish rebellion in Palestine than he had to gain from Herzl's offer of money. But there was a religious consideration. The sultan also happened to be the caliph, the keeper of Islamic religious law for the whole of the Muslim world. What would that world think of Abdulhamid if he turned over to the Jews Jerusalem, site of two of Islam's most treasured holy places—the Dome of the Rock shrine and the Mosque of Al Aksa?

In refusing Herzl's offer, the sultan did not waste an opportunity to express what turned out to be a farsighted estimation of the Jewish future in Palestine:

> The power of money can do anything. [The Jews] are not going to create a government today; it is a preliminary stage. It is an aim and a hope. They will commence their work now, and after many years, even if it will be a thousand years, they might be successful in their aim; and I think they will be.[39]

Jews entered Palestine on pilgrims' visas. When the visas expired, the pilgrims dissolved among the growing Jewish numbers in rural settlements and cities. Many entered the country illegally, usually through an overland route that took them from Egypt to Palestine. Some local government officials could always be bribed to ignore Istanbul's restrictions on immigration. Jerusalem's foreign consuls, led by the British, actively resisted these restrictions, seeing them as a violation of their own powers under the Capitulations. This had the effect of weakening local resolve to prevent Jews from entering the country. Often the deportation of Jews known to be illegal immigrants was prevented by Jerusalem's British consul, who acted on a policy enunciated by Foreign Secretary Palmerston in 1840—"to afford protection to the Jews generally."

At the start of the twentieth century local Arab reactions to the increased presence of Jews in Palestine were "primitive and nonpolitical."[40] Arabs complained that Jews fenced their land and failed to respect the traditional Arab practice of allowing animals to graze freely on land. Arab delegates to the Ottoman parliament in Istanbul complained about increased Jewish land purchases.[41] The news that land was being sold by Arab landowners to Jews, often against the wishes of the official Turkish governor of Palestine, appeared in the numerous Arabic language newspapers that arose in Palestine following the Young Turk revolution of 1908.[42] In the same year Ali Ekrem Bey, administrator of the Jerusalem district, urged the appointment of a Turk, not an Arab, as head of Jerusalem's Muslim court, for fear that an Arab would not protest land sales to Jews.

The first truly pointed political reaction to what was perceived as the "Jewish problem" of Palestine came from an Arab Christian writer in Lebanon, Negib Azoury, whose words were prophetic of a future clash:

> Two important phenomena, of identical character but nevertheless opposed, which till now have not attracted attention, are now making their appearance in Asian Turkey: these are the awakening of the Arab nation and the latent efforts of the Jews to reestablish, on an extremely large scale, the ancient Kingdom of Israel. These two movements are destined to struggle continuously, with one another, until one prevails over the other. The fate of the

entire world depends on the result of this struggle between the two peoples, which represent two contradictory principles.[43]

As Jewish settlements multiplied on Palestine's coast and in the Galilee in the early twentieth century, Arab newspaper writers mounted a campaign against Zionism. For the first time Arabs began using the Arab word *Filastin* to refer to the country. It was the beginning of a sense of distinct self-identity, uniting the Arab Christians and Muslims of Palestine.[44] Two newspapers in particular, *Karmil* in Haifa and *Filastin* of Jaffa, took the lead in warning of the dangers of Jewish immigration and land purchases. Anti-Zionist opposition erased the class lines separating peasants from town notables, and rose above the centuries-old divisions between Muslims and Arab Christians.

Raghib al-Nashasibi, prototype of the Jerusalem Muslim landowning urban notable class, on the even of his election to the Ottoman parliament in 1914, spoke for all of Palestine's Arabs when he declared, "If I am elected as a representative, I shall devote all my strength day and night to doing away with the damage and threat of the Zionists and Zionism."[45]

The historian Yehoshuah Porath writes that "As the anti-Zionism of the urban intellectuals increased, . . . [the intellectuals] began to organize the villagers for acts of opposition and sabotage against the purchase of land by Jews. Thus the seeds of hostility to Zionism fell on fertile grounds and were destined to sprout forth in years to come."[46]

The Jews' accomplishments alarmed the Arabs. Their ability to raise and spend vast amounts of money for the purchase of land; their agricultural productivity and communal self-sufficiency; the flying of the Zionist flag and the use of the Hebrew language; the establishment of schools, hospitals, and banks; their willingness to defend themselves with arms—all these things were seen by Arabs as proof that the Jews were bent on taking over the country. And Arabs knew from their own reading of Hebraic prophecy of the eventual restoration of Jewish government to Eretz Yisrael.[47]

Arab press criticism of Jewish activities led in 1910 to the formation of the first Arab anti-Zionist organization in Haifa. Its leader was Njib Nassar, Christian editor of *Karmil,* who invited Muslims to join in mounting an economic boycott against the Jews. In the same year a similar organization, the Patriotic Ottoman party, was founded by pro-Ottoman Muslims in Jaffa. They spoke of Zionism as "a flood" which threatened to engulf the country.[48] Although the language was hyperbole, the Arab sense of losing Palestine to the alien presence of Zionism was genuine and would increase with the years.

THE JEWISH IMMIGRATION to Palestine began a few years after Britain gained sole control of the Suez Canal in 1875, and about the time British troops, in 1882, began occupying Egypt as a protectorate. With that occupation, British strategists began to see Palestine as a necessary buffer for both the Suez Canal and Egypt, both vital to communication with the Persian Gulf and India. With Britain now desiring Palestine for herself, the perceived need for a stable, loyal community of Jews in Palestine grew proportionately. Britain saw in her "protected Jews" a valuable ally and tool in Palestine for enhancing her own imperial powers in the Middle East.[48]

The farsightedness of Lord Kitchener played a major role in the British reassessment of Palestine. As a young officer of the Royal Engineers, Kitchener participated in the mapping of Palestine in the 1870s and gained an appreciation of the value of the natural deepwater port of Haifa.[49] Haifa's usefulness as a naval base grew in Kitchener's mind as Britain began worrying at century's turn that Egypt might come under attack from Turkey or Germany. The possession of Haifa would give Britain a strategic naval, land, and air base for communications with Mesopotamia, Egypt, and the Suez Canal. Kitchener had also heard of France's plans to extend its military railway system into the Sinai, bringing French guns close to Egypt and the canal. Haifa was safe for Britain as long as the compliant Turk was in control of Syria and Palestine. But how long would that last?

Britain's seizure of Egypt was dictated by the strategic need to control the Suez Canal, gateway to the eastern Mediterranean and the Far East. The action effectively ended London's friendship with the Ottoman government. As British influence in Istanbul declined, Germany's grew. Through investment and diplomacy, Germany together with Austria forged a powerful new friendship with Turkey, capped by the sultan's decision to award Prussia contracts for the construction of railways throughout the Ottoman Empire, including the Berlin-Baghdad and Damascus-Mecca lines. This construction caused anxiety in Western capitals, concerned that a new Prussian-Turkish axis was forming. The new alignment threatened the international balance of power maintained since the Crimean War. The sultan, sensitive to Western fears and wary of appearing to be too deep in Germany's pocket, acceded to Western demands by awarding France a concession to build the Jaffa-Jerusalem rail line and to improve Palestine's ports. The decision momentarily postponed a confrontation of the Western powers over Palestine and the Middle East.

By 1914 Germany, Austria, and Turkey were in alliance to oppose Britain, France, and Russia. The stage was set for a world war whose outcome would change the map of the Middle East and cast the fate of Palestine for the remainder of the twentieth century.

PART THREE

The Land in Conflict

CHAPTER NINE

Allenby at Jerusalem's Gate

> If this splendid country is ever to be properly developed ... and still more if it is to be British, it is only the Zionists who can accomplish these two aims. . . . [The] blessed Arabs are a poor show in this country.
> —William Ormsby-Gore, 1918
>
> [Arabs] will not be content either to be expropriated for Jewish immigrants, or to act merely as hewers of wood and drawers of water to the latter.
> —Lord George Curzon, 1917
>
> British good faith ... is the most precious asset of our foreign imperial policy.
> —Herbert Sidebotham, 1934

Reversing what had been a losing war in southern Palestine, the British Expeditionary Force, newly commanded by General Edmund Hillary Allenby, early in 1917 crushed Turkish forces at Beersheba and Gaza. Later that year, on December 11, the army marched into a defenseless Jerusalem. In mid-1918 all of Palestine, after four years of hard fighting, was under British army control. The victorious advance continued northward, where the capture of Damascus in September 1918 effectively ended four hundred years of Ottoman imperial domination of the Middle East.

General Allenby was only the most recent conqueror in Jerusalem's three thousand years of history. But he wished to be regarded differently. No showy displays of kingly authority for him. No imitating Kaiser William II, who on a business trip in 1882, rode into the old walled town on a white charger and then proceeded from Jaffa Gate to the Church of the Holy Sepulchre on oriental carpets, palm fronds hailing his passage all the way to the church door. Allenby rode up to Jerusalem's ancient walls, dismounted, and walked unarmed like a pilgrim through Jaffa Gate to receive the city's surrender.

This gesture of reverence was shared in London. The taking of Jerusalem was announced in Parliament as a Christmas gift to the people. Next to their love of the Bible was the Britishers' love of the Land of the Bible.[1] They had not conquered Palestine but gratefully taken custody of their spiritual homeland.

These feelings were shared by General Allenby, a devout Scots Presbyterian who saw himself as trustee of a country cherished by millions of Christians, Muslims, and Jews throughout the world. He had freed the Holy Land and all of Syria from the cruel and corrupt Turk. He would govern these lands under Western standards of tolerant treatment of all peoples, through the just exercise of power. He left no doubt about this in the words he spoke at Jaffa Gate.

> . . . Since your country is regarded with affection by the adherents of three of the great religions of mankind, and its soil has been consecrated by the prayers and pilgrimages of multitudes of devout people of these three religions for many centuries, therefore do I make known to you the promise that every sacred building, monument, holy spot, traditional shrine, endowment, pious bequest, or customary place of prayer, of whatsoever form of the three religions, will be maintained and protected according to the existing customs and beliefs of those to whose faiths they are sacred.[2]

Well and good. But the general was also determined to govern in behalf of the British Empire. The government of native peoples frequently degenerates when it is the instrument of imperialistic expansion. British piety about the Holy Land was sincere enough; but British imperial policy had fixed on Palestine as a strategic asset. With that policy in mind, any promise could be made and unmade.

Less than two weeks before Jerusalem surrendered to Allenby, an extraordinary document was issued in London that affected the

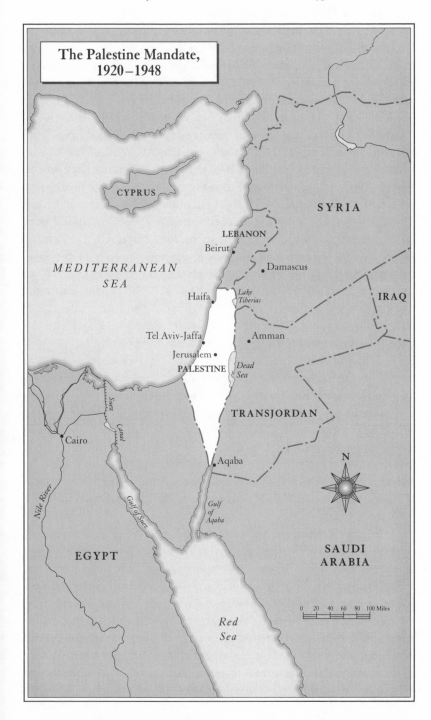

The Palestine Mandate,
1920–1948

CYPRUS

SYRIA

MEDITERRANEAN
SEA

LEBANON
Beirut

Damascus

Haifa

Lake
Tiberias

IRAQ

Tel Aviv-Jaffa

Amman

Jerusalem

PALESTINE

Dead
Sea

TRANSJORDAN

Suez
Canal

Cairo

Aqaba

N

Nile River

Gulf of Suez

Gulf
of
Aqaba

EGYPT

SAUDI
ARABIA

0   20   40   60   80   100 Miles

Red
Sea

future of Palestine for the next thirty years and more. It was a private letter written by Arthur James Balfour, Britain's foreign secretary, to Lord Rothschild, the most influential of Britain's Jews. In it Balfour, speaking for His Majesty's government, pledged support for the establishment in Palestine of a Jewish "national home."

We owe to the meticulous research of the late Israeli scholar Mayir Vereté an explanation of how the Jewish "national home" fitted into British imperial thinking at the time of World War I.[3] The goal of government leaders was obvious: to gain advantage in the Middle East upon the defeat of the Ottoman state and the breakup of its empire. Prime Minister Herbert Asquith and his successor, David Lloyd George, in 1916–1917 were concerned to protect Britain's lines of communication to vital interests in Mesopotamia, the Persian Gulf, and the Suez Canal. Palestine was seen as part of the land bridge connecting the Mediterranean Sea to the Persian Gulf. Were an enemy power or even a friend such as France to control Palestine, the vital Suez Canal entry to the Red Sea would be vulnerable. Better that Britain alone in Palestine sit astride the Suez Canal and thus exercise "continuity of territorial control from Egypt to India."[4]

British thinking about Palestine's strategic value had begun to crystallize in 1916, just after the government had entered into secret negotiations with France (the Sykes-Picot Agreement) over dividing Palestine between them in a postwar settlement. No sooner was the agreement signed than Britain began to look for a way out of it in order to keep all of Palestine for herself. It would not be simple. France had strong historic claims to the region then known as Greater Syria, which included Lebanon and Palestine. Nor would Russia care to see its own claims to the Holy Land set aside in favor of Britain.

For the British, the way out was Zionism. Vereté has made us aware of the British initiative to capitalize on her military occupation of Palestine by boldly using the Zionist movement as a diplomatic rationale for maintaining exclusive control of the country after the war. Upon the counsel of the chief imperial strategist for the Middle East, Mark Sykes, Prime Minister Asquith and Foreign Secretary Edward Grey decided in 1916 to throw the weight of the government behind the Zionist movement. It was thought that if the government "supported Jewish immigration to, and settlement in Palestine, this would afford Britain a considerable measure of influence sufficient to balance . . . the measure of respective French and Russian influence on the Catholic and Greek Orthodox sectors of the population. . . ."[5] Sykes argued that in the post-Ottoman Middle East, Britain had to support movements of national awakening as were occurring among Arabs, Armenians, and Jews. The trick was to find a way to make these national movements serve Britain's imperial objectives.

British leaders were well acquainted with Zionism through the turn-of-century visit of Theodor Herzl and the tireless campaigning of Chaim Weizmann, Nahum Socolow, and other Zionist Jews living in Britain. Reinforcing their sympathy with the Zionists was a memorandum circulated in 1914 by Herbert Samuel (the first Jew to sit in a prime minister's cabinet), arguing that the presence of a large and loyal Jewish settlement in Palestine would serve British interests.[6]

If France was one problem, the other was Woodrow Wilson. The American president, rightly suspicious that both Britain and France would use the defeat of Turkey to expand into the Middle East, issued his Fourteen Points in advance of the peace negotiations, calling for the "absolutely unmolested opportunity of autonomous development." Wilson, hoping for a "peace without annexations," endorsed the principle of self-determination for all small-nation peoples hitherto captive to the Ottoman Empire. If Britain and France wished to exercise influence in the Middle East, it could only be, in Wilson's view, with the aim of promoting eventual independence for small-nation peoples.

So Britain faced the problem of advancing their imperial interests in the Middle East without offending Wilson's doctrine of national self-determination. The solution took the form of an administrative vehicle, the trusteeship or mandate system. Introduced in 1919 at the Paris Peace Conference after World War I, the mandate allowed such powers as Britain and France to act as trustees of former Turkish provinces until such time as the peoples were sufficiently mature politically to decide their own future.

In late 1916, when Asquith was succeeded by David Lloyd George, the Zionist and mandate solutions were already part of British strategy for the postwar Middle East. If the use of Zionism was a matter of rational strategy for Asquith, Grey, and Sykes, none of whom paid much attention to its territorial goals, not so for Lloyd George and his Foreign Secretary Arthur Balfour, who were "Christian Zionists." They had religious feelings about the rightness of the Jewish Restoration and listened sympathetically to the Zionists' arguments that only in Palestine, and only with British cooperation, could the age-old question of Jewish security be answered.

Just here generations of British piety, ingenuity, and self-interest coalesced. The hundred-year-old British missionary involvement with the Holy Land had focused on Jews as the object of evangelical hopes. And the usefulness to Britain of a Jewish presence in Palestine could be traced all the way back to Foreign Secretary Palmerston's communication in 1841 to Lord Ponsonby, Britain's ambassador to Constantinople:

> There can be no doubt that very great benefit would accrue to the Turkish Government, if any considerable number of opulent Jews could be persuaded to come and settle in [Palestine]; because their wealth would afford employment to the People, and their intelligence would give a useful direction to industry; and the Resources of the State would thereby be considerably augmented.[7]

Now, more than a half century after Palmerston, it would be Britain, not Turkey, who would benefit from the immigration to Palestine of those "opulent Jews"—who would turn out to be not so opulent.

Zionism served not only Britain's long-term interests in the Middle East but her short-term interests as well. British leaders were convinced of the power of American Jews to influence President Wilson. Tending toward isolationism on the war issue because of the Western alliance with hated Russia, American Jews might join the war camp if Britain declared for a Jewish Palestine. A pro-Zionist declaration might also gain the support of Jews in Russia, where they were thought to be influential with the Bolshevik revolutionary leaders. Too, the British feared that if they did not soon signal their support of Zionism, Germany would do so—and strike a blow to the Allied cause. Of course, any number of influential Englishmen also believed that any policy which encouraged Jews to leave for Palestine was needed to rid Britain of the unwelcome burden of harboring the many Jewish refugees that had fled persecution and poverty in Russia.

ALLENBY'S ENTRANCE into Jerusalem was welcomed by Jerusalem's local church prelates—Greeks, Latins, Russians, Syrians, and Armenians—who were gladdened at the sight of the first Christian ruler to enter Jerusalem since the medieval Crusaders. But Sephardic Jews, who spoke Arabic and got along with the Turks, were none too pleased to see the passing of the old order. Their contentious brethren, the Ashkenazim, were of two minds: they could not cheer the arrival of a new gentile conqueror, but had not this conqueror defeated the wicked empire of Turkey, thus hastening (as the Prophet Daniel foretold) the day of the Messianic Redemption? The more secular-minded Zionists were, of course, elated by Allenby's entrance. News traveled fast among Jews. They had been led to believe that with the publication of Balfour's letter, Britain intended to establish a Jewish commonwealth in Palestine.

Muslims were cautious. Many were thankful to be rid of the imperious and venal Turks. The country had been bled white by the war. Much was expected from the British, who were known for their generosity. To those who had long memories, the sight of the British military was a reminder of the coming and going of conquerors. The British too would go in time. This land was not theirs. Muslims would tolerate Britain's trusteeship of the land as long as it served a useful purpose and as long as their own sense of ownership was not violated.

But already it seemed violated. Although General Allenby had suppressed announcement of the Balfour letter (an Arabic text of it was not published for two years), educated Arabs learned of it from the foreign press. This is what they read:

> His Majesty's Government view with favor the establishment in Palestine of a national home for the Jewish people, and will use their best endeavors to facilitate the achievement of this object, it being clearly understood that nothing shall be done which may prejudice the civil and religious rights of existing non-Jewish communities in Palestine, or the rights and political status by Jews in any other country.[8]

Arab reaction to what came to be known as the Balfour Declaration was noted by American intelligence officer William Yale:

> The Palestinians are very bitter over the Balfour Declaration. . . . They are convinced that Zionist leaders . . . intend to create a distinctly Jewish community and they believe that if Zionism proves

to be a success, their country will be lost to them even though their religious and political rights be protected.[9]

On any reading it is unclear even to this day what the British government intended by its declaration. Certainly it raised more questions than it answered. What was meant by a "national home"? What form of government was envisaged? Was the Jewish "national home" to be in part of Palestine or all of it? And what part? Balfour's letter makes no reference to any boundaries.

Arabs would later say that the establishment of a Jewish national home necessarily prejudiced "the civil and religious rights of the non-Jewish communities in Palestine." Why no mention of the national aspirations of the Arab people? Balfour's letter gave no answer. No English or Zionist official consulted with any Arab leader inside Palestine or elsewhere before the declaration.

Chaim Weizmann and his colleagues were elated with Balfour's letter. They would have preferred a commitment by Britain to a Jewish commonwealth or state. But the reference to a "national home" (recalling Herzl's words at the First Zionist Congress in 1897) was worked into the text by Nahum Socolow deliberately to suggest eventual statehood. Only Vladimir Jabotinsky was disappointed that the reference to a Jewish national home "in" Palestine and not "of" Palestine seemed to set limits to the territory. Weizmann believed that Zionists had no business talking of statehood until Jews constituted a majority in the land. Britain had opened the door to Jewish immigration; it was up to the Zionists to organize and develop it.

IN THOSE EARLY MONTHS of British military rule, Balfour's letter was not the only document on Arab minds. Many already knew or would later learn of another correspondence that contradicted in both letter and spirit the Balfour Declaration. As Britain in 1917 played its Zionist card to wrest Palestine from France, so months earlier, in 1915, British officials had played their Arab card to weaken Turkey militarily in the Middle East.

This other card involved a remarkable exchange of letters between Sir Henry McMahon, British commissioner of Egypt, and Sharif Husayn ibn Ali, emir of the Hijaz and custodian of the holy places at Mecca and Medina. The essence of the correspondence was an agreement: in exchange for Husayn's launching a military rebellion against Turkey, the British government would recognize and support his leadership of an independent Arab kingdom created out of former Turkish provinces. In this correspondence, as in Balfour's letter to Rothschild, the war situation confronting Britain played a major role.

The military reversal at the Turkish peninsula of Gallipoli in April 1915 was a blow to Britain and the Allies. The British newspaper magnate Lord Beaverbrook recalled the situation: "Germany was the military master of Europe. The French nation was exhausted. Russia was staggering to her doom. The British people were dispirited and a food shortage threatened the very existence of the nation."[10]

In those threatening times, British leaders worried about the security of their empire in Asia, particularly the loyalty of the Indian regiments that formed the bulk of the British army.[11] As soon as Turkey had joined Germany in war against the Allies, Ottoman Sultan Abdulhamid II, speaking as caliph, had called to his fellow Muslims to engage in *jihad* (holy war) against the Western infidel nations. Few heeded the call, but British leaders grew anxious that if Turkey were seen to be winning its war against the West, Britain's own Muslim subjects in India might revolt.

Britain's situation in the Middle East had also suffered when, in February 1915, Turkish troops, directed by their German advisers, crossed the "untraversable" desert of the Sinai and, after one failed cross-canal foray, took positions alongside the Suez Canal, Britain's lifeline to India. Britain countered by diverting badly needed troops to increase her canal defense force to 300,000.

In the midst of the Gallipoli debacle, with Turkey sitting across the canal, British Foreign Secretary Grey and War Minister Lord Kitchener searched for ways to neutralize the sultan's influence in the Muslim world. Britain's Cairo-based Arab experts, led by Reginald Wingate, D. G. Hogarth, Ronald Storrs, and Gilbert Clayton, proposed driving a wedge between Turkey and her Arab subjects. If the Arabs could be brought over to the Allied side of the war, Turkey, which was relying in battle on her Arab troops, would be greatly weakened. A defection of Arab soldiers from the Turkish flag would also call into question the caliphal legitimacy of the sultan and discredit his call for a Muslim *jihad* against the West.

Not everyone saw it this way. The generals administering India argued that a British-sponsored Arab uprising against the sultan might turn Muslims in the subcontinent against the government. Later, for the same reason, they opposed the Balfour Declaration.

The idea of using the Arabs against the Turks did not originate with the British but with the Arabs themselves. Even before Turkey joined Germany in August 1914, the sharif of Mecca, Emir Husayn, had sent his son Abdullah to sound out British military authorities in Cairo about support for an Arab insurrection against Turkey. Abdullah was initially ignored; but the idea of such an insurrection took on new meaning a year later when Britain's military situation in both Europe and the Middle East appeared suddenly bleak.

The Arab offer of revolt is not surprising if one recalls the history of Ottoman-Arab relations. Arab intellectuals and politicians shared the religion of Islam with the Turks, but little else. In the late nineteenth and early twentieth centuries, they had given voice to their resentment at being treated as culturally inferior subjects in the Ottoman Empire. Both Christian and Muslim members of the Arab intelligentsia formed secret societies and met regularly in Beirut and Damascus to express their hopes for an Arabic cultural revival that would lead to political independence from Turkey.[12]

These gatherings were well known to Sharif Husayn, who had his own political ambitions. Patriarch of the Hashemite tribe and blood descendant of the Prophet Muhammad's own sister, Husayn believed that he, not the Turkish usurper Sultan Abdulhamid II, could legitimately claim the title of caliph as spiritual-political successor to Muhammad. Husayn dreamed of leading an independent Arab kingdom. It was precisely to prevent the rise of such a kingdom in Arabia that Abdulhamid kept Husayn and his sons in elegant captivity in Constantinople for fifteen years. In the hope of gaining support for their new regime, the Young Turk revolutionaries freed the Arab noblemen in 1908 and sent them home to the Hijaz, where Husayn looked after the shrines in Mecca and Medina and plotted revenge. And so in July 1915 Sharif Husayn initiated the correspondence that included an offer of rebellion in exchange for British support of Arab independence. Counting on the support of a group of anti-Turkish Arab dissidents in Damascus, Husayn saw himself heading a single united federated Arab state, comprising sheikdoms embracing the Arabian peninsula, Iraq, and all of Greater Syria, including Palestine and Lebanon.[13]

The response from McMahon (who had been authorized by Foreign Secretary Grey to speak in behalf of the government) was positive but qualified as to the location and extent of territory that Britain would recognize as an independent Arab state. The qualifications arose from concern over Britain's own strategic aims in the Middle East and her relations to her war ally, France. Since the Entente Cordiale of 1904, when Egypt was conceded to Britain, France had focused her interests on Greater Syria, which then included Lebanon and Palestine. It would surely weaken the war alliance with France if Britain were seen promising to the Arabs the very lands that France would claim for herself in a postwar settlement following the defeat of Turkey. For that reason, in the crucial letter of October 24, 1915, from McMahon to Husayn, Britain ruled out any territory that was not "purely Arab," or in which France had a claim. The qualification was stated so: "The districts of Mersin and Alexandretta, and portions of Syria lying to the West of the districts of Damascus, Homs, and Aleppo, cannot be said to be purely Arab, and must on that account be excepted from the proposed delimitation."[14] "Around this single sentence," writes the historian Michael J. Cohen, "there has since raged an Arab-Zionist polemic as to whether the area later known as Mandated Palestine was in fact excluded from the areas assigned to Husayn in October, 1915."[15]

The polemic of which Cohen speaks focuses on the word "districts." The English authors of the letter used the ambiguous Turkish term *vilayet,* adapting it from the Arabic *wilayah.* Husayn and his advisers read *vilayet* according to its narrow meaning, which suggested that the area excluded from Arab independence represented a small territory a few kilometers west of Damascus, Homs, Hamma, and Aleppo. Since Palestine was understood not to be a few kilometers west of those towns but a sizable area well south of Damascus, readers of McMahon's letter assumed that Palestine was not excluded from the recognized areas of Arab independence.

From the British point of view this proved to be a wrong assumption. It seems that McMahon and the British "Arabic experts" who helped compose the letter *did* intend to exclude Palestine, but did not wish to state so explicitly. They expressed themselves so ambiguously and badly in Arabic as to bring about a misunderstanding that has lasted to the present day.[16]

The impression is that McMahon's letter was badly but carefully constructed, with deliberate ambiguity, to grant Arab independence in name only, without reference to any territorial borders of the proposed independent Arab state. "The McMahon letter of 24 October 1915," writes Cohen, "was little more than a cynical emergency measure, taken to lure the Arabs out of the Turkish camp."[17]

Husayn, however, wished to believe that Britain had made a solemn commitment to his project for Arab independence. He kept his part of the bargain in June 1916 by instigating a rebellion in the Hijaz region of western Arabia. A brigade of Arab Bedouin troops inflicted damage on Turkish rail facilities and harassed Turkish forces at several points. The brigade's military adviser was Colonel T. E. Lawrence, who would later become famous as Lawrence of Arabia. Turkish forces were diverted from their planned attack against the British on the Suez Canal. It was reported that Arab officers in Turkish uniforms deserted to the rebels.[18] While the rebellion was a blow to the Turkish war effort in Palestine, it was not a decisive event in ousting Turkey from the Middle East. Credit for that event goes to the courage and skill of the British army under General Allenby's command. But the Arabs had certainly played their part in behalf of Britain's cause and wanted their reward.

The McMahon-Husayn correspondence was on Sharif Husayn's mind in the fall of 1918, after the final defeat of Turkish forces in Syria. What he did not know was that in November 1915, almost immediately after the last letter exchanged between McMahon and himself, and months before the Arab rebellion, a series of secret meetings had taken place between Mark Sykes of Britain and François Georges-Picot of France. The aim of these meetings was to decide on the future of the Arab East. Ignoring the possibility of a large independent Arab state proposed in Husayn's first letter to McMahon, the negotiators agreed, with Russia's consent, to divide Turkish Middle Eastern provinces following the defeat of Turkey. Russia was promised control of Constantinople, the Bosphorus, and portions of Turkish Armenia; France would receive Lebanon and Syria, and Britain would rule Mesopotamia, Arabia, and Transjordan. But the British were as aggressive in their diplomacy as they were on the battlefield. As British leaders wriggled out of their "understanding" with the Arabs through the Sykes-Picot Agreement, so now they used the Balfour Declaration to control Palestine for the sake of empire.

WORLD WAR I had damaged and impoverished Palestine, and left the country diseased. Thousands had died from war and starvation. The population was reduced by a fourth, leaving 512,000 Muslims, 61,000 Christians, and 66,000 Jews. Two-thirds of the population consisted of peasants who lacked food.[19] Locusts swarmed in recurring plagues. Merchants had no money, and the currency was debased. Imitating the Romans, who had stripped the Judean hills of their trees to make battering rams for the siege of Jerusalem, Turkish soldiers had cut down every tree in sight to fuel their railway engines. There was little drinking water and no roads fit for carriage or car.

The British were not daunted by the task ahead of them. The Bible lovers would make the Land of the Bible breathe again. As King Herod the Great had done 2,000 years earlier, famine was ended by bringing grain from Egypt. The currency was revalued, and newly established banks made loans to peasants and merchants at 1.5 percent interest—instead of 20 to 50 percent that had prevailed.[20] Water pipes were laid and a new electrical grid built. Old roads were repaired and new ones cut; new hospitals, hotels, and schools were constructed. The city of Jerusalem was swept clean of filth, and newly appointed police provided a physical security that people had not known in living memory. Haifa's strategically valuable deep-water harbor (for whose possession alone Britain wanted Palestine) was rebuilt and further deepened. The return of health and prosperity was seen in the country's population growth to 757,000 by 1922.[21]

The early years of Britain's rule of Palestine under the mandate were the "good years of management," as the historian Elizabeth Monroe calls them, years in which Palestine satisfied the "British itch to administer maladministered peoples."[22] None were more grateful for British administration than Arab Christians, many of whom were employed by the government. Monroe writes:

> . . . Palestinians in the public service valued some of the British innovations and actively enjoyed working with the men who introduced them. This brand of respect, while it lasts, forges a human bond far more deeply felt than the impression created by roads, schools, hospitals, public security, mounting trade balances or im-

partial courts of law that all formed part of the [British] endowment. . . .[23]

From the beginning of their rule, British officials in Palestine took pains to cultivate relations with town dwellers, large landowners, and the educated political and religious elite of both Muslim and Arab Christian communities. Money, jobs, appointments, privileges, and powers were bestowed on them; largely ignored were the Palestinian peasants who were considered politically apathetic.

London politicians had decreed their pro-Zionist policy, but the military officers in Palestine, responsible for administering that policy, determined that vigorous support of Jewish immigration and land purchase would only inflame Arab passions and make the job of government more difficult. They knew that resentment of Zionist activity predated the Balfour Declaration. In the late 1870s Arab villagers had complained about the new Jewish agricultural settlers who purchased land at high prices, evicted Arab peasants, refused to allow free grazing on their land, kept to themselves, and generally acted as if the country belonged to them.

When asked about their tensions with the Jews, Arabs were quick to point out that they had no quarrel with the community of traditionalist Jews which had lived in Palestine for generations; their concern was rather with the new Jews who had begun to immigrate to Palestine under later Turkish rule. The Balfour Declaration fueled existing tensions, giving them a more specifically political character. Certainly relationships between Arabs and Jews were not helped by one of Weizmann's statements, often quoted in the Arab press, that Zionism aimed to make "Palestine as Jewish as England is English."

Within months of the issuance of the Balfour Declaration, Muslims and Arab Christians from the Greek Orthodox, Latin, and Greek Catholic churches met to talk of their grievances against the Zionists and to plan concerted action. Rapidly, chapters of a new Muslim-Christian Association opened in all of Palestine's major towns. It was an important moment in the communal history of the country. Forgotten for the time being were past expressions of hostility between Muslims and Christians. Now that the common enemy was the alien and growing power of the Zionists, no one wished to recall the violent rampage of Muslims against Christians in Nablus in 1848, or the 1861 massacre of Christians in Damascus.

This new alliance led to the establishment of political organizations, which gave Arab anti-Zionism considerable weight in the eyes of British military officers, strengthening their own anti-Zionist reports to their superiors in Cairo and London. Muslim-Christian clubs led shortly to the convening in February 1919 of the first Arab Congress in Jerusalem, whose Arab Executive Committee took the lead in organizing Arab opposition to Zionism. A propaganda campaign emphasized the uniquely Arab character of Palestine. Jews, it was argued, had enjoyed independence in Palestine only during the brief decades of the Davidic-Solomonic period; Arabs could trace their ancestry all the way back to the original Canaanite inhabitants of the land. Whatever claims Jews made on the land had been erased by the Islamic conquest of Palestine, which had given the country more than a thousand years of continuous rule. And Jerusalem too was a uniquely Arab city, with its abundance of Muslim and Christian shrines and scarcely any Jewish holy places.

The Zionists had provoked a counteroffensive from Palestine's Arabs. Still not clear was whether the new Arab organizations had a political goal larger than ridding the country of Zionism. Beyond calling for a halt to Jewish immigration and land purchase, could the Arabs propose an agenda for a future independent Arab state of Palestine?

FROM THE INCEPTION of British rule in Palestine in late 1917 until the ouster of Prince Faysal from Syria in June 1920, the Hashemite royal family was viewed by the vast majority of Palestine's Arabs as their natural leadership. They would have been content to see themselves rid of the Zionists, freed of the British, and governed by Sharif Husayn, instigator of the Arab revolt. But British policymakers did not want the right to govern Palestine in order to lose the country to its natives. They had no more wish to see an Arab Palestine than a Jewish Palestine. What they wanted was cooperation from both Arabs and Jews in governing a country technically under military occupation until the forthcoming Versailles peace conference, where it was expected that the League of Nations would vote Britain a mandate to govern Palestine.

Hoping to bring the hostile parties together, Britain approved the formation of the Zionist Commission, headed by Chaim Weizmann. The commission traveled to Palestine in March 1918 to act as a liaison between the British administration and the Jewish community, and to do whatever was needed to assure Arabs that Zionist projects would benefit Arabs as well as Jews.

In the same spirit of cooperation, Weizmann was persuaded to meet with Prince Faysal, a meeting arranged by Colonel Gilbert Clayton, chief political officer of the first military administration of Palestine. Clayton, an experienced Arabist and critic of Britain's pro-Zionist policy, was convinced that Zionism could make no progress in Palestine unless the Arab majority understood that Zionism meant not to harm or displace them. Clayton was also a realist and a pragmatist. Like many British officers posted in the Middle East, he believed Britain's promise of national independence to the Arab peoples, expressed through the McMahon-Husayn correspondence, had been violated in the Balfour Declaration. But he also recognized that however badly conceived the Balfour Declaration, it had become official British policy. It was his duty to square the circle through initiatives that might maintain order in what he knew to be a potentially violent situation.

If Britain was to retain a shred of honor in Arab eyes and establish a rational and stable policy of administering Palestine and other Arab-populated lands of the Middle East, a way had to be found to implement the Jewish national home without turning the Arab world against Britain. In Clayton's mind this meant seeking common ground between the Zionists and the Hashemite royal family. Clayton was convinced that the Zionist program could be carried out only if the Hashemites, led by Husayn and his sons Faysal and Abdullah, cooperated with the Zionists in recognizing and accommodating each other's goals.

The first meeting between Faysal and Weizmann, which took place on June 4, 1918, at Wadi Wahaida, on the Gulf of Aqaba, lasted but forty-five minutes. The atmosphere was cordial from the start. Faysal heard "Weizmann's promise of Jewish support for the establishment of an Arab kingdom in Syria with Feisal as monarch." According to the account given by Colonel P. C. Joyce, who was delegated to keep a record:

Dr. Weizmann pointed out that the Jews do not propose setting up a Jewish Government but would like to work under British protection with a view to colonising and developing the country without in any way encroaching on anybody's legitimate interests. Feisal did not want to discuss the future of Palestine "either as a Jewish colony or a country under British protection" because he feared Turkish and German propaganda, but he personally "accepted the possibility of future Jewish claims to territory in Palestine."[24]

Weizmann was elated by the prince's openness to the Zionist development, so different from the attitude of the Arab Palestine family elites, who regarded the country as exclusively their own and scorned contact with the Zionists. In Weizmann's eyes they were "a cancer ruining the country."[25] By contrast Weizmann found Faysal to be fully worthy of his princely title. Two weeks after his meeting at Aqaba he gushed to his wife about his new Arab friend:

> He is the first real Arab nationalist I ever met. He is a leader! He's quite intelligent and a very handsome man, handsome as a picture! He is not interested in Palestine, but on the other hand he wants Damascus and the whole of northern Syria. He talked with great animosity against the French, who want to get their hands on Syria. He expects a great deal from collaboration with the Jews! He is contemptuous of the Palestinian Arabs whom he doesn't even regard as Arabs![26]

Weizmann saw Faysal as a man of vision and honor, not at all like the corrupt Palestinian effendis who exploited the peasantry and turned them against the Zionists. With Faysal on his side, Weizmann could communicate to the Arab masses of Palestine that they would not lose but rather gain from the Zionists, who were bringing money into the country.

And Weizmann, it seems, made a convincing case for Zionism to Faysal. To Mark Sykes, Faysal wrote, "I have a perfect notion of the importance of the Jews' position, and admiration for their vigor and tenacity and moral ascendancy, often in the midst of hostile surroundings. . . . On general grounds I would welcome any good understanding with the Jews."[27]

The surprisingly favorable meeting caused Weizmann to assume that the Jews' "Arab problem" had been solved. He had no doubt that Faysal spoke for all Arabs of the region, including those of Palestine. All along Weizmann had taken the line that Arabs and Jews could live together and develop their respective communities in a country that did not lack for space.[28]

What followed, however, were machinations in which the British showed how serious they were about keeping Palestine. In September 1918 Allenby had begun his drive to remove Turkish forces from Syria. The sense of imminent victory over Turkey was strongly felt in London and Paris. In the Hijaz, Sharif Husayn looked forward to the British victory over Turkey as the beginning of Arab independence in the Middle East. He experienced some anxiety upon first learning of the secret Sykes-Picot Agreement. Embarrassed by the exposure of their "secret," British and French leaders hastened to reassure the Hashemites of the sincerity of their promise of independent Arab government in a joint declaration of November 7, 1918, emphasizing that the authority for such government would derive from the "initiative and choice of the indigenous populations."[29] This rank piece of duplicity was designed to ease Husayn's anxiety about independence and Wilson's penchant for self-determination. Neither Britain nor France intended to honor their common declaration.

In December, still trusting in Britain, Husayn sent his son Faysal to London to confirm Britain's commitment to Arab independence. But only a week before his arrival, British Prime Minister Lloyd George met secretly in London with his French counterpart, Georges Clemençeau, and sealed the future of the Middle East. In exchange for British support of French claims to Syria and Lebanon, France acceded to Britain's desire to control Palestine, Transjordan, and Iraq. Thus a united Syria, including Lebanon and Palestine, would not become part of an independent Arab state but would be divided between the two European nations militarily in control of the Middle East.

While in London, Faysal met again with Weizmann on December 11, 1918. From this meeting a document was produced on January 3, 1919, in which Faysal expressed approval of Jewish immigration to Palestine and recognized the country as the site of the Jewish national home.[30] That recognition entailed both Zionist and

British support for an independent Arab kingdom; without that support, Faysal made clear, he could not agree to Zionist claims on
Palestine.[31] But this exercise in diplomacy was made empty by the
prior secret agreement between Lloyd George and Clemençeau.
Whatever opportunities existed for future peace between Arabs and
Jews in Palestine had been sacrificed on the altar of European expansion into the Middle East.

That Britain had no intention of allowing a Jewish state to be
born in Palestine can be seen from the startled reaction of Arthur
Balfour when he learned in early 1919, before the peace conference,
that the Zionist leadership would press for a Jewish government of
Palestine. He wrote to Lloyd George: "As far as I know Weizmann
has never put forward a claim for the Jewish *Government* of Palestine. Such a claim is in my opinion certainly inadmissible and personally I do not think we should go further than the original declaration
which I made to Lord Rothschild."[32]

If Weizmann was eager to rationalize British coolness toward
Zionist ambitions, his Zionist colleague Harry Sacher was not.
Sacher felt that the British had clearly used the Zionists for their own
purposes and were prepared to ignore them when they were no
longer of use. Doubting that Jews would ever achieve independence
in Palestine, Sacher wrote: "We are left worse off than under the
Turks. We shall not get access to the land, and we shall be ruled by
anti-Semitic public school boys . . . with a pro-Muslim bias. . . . The
blunt truth is that we have been done. We have helped to give England Palestine and with that our usefulness is exhausted."[33]

Together Britain's refusal to support Faysal's claim to a united
Syria, the detachment of Palestine from Syria, and the Balfour Declaration threw the Hashemite prince into the lap of the anti-Zionist
nationalists of Damascus. The First Syrian Congress of July 1919 declared its rejection of Zionism and demanded that Syria and Palestine remain united and be recognized as an independent state under
the rule of Faysal.[34] The agreement between Weizmann and Faysal
disappeared in the blizzard of anti-Zionist rhetoric that followed the
Congress.

Colonel John French, the British intelligence officer in Cairo,
expressed to Lord Curzon in August 1919 the view that "Dr. Weizmann's agreement with Emir Feisal is not worth the paper it is written on or the energy wasted in the conversation to make it."[35] French

was certainly thinking of the fragile character of any Arab-Zionist agreement. He knew that the Arabs of Palestine would oppose any agreement by which an Arab leader conceded Palestine to the Zionists for a Jewish state. He knew that Palestine's Arabs would have regarded any deal with Weizmann involving their country as a betrayal of trust.[36] He also knew that Faysal had never visited Palestine and that his sole interest was to advance his family's territorial ambitions. But what he also knew, did not say, and might even have found offensive, was that the secret dealings of Lloyd George and Clemençeau had rendered any Arab-Zionist understanding useless.

And so there is room to wonder about what might have happened to Palestine if Britain had not acted with empire in mind. What if she had thrown her weight behind the Weizmann-Faysal agreement? What if she had been willing to promote a political division of the country to allow for an Arab-Hashemite government in one part of it and a Zionist-led Jewish government in another? Would the ensuing Arab-Jewish conflict, as we know it, ever have occurred? One should not forget that at the time of the Faysal-Weizmann meetings, blood had not been spilled.

The pity is that following the ouster of Faysal from Damascus, Weizmann did not make greater efforts to come to terms with local Arab leaders in Palestine. Weizmann had little use for these Arabs. Like the English, whom he loved and imitated, he judged people by their class. Born to humble parents in a dusty shtetl in a scorned part of the Russian Pale of Settlement, he had risen high above his origins and now preferred the company of British and Arab aristocrats to those who would ultimately make the difference in the future of Arab-Jewish relations in Palestine.

Fifteen months after the London meeting of Faysal and Weizmann, at the conference in the Italian Riviera town of San Remo in April 1920, legitimacy was bestowed on the secret Anglo-French agreement by the mandates granted by the League of Nations. France would govern Syria and Lebanon, and Britain would exercise sole government in Iraq and Palestine. These mandates, whatever their noble purpose in the minds of the various nations represented at the peace conference, proved to be fig leafs to cover the naked exercise of power and territorial expansion that Woodrow Wilson had warned against.

Incorporated into the preamble of the mandate awarded to

Britain for governing Palestine was the entire text of Balfour's letter to Lord Rothschild. Thus the deliberate (but false) impression persisted that Britain had undertaken to govern Palestine in order to administer a pro-Zionist policy. Reinforcing that impression, Article 4 of the mandate document specifically named a "Jewish Agency" to facilitate the execution of that policy—thus awarding quasi-governmental status to the Zionist organization.

The publication of the mandate document enraged Palestine's Arabs. They had only to remember the words of the covenant of the League of Nations, declared a year earlier. Paragraph 4 of Article 22 of the covenant stated:

> Certain communities formerly belonging to the Turkish Empire have reached a stage of development where their existence as independent nations can be provisionally recognized subject to the rendering of administrative advice and assistance by a Mandatory until such time as they are able to stand alone. The wishes of these communities must be a principal consideration in the selection of the Mandatory.[37]

Arab Palestinian leaders would turn to the covenant as proof positive that Britain's mandate for governing, incorporating as it did a Zionist policy, had no legitimacy. To them there was an appalling contradiction between what the covenant promised and what the British government was doing in declaring its commitment to the Jewish national home in Palestine without consulting their "wishes" as the majority population of the country.

The granting of the mandates at San Remo sounded the death knell for the independence movements led by the Hashemites. In July 1920 Britain, deferring to the new political order, allowed France to oust Faysal from Damascus. Later Britain bestowed on Faysal the consolation prize of ruling Iraq as its king. This was followed by the decision in 1922 to detach Transjordan from the original mandated territory of Palestine and give it to Prince Abdullah to rule as an emirate under British supervision.

Thus did Britain "honor" her 1915 promise to support the Hashemite dream of ruling a united Arab kingdom. Greater failure befell the patriarch, Sharif Husayn, who in 1924 lost control of the Arabian holy places to his rival, Ibn Saud. Britain, no longer needing the old monarch but still grateful for services rendered, rescued

Husayn from Ibn Saud, bringing him to Cyprus, where he died in 1931. At the insistence of his sons, his body was brought for burial to Jerusalem's Haram esh-Sharif.

Out of the disintegration of the Arab national movement emerged a new political focus for the Arabs of Palestine. After the humiliating eviction of Faysal from Damascus, they began to look to themselves for solutions to their problems with the Zionists. It was the beginning of a political evolution which would turn the Arabs of Palestine into "the Palestinians," slowly leading to a new national self-identity. But in the 1920s Arab leaders were united only in their wish to be rid of the Zionists.

THE MILITARY ADMINISTRATION of Palestine began the day General Allenby walked through Jerusalem's Jaffa Gate to accept the surrender of the city. The officers he appointed to the administration of the country enforced his pledge of religious freedom for all the communities of Palestine. But, believing it to be unworkable, they did much to subvert the pro-Zionist policy to which the government had officially committed itself.

In the thirty-four months of Britain's military administration, a succession of three commanding generals engaged in partisan politics in favor of the Arab cause and sought to persuade their civilian superiors in London to rescind the Balfour Declaration. Frustrated in their efforts to abandon their government's official pro-Zionist policy, the generals often took matters into their own hands by limiting Jewish immigration to Palestine, discouraging land transfers, and favoring the hiring of Arabs over Jews in administrative jobs. They did this with the confidence that their chief, General Allenby, headquartered in Cairo, largely agreed with their anti-Zionist attitudes.

Thus from the beginning a contradiction existed between the policymakers in London, led by Prime Minister Lloyd George and Foreign Secretary Balfour, who supported the Jewish national home, and the military administrators in Palestine, who opposed it. The Zionists were caught between London and Jerusalem.

What troubled the Zionists was not opposition to their movement, for they had faced that even from fellow Jews, but expressions of anti-Semitic contempt. It was known that copies of the tsarist anti-Semitic forgery, Protocols of the Elders of Zion, could be found in the knapsacks of British field soldiers. The generals responsible for the administration of the country allowed their anti-Zionism to degenerate into anti-Semitism. Typical was the attitude of the first military governor, General Arthur Money, who described Jews "as a class inferior morally and intellectually to the bulk of the Muslim and Christian inhabitants of the country."[38] He believed that Zionists lacked ideals and devoted their political movement to acquiring wealth.

> The trouble about all these Jewish schemes is that, however skillfully ruled, they are rather open to the suspicion of having some financial end in the background, as the Jew is not in the habit of going to out of the way parts of the world solely for the benefit of his health.[39]

In words soaked with contempt, Money described the pious (non-Zionist) Jewish traditionalists of Jerusalem:

> Pharisees of the New Testament, insistent on the letter of their religion, and bringing up their rising generation in their schools to be dirty idle wasters. . . . Their men turn out more idle wasters and their women more prostitutes than the rest of the population put together.[40]

Money's successor, General H. D. Watson, remarked:

> The great fear of the people is that once Zionist wealth is passed into the land, all territorial and mineral concessions will fall into the hands of the Jews whose intensely clannish instincts prohibit them from dealing with any but those of their own religion to the detriment of Moslems and Christians.[41]

Not surprisingly, the Britishers' anti-Semitic disdain passed on to Palestine's Arabs, who had not been known to express anti-Semitic views. Establishment of an organized Arab opposition to Zionism, in the form of the Muslim-Christian Association, was encouraged by British officers who wished to counter the semi-official authority exercised by Zionism under the mandate. Some observers thought that British officers encouraged Arabs to make public demonstrations of their opposition in the hope that London could be persuaded to rescind its pro-Zionist policy.

In this climate of growing tension, a violent confrontation was perhaps inevitable. It happened on April 4, 1920, at the Nebi Musa festival near Jerusalem. In the past this annual festival, expressing Muslim reverence for the prophet Moses, was meant to coincide with Eastern pilgrimage festivities. It served as an opportunity for the Muslim leadership of the country to demonstrate its power to Arab Christians. Muslims would conduct a long pilgrimage walk from Jerusalem to what local Islamic tradition held to be the burial site of Moses, a few miles south of the city, on the road to Jericho. Often, as Muslim pilgrims marched past Jerusalem's churches, they shouted taunts at Christians; fights broke out, sometimes a riot occurred.

On this occasion the holding of the Nebi Musa festival, intended to impress the British officials and intimidate the Zionists, was a fresh show of Arab Muslim power. Arab feeling had been building for several years; the mood was now euphoric. Only a month earlier, the General Syrian Congress had proclaimed Faysal king of Syria. The popular expectation was that Faysal would extend his power into Palestine and put an end to Zionist activities.

Military officials were aware of the potential for danger at the festival and warned Muslim leaders against inflammatory speeches that might provoke disturbances. Yet few security precautions were taken. No army troops were stationed in the city, and the regular police were all Arabs with known anti-Zionist sentiments. Official requests made by Jews to the British administration for permission to arm their community against possible Arab attacks were rejected as unnecessary. Members of the Jewish battalions that had served under British command in the war against Turkey were turned down as a defense force. Still, in anticipation of anti-Jewish riots that might occur at the festival, some six hundred Jews secretly received small-arms training in Jerusalem under the direction of Zionist ideologue Vladimir Jabotinsky.

On the morning of April 4 the procession took place. An Arab band marched through Jerusalem. Muslim pilgrims arrived from throughout the country to participate in the festivities. Complying with British instructions, the Arab political writer Aref al-Aref rode up and down the procession on a white horse to calm the crowd. Then someone raised a portrait of King Faysal, and the pilgrims responded. Inflammatory speeches ensued, including an incendiary anti-Jewish declamation by a young Muslim patrician firebrand named Haj Amin al-Husayni, a nephew of Jerusalem's mayor. Shouting led to shoving, and fights broke out. Within minutes a riot had begun. Arabs ran through the narrow alleys of the Jewish Quarter, beating people where they found them. Looting followed. In four days of bloody rioting, 5 Jews and 4 Arabs were killed; 211 of the 244 wounded were Jews. Arab police who were called to the riot sided with the rioters. It did not matter to the Arab attackers that a majority of their victims were anti-Zionist Orthodox Jews.

Some of the rioters were caught and punished, but no police were charged for failing their duty. Musa Khazim Pasha al-Husayni was dismissed as mayor and replaced by the head of a rival notable family, Ragheb Bey Nashashibi. Both Aref al-Aref and Haj Amin al-Husayni fled the country and received in absentia prison sentences of ten years. A bitter humiliation to the Zionists was the arrest of Vladimir Jabotinsky, who had secretly trained Jews to defend themselves against an Arab mob; he was given a long prison sentence for violating a British ban against bearing arms.

There had been skirmishes before—rock throwing, the roughing up of a few Jews—but never a bloody riot in which Jews were murdered. It was a new and ugly milestone in Arab-Jewish relations.

The Jerusalem riot of April 4, 1920, produced major political repercussions. An official inquiry found the British military administration lax in its duty to maintain order and infected with anti-Semitic hostility. Colonel Ronald Storrs, the governor of Jerusalem, was criticized for negligence of duty. The committee of inquiry blamed the Zionist Commission for provoking the Arabs and blamed the Arabs for being provoked. Apart from Storrs no military administrators were blamed for the riot, even when they were found to be pro-Arab, anti-Zionist, and anti-Semitic.

By their actions, British officials in Palestine had shown they could not be trusted to carry out the provisions for a Jewish national home. And the Zionists learned that their goal of statehood would not be achieved without a capacity for physical self-defense.

Zionists realized that if they were to continue to build the Jewish community of Palestine, they would have to come to terms with the Arab Palestinians. They could no longer afford the patronizing attitude of a Weizmann, who tended to ignore them.

Finally the riot, while demonstrating Arab hostility toward Zionism, did not advance the cause of Arab political independence from Britain. London reacted strongly in favor of the Zionists. The mandate awarded at San Remo a few weeks later allowed the government to end the military administration and replace it with a civil administration. To their consternation, the Arabs learned that Palestine's first civilian high commissioner would be Herbert Samuel, the English patrician and politician who happened also to be a Jew and an ardent Zionist.

CHAPTER TEN

Herbert Samuel Changes His Mind

> We are pushing an alien and detested element into the
> very core of Islam, and the day may come when we
> shall be faced with the alternative of holding [Palestine]
> either by the sword or abandoning it to its fate.
> —Colonel Gilbert Clayton, 1924
>
> Palestine is a country inhabited largely by
> unreasonable people.
> —William Ormsby-Gore, 1928

For two and a half years the British military officers governing Palestine paid lip service to the official Jewish "national home" policy. So the sudden outbreak of Arab rioting in April 1920 was unexpected and embarrassing both to the army command in Jerusalem and to political leaders in London. The riot occurred just a few days before the San Remo conference, where the Council of the League of Nations voted Britain the mandate to govern Palestine. The question in everyone's mind was how Britain would administer a country under a mandate that proposed to benefit Jews without harming Arabs.

The military's habit of appeasing Palestine's Arabs with words, jobs, and bribes had only emboldened them to act violently against Jews. After the riot, London knew it was time to replace the military administration of Palestine with trained civil servants. It was also necessary to reassure Jews that Britain was firmly committed to advancing their national home. British policymakers would not be budged from their strategic objectives in Palestine by gangs of Arab ruffians.

In the minds of Lloyd George and Balfour, the civilian needed to replace the military governor of Palestine had to be a man who could juggle three goals: implement the Jewish national home provision of the mandate document; defend Arab rights while reconciling the Arabs to the government's Zionist policy; and accomplish both of the above without forgetting that Britain was in Palestine above all to safeguard her imperial strategic lifeline at the Suez Canal.

Britain's man for Palestine turned out to be Herbert Samuel, an English-born Jew and a champion of the Jewish return to Palestine. Oxford educated, patrician, politician, religiously observant, Samuel was the first nonbaptized Jew to sit in a government cabinet. Before Samuel there had been only the Jewish-born Benjamin Disraeli, who, for reasons of career, had been baptized into the Church of England. In London's governing circles, Samuel was thought to be just the sort of man who could persuade Arabs that Britain's pro-Zionist policy would attract so much international Jewish money to Palestine that it would be worthwhile for them to share the country with Jews.

On June 30, 1920, Herbert Samuel became the first Jewish head of the country since Simon Bar Kochba of Roman times. Samuel took office temporarily at the August Victoria Hospital on the Mount of Olives, while a permanent dwelling was under construction on a prominent rise of ground named the Hill of Evil Counsel.[1] Before completing his term of service five years later, Commissioner Samuel would have reason to reflect on that ominous name.

On that first July Jewish Sabbath, under Jerusalem's sunny and cloudless summer morning, it seemed that all the Old City's Muslims, Christians, and Jews had gathered on their rooftops to watch the new high commissioner walk slowly down the slope of the Mount of Olives to the services at the Hurva synagogue in the Jewish Quarter, two miles away. Dressed according to Orthodox Jewish custom in long black coat and tall black hat, no one like him had been seen in the country since the visits of Sir Moses Montefiore, a half-century earlier. Jerusalem's Jews later said that the sight of Samuel walking to Shabbat services made them think of a latter-day Judaic prince come to honor the religion of his ancestors in Zion, the capital city of the Land of Israel.

Samuel arrived in Jerusalem with no illusions about the task before him. During a short visit to Palestine just two months before his appointment, an outspoken Arab warned him: "If the Zionists are going to immigrate into the country a terrible revolution will break out."[2] Samuel was a rational and compassionate man, a "liberal imperialist," the historian Bernard Wasserstein calls him. He would implement the government policy on the Jewish national home but not force it down the Arabs' throat.

Samuel's first administrative appointments made it clear that the high commissioner intended to hear from all sides. The top post of civil secretary went to Wyndham Deedes, a devout evangelical Christian who believed that the return of the Jews to the Holy Land was a prelude to the Second Coming of Christ. As chief legal counsel, Samuel picked Norman Bentwich, a pro-Zionist Jew who was the husband of his niece. Zionists, obviously happy with these appointments, were disappointed to learn that Samuel retained on his staff many of the officers who had made no secret of their disdain for the Balfour Declaration, including Colonel Storrs.

Under the terms of the mandate, Palestine technically was a trusteeship; yet the country was administered as a crown possession, out of the British Colonial Office. While all senior appointments were assigned to career British civil servants, lower-level bureaucratic jobs went to a few Jews and some Muslims, but mostly to Arab Christians, who were considered well educated, loyal, and eager to serve the first Christian power to rule the Holy Land since Crusader times.

Arab police guarded Jerusalem and most of the other major cities; only Jewish police were assigned to the new enlarging northern suburb of Jaffa called Tel Aviv. Comparing the two police forces, one English administrator wryly noted that the Arabs were taller but the Jews brainier.[3]

Samuel acted quickly to heal the wounds caused by the April riot. He granted amnesty to Aref al-Aref and Haj Amin al-Husayni, the two activist Arabs who had fled to Syria in the wake of the riot. Aref now settled in Jerusalem, accepted a government job, and spent the rest of his life writing books on Arabic Palestinian culture. Haj

Amin, who became Jerusalem's mufti (chief jurist-interpreter of Shari'a law) and the most powerful Muslim in Palestine, proved to be a thorn in the sides of both the government and the Zionists.

To benefit Jews, Samuel lifted the suspension on immigration and renewed permission for Jewish land purchases. He took another large step toward reconciliation with the Jews by releasing from prison Vladimir Jabotinsky and nineteen other Jews who were serving prison sentences for illegally organizing and arming Jewish fighters at the time of the April riot. And to the great satisfaction of Zionist culturalists, he authorized the modern Hebrew language to appear alongside English and Arabic as one of the three official languages used in public documents. With the high commissioner's encouragement, plans were made for building on Jerusalem's Mount Scopus the first secular Hebrew-language university.

Samuel, the "liberal imperialist," followed the tested British colonial practice of cultivating native elites and ruling through them. Village sheiks and town notables; Muslim, Jewish, and Christian religious leaders; all the educated, important, rich, and powerful were at various times consulted, flattered, and wined and dined at receptions at the high commissioner's residence.

The ample evidence of corruption, exploitiveness, and destructive factionalism among the elites meant less to British rulers than the willingness of the Arabs to cooperate with this government, which operated under the severe constraint of the Jewish national home policy. As long as the Arabs showed no active signs of hostility, as long as violence was a matter of passing incidents, Samuel, like those who followed him in the mandatory government, assured themselves that British government was effectively keeping the peace and fulfilling Britain's strategic purposes in Palestine. In behalf of those purposes, the government turned a blind eye to the growing alienation between poor Arab villagers and rich town notables, which had begun in the nineteenth century and worsened in the twentieth.

In the ten months between his appointment in late June 1920 and May of the following year, Samuel worked with apparent success in bringing his message of reconciliation to Arab and Jew alike. He emphasized the economic benefits of Jewish investment to Arab society. New money had begun to flow to Arabs for Jewish land purchases and as salaries for work on Jewish farms and in

Zionist-funded construction. With the aim of improving Palestine as a military base, the government began to spend large sums on local engineers and workers to modernize the country's infrastructure of roads, harbors, bridges, airfields, telephone, and telegraph.

Suddenly, however, in the midst of this economic upswing, Samuel's honeymoon with Palestine came abruptly to an end. An unexpected outbreak of rioting occurred in Jaffa on May Day, 1921. It had a bizarre beginning in a scuffle between two rival groups of Jews: socialists parading in celebration of May Day were confronted by Jewish Bolsheviks, who carried banners in Yiddish calling for a Soviet Palestine.[4] The police "drove the communists back to an open space of sand dunes separating Jaffa from Tel Aviv." Arabs in the neighborhood, who had come out to watch the fracas, seized the occasion to attack Jewish shops. Then Arab police armed with rifles joined the rioters. A senior Arab police officer who had witnessed the attack from the outset and might have prevented violence, decided it was time to go home for lunch.[5] The rioting continued for six more days and spread to Petah Tikvah, Kfar Saba, Rehovot, and other Jewish towns. By May 7 the riot statistics showed 47 Jews killed and 146 wounded, and 48 Arabs killed and 73 wounded.

The May riots proved to be the critical juncture in Samuel's administration of Palestine. However personally sympathetic he was to the Zionist cause, he was more firmly a British governing official who saw his highest administrative duty to be the maintenance of civil order. He knew that the jailings of lawbreakers would be a mere bandage applied to problems that were deeper and more explosive than the question of obeying civil law. He correctly perceived the problems to be political. Thus only a demonstration of British willingness to heed Arab complaints about Jewish immigration would prevent future rioting. And so the arrest of lawbreaking Arabs was immediately followed by another suspension of Jewish immigration.

Samuel's action had sad consequences for one small ship loaded with refugees from anti-Jewish pogroms in the Ukraine. The ship was turned back to Constantinople, where Turkish authorities ordered the captain to prepare immediately to steam back to Russia. A second incident involved a ship loaded with Christians and Jews which dropped anchor off the Jaffa shore. According to Wasserstein, "The boatman refused to take ashore any passengers until they had been examined by a doctor and certified to be non-Jewish."[6]

Zionists were incensed to learn that the high commissioner had ordered the suspension of Jewish immigration on the advice of the elderly leader of the powerful Jerusalem-based Husayni clan, Musa Khazim Pasha al-Husayni. To the Zionists, Samuel's appeasement of the Arabs would only bring more violence. Weizmann complained directly to Samuel that he took Arab agitation too seriously and treated it too leniently. Samuel replied, "You have not recognized the force and value of the Arab nationalist movement. . . . It is very real and no bluff."[7] To those Zionists who expected the establishment of a Jewish state in their lifetime, Samuel warned that "to attempt to realize the aspirations of a Jewish state one century too soon might throw back its actual realization for many centuries more."[8]

It seems that the May riots changed Samuel's mind about the possibilities of British policy in Palestine. Now he took a gradual approach, allowing the Jewish national home to develop slowly, by small steps, without alarming or harming the Arab majority. Jewish immigration was restored, but with fewer annual immigration permits issued.

Jewish disillusionment with Samuel deepened a month after the riots. In a speech on June 3, 1921, the high commissioner offered his own interpretation of the Jewish national home provision of Britain's mandate for governing Palestine. He began by denying that Britain's sponsorship of the Jewish national home meant that his country intended a Jewish government to rule over the Arab majority of the country. What then did Britain intend? Samuel answered by first acknowledging that in immigrating to Palestine, Jews were returning by historic right to their ancestral home. Then, to the astonishment of Zionists, he added: ". . . that some [Jews] among them, within the limits that are fixed by the numbers and interests of the present population, should come to Palestine in order to help by their resources and efforts to develop the country, to the advantage of all its inhabits."[9]

Here indeed was a signal change in Samuel's thinking. If future Jewish immigration were now connected to limits "fixed by the numbers and interests of the present population," the Jewish national home would be linked to Arab acceptance. The practical outcome of that linkage was that Zionists would not be completely free to plan and fund Jewish immigration to Palestine. In Zionist eyes, Samuel's speech made shambles of the Zionist dream of a Jewish majority leading to an independent Jewish state in Palestine. One facetious Jew noted that if taken at his word, Samuel had revised the Balfour Declaration to mean that the Jewish national home had become the Arab national home.[10]

Chaim Weizmann was now more convinced than ever that Samuel's lack of firmness with Arab agitation would spark more anti-Jewish violence. Meeting with Samuel after the speech, Weizmann became angry when he was asked to reassure Arabs by announcing that the Zionist leadership had no intention of establishing a Jewish state in Palestine. He refused. To Weizmann, the evolution of the Jewish national home into a state was the essential aim of Zionism. To have Samuel, under the pressure of Arab agitation, suggest otherwise was outrageous. It was also betrayal. For Weizmann appreciated more than most that Herbert Samuel was an ardent Zionist, an early advocate of the Jewish restoration in Palestine, a man who had once even suggested rebuilding Jerusalem's Jewish Temple.[11]

If Samuel and his superiors in London began to modify their commitment to the Jewish national home, they could not abandon it even after the General Staff advised in 1923 that Palestine was no longer needed for the defense of the Suez Canal. To have done so would have been a blow to Britain's prestige and status as an international power. For the Jewish national home conferred legitimacy on British government in Palestine. There was also a question of respect—perhaps exaggerated—for Jewish wealth and influence. As a cabinet minister stated in August 1921, "The honor of the Government was involved in the Declaration made by Mr. Balfour, and to go back on our pledges would seriously reduce the prestige of this country in the eyes of Jews throughout the world."[12]

Jewish objections notwithstanding, Samuel's strategy of conciliation and appeasement prevailed. It shaped the substance of a White Paper in June 1922, issued over Colonial Secretary Winston Churchill's signature. This policy statement, which guided British policy in Palestine for the next ten years, was described as a "cunningly balanced document" that reaffirmed the government's commitment to the Jewish national home while reassuring Arabs that this commitment did not pose a threat to their survival, prosperity, and independence in Palestine. The White Paper asserted that there was no intention to convert Palestine into the Jewish national home, only that the national home "should be founded in Palestine."[13] With this new policy statement, the government for the first time since the issuance of the Balfour Declaration set official limits to Jewish immigration. Henceforth it would be allowed only within the country's "economic absorptive capacity," leaving it to the mandatory government itself to give content and meaning to those vague words.

HAVING EXPERIENCED two major riots that challenged the mandate and drew negative attention to Britain, government officials in London and Jerusalem were concerned to avoid a repetition of the disorders. Army officers were instructed to keep their anti-Zionist opinions to themselves and to do nothing to encourage Arab agitation. Any evidence of antigovernment actions on the part of Arabs led to imprisonment. The new firmness, combined with the policy of appeasement that Samuel set forth, produced eight uninterrupted years of peace in Palestine, from the riot of May 1921 until 1929.

The 1920s were a fertile period in the buildup of the Jewish national home. World Jewry was enlisted for financial support, and great sums of money were provided for the purchase of land and for funding agricultural estates, building homes, starting businesses, founding banks, and opening schools and hospitals. As the organizing center of Palestine's Jewish community, the Zionist Agency (later the Jewish Agency) was established with the support of 90 percent of Palestine's Jews. The other 10 percent comprised the ultra-Orthodox community, which rejected secular Zionism but after the riots of 1920 and 1921 did nothing to oppose it.

Samuel approved the establishment of a Jewish representative assembly, Assefat Hanivaharim, in October 1920 and held meetings with members of the executive body, the National Council, Va'ad Leumi. These institutions, together with the Jewish Agency, created a semi-autonomous government for the Jewish community of Palestine. And mandatory officials were not unhappy to see the growth of this Jewish "government within a government," for while Jews remitted their taxes to the British government, they were also willing and able to pay for the development of their own community.

Increased building construction led to more members for the newly founded Jewish labor organization, the Histadrut. And because the riots of 1920 and 1921 had sobered Jews about the willingness of the British government to defend them against Arab attacks, a small underground Jewish militia, the Haganah (for "defense"), was formed as the fighting arm of the Histadrut. The Haganah grew in numbers and strength as anti-Jewish violence continued.

Despite the temporary suspension following the riots, Jews continued to immigrate, but not in the great numbers that Zionists had hoped for. From 1920 to 1923, rarely more than 8,000 arrived annually. In the years 1924–1926, because of anti-Jewish legislation in Poland, the figures rose to 34,000. But in the late 1920s, when Palestine suffered an economic depression, more Jews may have left the country than entered it. In 1922 a government census recorded some 84,000 Jews in Palestine; that population doubled by 1931, bringing the New Yishuv to 175,000.[14]

The Jewish immigrants were young—their average age was twenty-seven. They settled on the narrow coastal strip from south of Jaffa and due north to Haifa, and in the Esdraelon plain, the Jezreel Valley, and the lower and eastern Galilee. Reversing historic patterns, they farmed, did manual labor, and worked as stone masons and in factories. And they built. On an empty strip of seacoast sand they built the all-Jewish city of Tel Aviv, which had been founded in 1910 as a northern suburb of Jaffa. By 1936 Tel Aviv grew to a population of 150,000 and became Palestine's largest city.

They learned to read and write the modern Hebrew language—perhaps too well. They learned little if any Arabic. Their contacts with Arabs, most of them villagers hired as seasonal laborers, were minimal.

The establishment of schools throughout the country was crowned with the opening in 1925 of the Hebrew University of Jerusalem and later a university for scientific research at Rehovot. The system of primary and secondary schools made Jews the most literate people in the Middle East. Advanced medicine also resulted in the lowest birth mortality rates for Jews anywhere in the region.[15]

An important aspect of the new Jewish immigrant society was its spirit of political pluralism. Beyond the commonly held axioms of free immigration and national independence, Zionists disagreed about what independence should consist of and how best to deal with both Britain and the Arabs. The majority, following the leadership of the London-based Weizmann, were General Zionists. They trusted that Britain held the key to the Jewish national home in Palestine. Loyal support of Britain and close cooperation with its government would ensure the immigration that could create a Jewish majority and eventually make an independent state of the national home. But Weizmann and others had learned from experience that any use of the words "Jewish majority" and "Jewish state" only inflamed the Arabs and embarrassed the British, and so they avoided such words. Weizmann stressed the economic argument that the wealth brought to Palestine for building the Jewish national home would also benefit Arab society and reduce tensions between the two peoples. David Ben-Gurion, who in the 1920s was rapidly establishing himself as a major voice among Palestine's Jews, seemed sincere when he said that the Jewish national home could be developed "without wronging a single Arab child."[16] Not to dominate or to be dominated was the commonly shared conviction of all the Zionists.

Contradictions within the ideology of the Zionist movement showed up in the attitude toward labor, and particularly toward the many Arab workers who were employed in the years of Jewish agricultural development. Many of the Russian-born Zionists were socialists who believed in the solidarity of workers, which in Palestine meant that Arabs were as fully entitled to their labor and to fair wages as Jews. But from the beginning of Zionist-sponsored immigration this principle of worker solidarity came into conflict with another ideal, the "conquest of labor," which called for Jewish self-sufficiency. In order to reverse centuries of European urban-ghetto dependence, some argued, Jews should redeem themselves through the Land of Israel. They should plow their own fields and milk their own cows without relying on others to do it for them.[17]

Arab spokesmen, who knew little about the subtleties of socialist or Zionist ideology, saw the rejection of Arab labor as discriminatory and evidence of the Jewish desire to win exclusive control of the land. The conflict between the "solidarity of labor" and the "conquest of labor" would plague the Histadrut for years, stymieing its repeated efforts to enlist Arab workers.

Ben-Gurion may have believed that the Jewish national home could be developed without harming a single Arab child; but others, a small minority, took the view that Jewish immigration, land purchase, and national independence inevitably would lead to domination of the Arab society. The most prominent of these Jews was Zev Jabotinsky, firebrand of the Revisionist party, established in 1925. Jabotinsky made no secret of his ambitions to see a powerful Jewish majority ruling over an Arab minority, not just in Palestine but in Transjordan as well. The Revisionists were so called because they insisted on reinterpreting the original resolution of the First Zionist Congress, which called for the establishment of "a Jewish home in Palestine secured by public law." To the Revisionists, the word *Palestine* had to apply to Transjordan, because the Biblical patrimony from the time of King David extended eastward of the Jordan River, and because the British mandate included Transjordan as well as western Palestine. Thus Jews had every right and obligation to settle in Transjordan. The sharp difference between the General Zionists and Revisionists is seen in their attitudes toward the British decision in 1922 to cede Transjordan to the Emir Abdullah. For reasons of politics, the General Zionists acquiesced; for reasons of principle, the Revisionists organized in opposition.

If the Revisionists were on the far right of the *yishuv*'s ideology of nationalism, the far left was held by the small party called Brit Shalom (Covenant of Peace), also established in 1925. Composed mainly of Jewish intellectuals, Brit Shalom, while endorsing the Zionist axioms of immigration and national independence, worried that Zionist development might lead to Arab dislocation. Believing that a Jewish state could not be imposed on an unwilling Arab majority, adherents of the party took the position that only a single, binational Arab-Jewish state was justifiable in Palestine. Criticizing Weizmann and his colleagues for overdependence on the British, Brit Shalom ideologues stressed the priority of Jewish-Arab relations. Better an Arab friend than a British patron was the right attitude. Unfortunately, save for a few farsighted Arab intellectuals, Brit Shalom found few supporters of binationalism among the Arab ruling elite.

On the margins of this dispute were the few thousand pietistic Jews, descendants of the Hasidim and Perushim who had immigrated to Palestine in the nineteenth century. Theologically they opposed the Zionists and the idea of a secular-based Jewish state, believing that the only true Jewish state would be brought into being by God in the days of the messianic redemption. Awaiting that blessed event, ultra-Orthodox Jews kept the Zionists at arm's length but also depended on them for protection against Arab rioters.

None of the Zionists liked the limitation on Jewish immigration in Churchill's White Paper, but they acquiesced in it for the sake of good relations with Britain. Palestine's Arabs rejected the White Paper as they would reject all of Herbert Samuel's later efforts (1921–1923) to provide for constitutional and legislative self-government for Arabs and Jews. The Arab position was simple: cooperation with Britain in schemes of self-government that included Zionists meant endorsement of the mandate and its Jewish national home provisions—both of which were unacceptable. Arab leaders were prepared to establish a national government in Palestine based on majority rule, in which Jews as a minority would take their place. But to effect this Britain had first to renounce the Balfour Declaration and recognize the right of political self-determination by the Arab majority of Palestine. Nothing less than this had been promised in the correspondence between McMahon and Faysal in 1915 and repeated in the Anglo-French Declaration of 1919. Awaiting fulfillment of their right to self-determination in Palestine, Arabs believed that Britain ruled in Palestine not by right but by might, as a conqueror. The Arabs of Palestine would not confer moral or political legitimacy on the conqueror by accepting any scheme of self-government offensive to the majority of the country.

But Jews too were wary of Samuel's efforts to promote Arab and Jewish self-government. As a tiny minority, they were anxious about being overwhelmed in a democratically based assembly or legislature. Jabotinsky declared candidly that if there were a democratic institution of self-government responsible to the "majority," the Jews themselves would either be prevented from entering the country or evicted from it. So it came as some relief to the Zionists that not they but the Arab leaders formally rejected Samuel's proposals for self-government.

Did Arabs make a wise decision in so doing? Probably not. It is true that Arab cooperation with Samuel's arrangement for constitutional government would have conceded legitimacy to Britain's mandate, and implicitly to her right to govern Palestine under the Jewish national home provisions. But it is hard to see how that "legitimacy" would have weakened the Arab desire for political self-determination in all of Palestine. Quite the opposite. Cooperation with Samuel would have forced the Arabs to look beyond their own factionalism and regional rivalries in a common effort to govern the country. Certainly the Arabs' later political chaos, which made effective national leadership impossible, might have been avoided. Had the Arabs participated with the British and the Zionists in early efforts at self-government, they and their interests (as Jabotinsky saw) would have prevailed irrespective of the vote on any given issue. They would have shaped the future by the weight of their numbers and their influence. What the Zionists most feared—defeat through parliamentary power—would have come to pass. Arabs could have brought early parliamentary pressure on Britain to limit Jewish immigration to the country and land sales to Jews, and they could have taken a major step toward a future independent national Arab government. In refusing to participate in a British-sponsored government of both Arabs and Jews, Arab Palestinians created a political vacuum that was filled by family clan rivalries. The result was chaos and the indefinite postponement of national independence.

If their refusal to cooperate in representative government was a failure for the Arabs, a second failure lay in not using the tactic of civil disobedience to press demands on the British. From the moment of the issuance of the Balfour Declaration, London was unsure of how to achieve the Jewish national home. It was extremely sensitive to the opinions and actions of the Arab majority, which made no secret of its total opposition to Zionism. In the riots of 1920 and 1921 the government was forced to confront lawless violence with police measures. But had the Arab leadership acted after these riots with an organized campaign of civil disobedience, including the refusal of tax payments, British leaders might have had to rethink their commitment to the Jewish national home. That the Arabs did not act in such fashion is explained by the absence of leadership. Until the rise of Haj Amin al-Husayni, Palestine's Arabs lacked effective national leadership because of continuing family feuds. But there was also considerable ambivalence among the Arabs generally about their relationship to the mandatory government. They resented the government for supporting the Zionists but were willing to accept administrative appointments and other well-paying jobs that might be endangered by acts of civil disobedience.

The Jaffa riots of May 1921 proved to be a turning point in the evolution of the Arab Palestinian nationalist movement. A few weeks before the riots, Jerusalem's influential mufti, Kamal Effendi al-Husayni, died. Tradition demanded the election of a new mufti according to procedures formulated by the Ottoman government. The British mandatory authority, acting in place of the Ottomans, decided to exercise the right to appoint one of the four candidates who would win the greatest number of votes. It was a delicate moment that put High Commissioner Samuel squarely in the middle of the generations-old rivalry between two of Jerusalem's most influential family clans, the Husaynis and the Nashashibis.

The patriarch of the Nashashibi clan, Ragheb Bey, had been appointed mayor of Jerusalem after the government had dismissed the previous mayor, Musa Khazim Pasha al-Husayni, for participating in the April 1920 Jerusalem riot. The Nashashibis were concerned to enlarge their powers by gaining the office of Jerusalem's mufti; the Husaynis were determined to prevent that. To maintain the political balance within the world of local Arab politics, the government leaned toward Haj Amin al-Husayni, one of the candidates and the younger brother of the former mufti Kamal al-Husayni.

But Amin could win no better than fifth place on the voting list and was thus ineligible for appointment. Now the Husayni clan launched a campaign of vituperation, accusing Arab partisans of the Nashashibis of being in league with the Zionists in an effort to discredit Haj Amin. Samuel was pressed to recognize that the office of Jerusalem's mufti had been a virtual Husayni hereditary property for generations. Samuel, however, had already determined that the most effective way to gain Arab support for the mandate was to coopt its leaders. In Samuel's mind, Haj Amin was ripe for cooption. He was beholden to the high commissioner for being allowed to return to the country after the April 1920 Jerusalem riot. If he were now favored over his rivals for the office of Jerusalem's mufti, he and his powerful family could be a force for Muslim moderation in Palestine. Samuel's calculation proved correct in the short run—disastrous in time.[18]

The May Jaffa riot occurred after (and despite) a private conversation in which a compliant Haj Amin offered assurances to a grateful Samuel of peace and order. Amin kept his word. He saw to it that no rioting occurred in Jerusalem during the seven days of disorder in Jaffa and elsewhere. Now Samuel believed that he had his own man in the Muslim community and wasted no time in bribing the leading vote-getter, a pro-Nashashibi member of the Jarallah family, to resign, clearing the way for the appointment of Amin.

In his less than subtle effort to win the support of the Husayni clan for the government's policies, Samuel invented the new and hitherto unknown title of grand mufti of Palestine. Now, to the dismay of older Muslim religious officials throughout the country, he bestowed it on Haj Amin, a youth in his late twenties with the honorable title of Haj but with little experience in the administration of Muslim religious law.

Muslim leaders had rejected Samuel's proposal for the establishment of an Arab Agency to parallel the officially recognized Jewish Agency. But Haj Amin and others came forward with their own suggestion that instead of an Arab Agency the government establish a Supreme Muslim Council, to be headed by Jerusalem's mufti. Samuel, following his policy of appeasement, readily consented. The office of the Jerusalem mufti would be salaried by the government and ultimately accountable to the high commissioner; otherwise the mufti and the other Supreme Council members would be free to manage the affairs of Palestine's Muslims, and its shrines, estates, and endowments, without interference from British officials.

In agreeing to the Arab request, Samuel (without fully realizing it) made Amin potentially the single most powerful Arab in Palestine. He had only to draw on the immense resources of the Muslim religious trust to enlist political support for himself and his family over his rivals among the Nashashibis and other clans—which is precisely what he did.

In the remaining four years of his administration, Samuel seemed to make wise decisions in the wake of the Jaffa riots. In sponsoring communal autonomy for Arabs and Jews, he provided a measure of stability and peace in the country that lasted through the administration of his successor, Lord Plumer, until nearly the close of the 1920s. It was precisely this communal autonomy for Arabs and Jews, the alternative to representative government, that in Wasserstein's judgment "opened the door to the partition of the country."[19] Without realizing it or wanting it, High Commissioner Samuel had in effect provided the only logical solution to the problem of how two peoples can coexist in one country that they cannot or will not share. But he had also assured future conflict.

AFTER IMMIGRATION, land ownership was the major preoccupation of Zionist planners, who set up two organizations, the Jewish National Fund (Keren Kayemet) and the Palestine Foundation Fund (Keren Hayesod), to help accomplish this objective. Both Jewish purchases of land and Arab complaints about them began well before the Balfour Declaration. In late Ottoman times, Jewish settlements at Hadera, Zichron-Yaacov, Rosh Pinna, Tel Hai, and eighteen other locales were on estates purchased privately from Arabs. Kenneth Stein notes that these purchases, paid for mainly by Baron Edmond de Rothschild, comprised 20 percent of all Jewish-owned land at the end of the mandate period. But the increase of Jewish population from 24,000 in 1882 to more than 60,000 in 1914 created a need for still more land.[20]

Article 6 of the British mandate for Palestine called for "close settlement by Jews on the land, including State lands and waste lands not required for public purpose." But Article 11 charged Britain with the responsibility to "introduce a land system appropriate to the needs of the country having regard . . . to the desirability of promoting the close settlement and intensive cultivation of the land." The first article affecting Jewish settlement was faithfully adhered to; the second, which most directly affected the Arab rural population, was largely ignored.

In his meetings with Prince Faysal, Weizmann had stressed that Jewish development of Palestine would benefit the Arabs and that land purchases would not displace the peasantry. And Faysal acknowledged that there was sufficient land in Palestine to allow for Jewish development. In the protocol they signed in January 1919, the two men "agreed to uphold the rights of the Arab peasantry to remain on the land they cultivated." But Weizmann's sincerity on the Arab land question was put in doubt because, just a year before his first meeting with Faysal, he had opposed British loans to Arab peasants.[21] Since it was precisely the peasants' need of money that led to land sales to the Zionists, it was best to keep them poor.

As early as April 1918, William Ormsby-Gore, British liaison officer to the Zionist Commission, who was personally sympathetic to Zionist aims, warned of the continued land transfers. The removal of the tenant farmer would create a landless peasantry, Ormsby-Gore noted, which could become an economic and political burden for Britain.[22]

Rarely did an Arab landowner refuse to sell land if a Jewish buyer was willing to pay what was often an inflated market price. Stein tells us that "the quantity of Arab land offered for sale was far in excess of the Jewish ability to purchase."[23] Throughout the 1920s Jews bought large tracts of land chiefly from a handful of absentee landowners living in Beirut or Damascus. The single purchase of a huge estate of fifty thousand acres from the Sursuk family of Beirut in the years 1921–1925 provided Jews an agricultural foothold in the Jezreel Valley of the lower Galilee. Some 35 percent of all Jewish land purchases during the mandate came from sales by absentee Arab landowners, most of them in the 1920s. The remaining 65 percent was purchased in the 1930s from smaller Arab landowners, many of them strapped for cash because of a series of crop failures. Arab land sellers included members of some of the country's most prominent families, including the Shawas of Gaza, the Abdul al-Hadis of Nablus, and the Nashashibis and Husaynis of Jerusalem.

As long as the sale of their lands remained secret, Arabs had no reluctance to take the large sums of money that such sales brought. And British officials as well as Zionist land purchasing agents were more than willing to keep the names of Arab land sellers secret. Michael Cohen observes: "The rising land values that Zionist demand engendered enabled the effendi (landowning) class to maintain a certain life-style and statue so long as they were permitted to manipulate the market at will, which they did in full collaboration with the Jews."[24] Stein adds that "a group of speculators, brokers, and middlemen grew wealthy from land sales and drove up land prices considerably as a result of applying their fees. Both Jewish and Arab brokers made little, if any, distinction between the sources of their income and the political ramifications of their actions."[25] Ironically the most vocal Arab critics of land transfers to Jews were land sellers themselves. In 1933 the German consul declared that there were Arabs "who in daylight were crying out against Jewish immigration and in the darkness of the night were selling land to the Jews."[26]

In fact, Arab peasants had already lost much of their land to wealthy Arab families. The arrival of Zionist land purchasers in the late nineteenth and early twentieth centuries only accelerated a trend begun generations earlier.

Zionists denied charges that their land purchases were dispossessing the Arab peasantry. They argued that they were buying uninhabited or sparsely inhabited land, and that the few peasants vacated were fairly compensated. A 1936 Jewish Agency report showed that fewer than seven hundred Arabs were dispossessed but also compensated for their land by Jewish purchasers.[27] Zionists argued that the large tracts purchased from absentee landowners were swampy, infertile lands that were rendered arable by Jewish labor, money, and ingenuity.

Yet Stein informs us that purchase agreements were written with provisos that the Arab landowner had first to remove the peasants from the land before the sale to the Jewish purchaser could be completed. In some instances whole villages were dislocated because of land transfers.[28] A customary practice was for the Arab land seller to compensate peasants for leaving the land either with money or with the offer of alternative land. The peasant, who was indebted to the landowner, had little choice but to accept the offer. And it was not uncommon for the Arab landowner to raise the rent on the peasant tenant and thus force him to leave the land prior to its sale. The end result of land transfer was the migration of thousands of peasants to the cities, where they became a newly emerging proletariat. According to Ylana Miller, "The growth of the Muslim population in Haifa, Jerusalem, and Jaffa between 1922 and 1931 was approximately 74 percent, with a subsequent rise of 49 percent between 1931 and 1944," most of it due to internal migration.[29]

The political implications of the land transfers were obvious and powerful. Palestinians steadily lost control of their own destiny, while, as Stein puts it, "Zionists grasped at greater control of their own fate."[30] Looking at the statistics, we can well believe that the Arab peasantry came to fear the Jews as wanting to seize their land and become their overlords.

British government officials expressed sympathy for the hardships caused to Arab peasants by the loss of their land, and made halfhearted efforts to suspend the purchases. But in fact they welcomed the land transfers because they brought into the country much badly needed money, which helped pay the cost of administration. Michael Cohen observes: "The British relied heavily on imported Jewish capital, not only to fuel the economy but also to pay for the Jewish community's social services and, so long as security expenditure could be kept down during tranquil periods, to keep the Palestine budget in healthy surplus."[31]

Cohen further argues that the unwillingness of the British government to invest in the reclamation of Palestine exacerbated the country's problems, for which they then unfairly held the Zionists responsible.

With their paternalistic, yet parsimonious policies, the British increasingly blamed the Zionists for unsettled conditions in Palestine, thus diverting attention from their own frugality and the Arab effendis' own collusion in the [land] sales. But a thorough reform of the Arab agrarian economy, enough to have made it at least self-sufficient, would likely have required an investment far beyond that which any colonial power was willing to make.[32]

To rescue rural Palestine from its malaise, Britain would have had to formulate and fund a major plan involving loans to the peasantry, the reform of tax policy, and professional training of the peasantry in modern agricultural machinery and methods. It would have been a plan as ambitious and costly as Britain's strategic-military investment in Palestine's roads, airfields, and harbors—and an investment the government was unwilling to make. Without aid, the impoverished peasant became increasingly alienated and more vulnerable to the extremist, violence-prone politics that arose as the mandate wore on.

Britain's sorry record on the land question should not obscure its few positive measures. The government enacted laws against usury and in 1928 compiled a land registry; taxes were reduced on grain, and new roads were cut to move farm produce more efficiently to the cities. Peasants were offered low-interest loans to break their dependence on moneylenders.

But just as Britain failed to protect Palestine's peasantry from the loss of land, so she failed to provide the quality of education needed to lift the peasantry out of its malaise. Where Jews could rely on outside capital to fund their schools, Arab peasants (mostly Muslim, comprising 70 percent of Palestine's total population) had to depend on the British government for teachers and school buildings, as they had earlier relied on the Ottoman government.

Early in the mandate it became clear to the peasants that the British government would spend little money to improve their villages and educate village youth. Villagers could not trust elders who enforced British laws and extracted taxes but did little for them. One report blasted the government for its failure to support Arab rural education:

> If a school is needed, the village has to build it and provide the furniture. Government may or may not contribute but never con-

tributes more than a small amount of the total cost. . . . So many of these fine sturdy people [villagers] are drafted into the services and the police that it is difficult to understand why they remain silent when they know the needs of their people and see how Government provides social services for the towns and neglects the villages.[33]

During three decades of British rule there was little evidence that Arabs advanced much beyond the illiteracy and ignorance known in Turkish times. In 1945 an official evaluation found that since 1918 the government had built at its own expense only five elementary schools; all other schools were built by the Arabs themselves. It was not uncommon for Arab women to sell their jewelry to contribute to school building funds. A chronic lack of trained teachers characterized a period in which school-age children doubled in number. Well into the 1930s more than 80 percent of the Arab peasantry were illiterate. By the end of British rule in 1948, only 34 percent of Arab children attended school, and a literate village girl was considered a rarity.

The political implications of these conditions were described by the country's director of education.

It is impossible to move among the Arab villages in any part of the country without being impressed by the sincerity of the desire of the peasantry that their children shall have fuller opportunity for education. . . . There have already been numerous indications that the nationalist politicians seek to turn the general impatience at the slow spread of the Arab public schools system to their own profit.[34]

The gap between Arab and Jewish levels of literacy, income, and living standards also had profound implications. The lack of qualified Arab engineers, artisans, and technicians meant that the future of the country would be shaped by Jewish hands. As one Arab commentator put it, "If the East is to meet the West on comparable terms, and particularly if the standard of living of Arabs in Palestine is to be brought near to that of the Jews, it is essential that intensive efforts should be made to improve the quality of Arab engineers and technicians."[35]

The exceptions in Arab education were the select Arab young men, mainly Christians, from well-known urban families, who were educated in privately funded church schools. They found employment readily because their skills were needed for government administration.

Why didn't the British government of Palestine support Arab rural education? According to Ylana Miller, the government feared that an educated, historically conscious generation of Arabs would inevitably oppose the colonial-style government that Britain had brought to Palestine. She writes: "Without literacy and historical awareness on the part of a leadership, the impulse to act is rarely disciplined enough to be effective."[36]

Believing that any reminders of the glory of the Ummayad Empire or the courage of Saladin in turning back the Western Crusaders would encourage nationalism and anti-British hostility, the government-approved curriculum deliberately neglected Arabic history. Ironically the government did fund the formation of units of Arab boy scouts, only to see these scouts, under the guidance of their scoutmasters, become the young spear points of nationalistic opposition to both Zionism and Britain.[37]

British officials, whom one historian has called "paternalistic and parsimonious," viewed Palestine's peasants as sociable, generous, illiterate, and ignorant. Keep the peasants on the farm, was the attitude. An overdose of education would only ruin the peasant, driving him to the city where he would hunt for a job and make trouble. But here was another contradiction in British practice. To retain a stable and backward rural population, one had to make sure that it prospered materially; but British collusion in the land transfers with both Zionist purchasers and Arab landowners worked to impoverishing the peasants, forcing them off the land and into the city, where they were indeed poor, resentful, and prone to violence. From 1922 to 1936 the population of Arab towns increased from 200,000 to 300,000, chiefly from dislocated peasants. The poverty of this population was dramatized by Haifa's "tin town" of more than 10,000 Arabs living in huts made of petrol cans.

British neglect led to a breakdown of traditional authority, with villagers wanting "direct control over their own lives."[38] By the mid-thirties, given poverty, illiteracy, and dislocation, the Arab Muslim peasantry was ripe for revolution, willing and eager to follow leaders urging them to fight all their oppressors—Britishers, Zionists, and Arab notables alike.

WHEN HERBERT SAMUEL left the office of high commissioner on June 30, 1924, five years to the day after he had assumed it, he could say that his policies had worked. After the May 1921 riots he had succeeded in keeping the peace. He had mollified the Arabs by slowing the Zionist enterprise. He had angered but not alienated the Zionists by showing them that a slowed Zionism was not a derailed one. The shrewder of the Zionists came to recognize that Samuel's deliberate scaling-down of government financial support for Jewish settlement worked to make Jews more economically self-reliant and stronger.

In the five years of his stay, Samuel had fallen in love with the country. He wanted to continue living there after leaving office, in a house on Mount Carmel, and to devote his retirement years to contemplating philosophical issues and the writing of books. Probably he would have if Lord Plumer, his successor, had not discouraged him. Plumer did not need Arabs or Jews running to Samuel with every disappointment coming out of the office of the new high commissioner.

Whatever Samuel's successes, he had not removed the source of Arab fury against the growing Jewish presence. November 2, 1921, the anniversary of the Balfour Declaration, had seen renewed rioting during which five Jews and three Arabs were killed in Jerusalem. That Balfour Day would each year bring some degree of Arab rioting to Palestine was a virtual certainty. But no one could have predicted the massacre of August 1929, which changed Palestine's history forever.

CHAPTER ELEVEN

Nobody Wants a Palestinian Flag

All British officers tend to become pro-Arab, or,
perhaps more accurately, anti-Jew. . . .
—John Hope-Simpson, 1930

There are three national flags flown in Palestine—
the Union Jack; the red, white, green and black Arab
flag; and the blue and white banner of Zionism. No-
body wants a Palestinian flag. . . .The disease from
which Palestine is suffering is so deep-rooted that the
only hope of a cure lies in a surgical operation.
—Royal Commission Report, 1937

High Commissioner Samuel and Chaim Weizmann were in the
majority among British and Zionist leaders (Vladimir Jabotinsky was the rare exception) who believed that the material prosperity
brought to Palestine by Jews would reconcile the Arabs to Jewish immigration and land acquisition. But the opposite happened. The proliferation of Jewish immigrants, the evidence of their enterprise,
skill, and money, prompted the Arabs to fear the loss of a country
they considered their own.

This misjudgment of Arab feelings extended to Samuel's successor as high commissioner once removed, Sir John Chancellor. The
absence of serious clashes between Arabs and Jews for eight years

(following the May 1921 riot) convinced him that relations between the two peoples had improved. His delusions were shattered when violence erupted in Jerusalem in late August 1929 and spread like wildfire across the country.

This new riot marked a more deadly watershed in Arab-Jewish-British relations. Suddenly there was a new awareness on all sides. Arabs learned that violence was more effective than diplomacy in gaining the attention of British leaders; Jews realized that behind the Arab rabble-rousers was a nationalistic movement in the making; the British awoke to the blunder of governing an Arab-populated country under the lopsided pro-Zionist stipulations of the mandate.

The troubles began a year before the riot. On the Jewish holy day of Yom Kippur, 1928, Jews brought a wooden screen to the Western Wall, intended to separate men and women according to traditional Jewish worship practice. But the addition of the screen was inconsistent with official regulations regarding what Jews could bring to the Wall, regulations intended to prevent any Jewish claim of ownership of it. Although the British police removed the screen the next day, Mufti Haj Amin and the Muslim Supreme Council seized the occasion to campaign against the Zionists. Rumors circulated that the Jews were using their services at the Wall to prepare for a seizure of the Wall and a takeover of the adjacent Muslim shrines.

Muslims were again provoked in mid-August 1929, when a group of highly nationalistic Jewish Revisionist youth from Tel Aviv showed up at the Wall, unfurled the Zionist flag, and sang the Hebrew national anthem, Hatikvah. The demonstrators left peacefully, but the mufti used the demonstration as a reason to intensify a campaign of incitement, which now included cries that the Jews were planning a massacre of Muslim worshipers at the mosques.[1]

The troubles resumed on Friday afternoon, August 23. Once again it was the eve of the Jewish holiday of Yom Kippur. Muslims armed with sticks and swords left their midday prayers at Al Aksa mosque and proceeded to attack Jews in the Mea Shearim quarter north of the old city. As in the 1920 Jerusalem riot, Arabs found a convenient target in the neighboring community of pious, ultra-Orthodox Jews who were defenseless and theologically opposed to the Zionist movement.

Violence quickly spread to Hebron and Safed, where more reli-

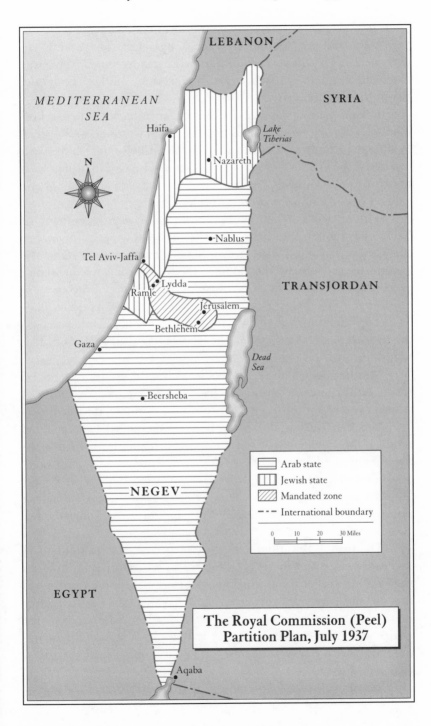

The Royal Commission (Peel)
Partition Plan, July 1937

gious Jews were massacred. When the hostilities ended a week later, 133 Jews had been found murdered by Arab rioters and 339 wounded; Arab killed numbered 116, with 232 wounded.[2] This was surely the deadliest confrontation between Arabs and Jews under the British rule of Palestine.

Behind the riot was an explosive combination of politics and religion, nationalism and ritualism, centered on Jerusalem's Western Wall and Haram esh-Sharif area. The bloodshed might have been avoided if Jerusalem's mufti, Haj Amin al-Husayni, had not set a match to the combustible elements. The charred remnants of the conflict would haunt the country for decades.

The Western Wall, which Jews revere as the remnant of Solomon's Temple, also happens to be the southwestern support of the Haram esh-Sharif (the Noble Sanctuary) on which stand the mosque of Al Aksa and the Dome of the Rock shrine, two of Islam's most revered monuments. For Muslims, the sanctity of the area extends even to the Western Wall itself. For Islam honors the Wall as al-Buraq (Lightning), the name of Muhammad's horse, who, according to tradition, was tethered to the Wall before the Prophet's miraculous Heavenly Ascent.

Muslim ownership of the Wall has been officially recognized through the centuries, but so also has been the right of Jews to worship at the sacred site. In the early twentieth century a dispute developed between Muslims and Jews about which religious articles Jews might bring to worship at the Wall. Turkish and, later, British authorities allowed Jews to bring with them Torah scrolls and prayer books. Trouble began in the late 1920s when Jews also began bringing with them benches and chairs, which obviously had a practical purpose for worshipers fasting and praying for hours under the hot August sun.

To Muslims the additional objects represented a sinister departure from customary practice, designed to secure a Jewish hold on the Wall. In earlier times Muslims had complained to Ottoman authorities about Jewish "deviations" at the Wall and had won decrees in 1840 and 1911 which specifically forbade Jews to place benches, chairs, and a sun-shielding tent at the Wall. Jews persisted in bringing the proscribed objects because local police could usually be bribed to overlook them.

The unwritten law governing Palestine's holy places was a vari-

ation of squatters' rights: whoever uses or protects or acts as custodian of a sacred site is recognized as the proprietor of that site. In
Muslim eyes, the benches, chairs, and other such objects brought to
the Western Wall by Jews were seen as the first stage in the establishment of a synagogue. With a functioning house of worship at the
Wall, Muslims feared that Jews would exercise a counterclaim of
ownership over the sacred area.

It was never easy for Jews to worship at the Wall. Making their
way there from an alley at the south end of the Arab market, they
were pelted with rocks from rooftops. When they reached the Wall
they had to wade through garbage habitually thrown on the outer
pavement by Muslims living in the Mughrabi quarter adjacent to the
Wall. Animals were driven down the narrow passageway in front of
the Wall. Worshipers often had to wipe animal excrement from the
stones of the sacred Wall, recalling the practice of medieval Christians who would "empty their slop pails [on the Temple Mount] as a
special token of contempt for the Jewish religion."[3]

These difficulties led to Jewish efforts before and after World
War I to gain control of the area. Jews applied to the Turks and later
to the British for permission to pave the passageway in front of the
Wall, knowing that if permission were granted a claim of ownership
could be made. Permission was repeatedly denied. At one point
Baron Edmond de Rothschild tried to purchase the passageway and
the adjacent Mughrabi quarter. His efforts failed only because Muslim officials set too high a price on the properties.

The Jewish-Muslim controversy over the Western Wall acquired a new dimension when Mufti Haj Amin exploited the historic controversy to advance his own political agenda. Spreading
fears about Jewish threats to the Western Wall and to the Haram was
a way of gaining international Muslim money and support—and not
incidentally a way of elevating himself as a world Muslim leader.

Amin Husayni was a distinctive personality, whose record of
subversion and survival is unique in the history of the mandate. Although handpicked by the British to be mufti of Jerusalem and all
Palestine, Haj Amin had a mind of his own and could not be domes-
ticated by the government.[4] His intelligence and energy were apparent. He shrewdly balanced his government-secured office with his
nationalistic activities. And he possessed superb organizational and
propaganda skills, knowing just how much trouble to provoke and

when to sit back and let the flow of events accomplish his objective. Under his leadership the mosques and monuments of Jerusalem and Palestine gained worldwide Muslim interest; simultaneously he rallied the Islamic world against Zionism and in defense of Arab Palestine. In the long-simmering Western Wall controversy, the mufti saw a way of accomplishing both his religious and political objectives.

To focus attention on Al Aksa mosque and the Dome of the Rock, Amin launched a campaign to discredit Jews, whom he accused of immigrating to Palestine to dispossess Arabs of their country, and of using the Western Wall as a stepping-stone to an eventual seizure of the Haram esh-Sharif. The campaign met with success in 1922–1925, when the government repeatedly prevented Jews from bringing tables, chairs, and other proscribed articles to the Wall. Meanwhile, Muslim delegations were sent abroad to promote interest in Palestine and to preach the message of anti-Zionism. The Muslims made shrewd use of a Jewish picture which showed the Star of David atop the Dome of the Rock. Jews explained that the picture was merely decorative and was used by Jerusalem's religious academies to raise money among Jews living abroad.[5] The explanation was wasted on the mufti, who saw in the picture a unique opportunity to discredit Zionism and the entire community of Palestine's Jews. He began by circulating the picture throughout the Muslim world as evidence of Jewish ambitions to dominate the country. Then he called on Muslims everywhere to rise up against the Zionist menace.

Once the Western Wall controversy was linked to Zionist threats against the Haram esh-Sharif, the Supreme Muslim Council had no trouble enlisting support for the Palestinian cause from Muslim villagers who would not have been moved merely by squabbles over how Jews prayed at the Western Wall.[6] This same link between politics and religion brought in money from Muslims throughout the Middle East for the cause of their brothers in Palestine. The organized opposition to Jewish practices at the Wall ended in 1929 with the massacre of Jews in Jerusalem, Hebron, and Safed.

Mufti Husayni and officials of the Supreme Muslim Council disclaimed any responsibility for the riots of 1929 and deplored the killings that occurred. But months later individuals who had been arrested, convicted, and executed for the killings were hailed by leading Muslim officials, including the mufti, as heroes. Muslim feeling about the riot was expressed by one follower of the mufti:

Today is the anniversary of the August uprising . . . the flames of which were borne high on this day in 1929. That day was a day of brilliance and glory in the annals of Palestinian-Arab history. This is a day of honor, splendor and sacrifice. We attacked Western conquerors and the Mandate and the Zionists upon our land. The Jews had coveted our endowments and yearned to take over our holy places. In our silence they had seen a sign of weakness, therefore there was no more room in our hearts for patience or peace. . . . No sooner had the Jews begun marching along this shameful road than the Arabs stood up, checked the oppression, and sacrificed their pure and noble souls on the sacred altar of nationalism.[7]

While the 1929 riot did not end Jewish immigration to Palestine, it did pressure the British government into once again setting limits to entry. The mufti, to the consternation of his Nashashibi rivals, was credited for the change. For years moderate Arabs such as Ragheb Nashashibi had argued unsuccessfully with British leaders in Palestine and London to end Jewish immigration and rescind the Balfour Declaration. Now a thirty-four-year-old Muslim cleric had demonstrated how vulnerable the British government was to violence and how eager it would be to appease the violent.

The official commissions of inquiry that followed the riot showed that the government had now begun to wonder if its pro-Zionist policy was damaging British interests. To the shock of the Zionists, who expected condemnation of the mufti and his supporters, the Shaw Commission report of March 1930 blamed the riot not on anti-Jewish incitement but on the effects of Jewish immigration and land purchases. Ignoring the campaign of religio-political vituperation waged by the Supreme Muslim Council, the commission exonerated Mufti Haj Amin of any responsibility for the rioting. Arabs, said the commission, were provoked to violence by a growing Jewish presence and their fear of a power that would soon dominate them.

A Labor member of Parliament, Sir Harry Snell, was the one dissenting voice on the Shaw Commission. Snell, who directly faulted Arab leaders, believed the situation demanded not political concessions to the Arabs but, as he put it,

a change of mind on the part of the Arab population who have been encouraged to believe that they have suffered a great wrong and that the immigrant Jew constitutes a permanent menace to their livelihood and future. . . . [For] on any long view of the situation the Arab people stand to gain rather than to lose from Jewish enterprise.[8]

Snell went on to single out Mufti Amin for using religious rhetoric that was intended to have violent consequences:

I therefore attribute to the Mufti a greater share in the responsibility for the disturbance than . . . in the report. I am of the opinion that the Mufti must bear the blame for his failure to make an effort to control the character of an agitation conducted in the name of a religion of which . . . he was the Head.[9]

The conclusions of the Shaw Commission so provoked the Zionists that the government was reluctant to act on it. Another inquiry was called for, this one focused on the land question. Carried out in 1930 by John Hope-Simpson, the new inquiry proved no more sympathetic to the Zionist point of view than the Shaw report. Hope-Simpson asked rhetorically whether there was any land available in Palestine for the continued building of the Jewish national home that would not at the same time injure Arab interests. The answer was, very little. "If all the cultivable land in Palestine were divided up among Arab agricultural population, there would not be enough to provide every family with a decent livelihood." Concerned about Arab unemployment as well as land scarcity, Hope-Simpson called for severe restrictions on Jewish immigration and land purchases.[10]

The British government accepted the conclusions of the Hope-Simpson report and incorporated them in the form of a White Paper policy statement in October 1930. Zionists, seeing betrayal, reacted with fury. How could a government pledged to the Jewish national home call for limitations on the building of that home? Many Zionists felt that the Arab voice was now being heard in ways that would fundamentally change the political balance in the country. In a furious protest against the White Paper, Chaim Weizmann resigned his dual position as president of the International Zionist Organization and head of the Jewish Agency of Palestine. Although he later withdrew his resignation, the troubles stemming from the 1929 disturbances marked the beginning of a deterioration of his influence with both British leaders and his fellow Zionists.

Still the Zionists would not be deterred by commissions and their reports. As in the past, they sought to regain in London what they had lost in Jerusalem. They wasted no time in fighting to rescind the White Paper. Putting researchers to work, they challenged the Hope-Simpson conclusion on the scarcity of land for Arab cultivation, pointing to large quantities of state-owned land that could be made available to the Arab peasantry. Enlisting support from Lloyd-George, Balfour, Jan Smuts, and many old pro-Zionist friends in the British Conservative party, Weizmann and his colleagues pressed the minority government of Prime Minister Ramsay MacDonald, who was now confronted with a Palestine issue that threatened to divide British political parties along the lines of the Arab-Jewish split. Seeking to avoid that division, MacDonald made an historic decision. He won back Zionist support by sending an official letter to Weizmann on February 13, 1931, offering a new "interpretation" of the White Paper which stripped it of its anti-Jewish tone and content.[11] The new approach restored Jewish land purchases and allowed Jewish immigration to continue in accord with the economic absorptive capacity of the country, as stipulated in the Churchill White Paper of 1921. The Zionists had succeeded in rescuing the national home from fatal damage.

MacDonald's letter showed that whatever troubles Britain was encountering in Palestine, it was not prepared to turn its back on the Jewish national home. Britain was committed to her obligations under the mandate, concerned about the public image of her trustworthiness, and desirous of the goodwill and support of world Jewry. A full-scale Arab rebellion and another world war would ultimately change those views.

THE SERIES OF INQUIRIES beginning with the Shaw Commission and ending with the White Paper were a sobering experience for the Zionist leadership in Palestine. All these documents had been influenced by High Commissioner John Chancellor, for whom the 1929 riot had the same transforming effect as Herbert Samuel had experienced with the 1921 disturbance. Chancellor, who was less pro-Arab than anti-Jewish, blamed the 1929 riot on Jewish provocations.[12] His effective influence on the official investigating bodies showed that Britain, while not actually rescinding the national home, was inching back from it. After the 1929 riot the government insisted that its mandate for administering Palestine called not only for support of the national home but for the protection of Arab political and economic rights—this despite the obvious priority given to the national home in the mandate document. It was the beginning of a British policy of duality. But just how the government would "support" the Jewish national home and still "protect" Arab rights was not made clear.

Arab leaders, stunned by the turnabout in London, dubbed MacDonald's communication to Weizmann the "black letter," and grew increasingly bitter about what they believed to be the growing loss of their country to the Zionists. The more extreme of the nationalists talked of revolt, and in the villages there were those who saw in MacDonald's letter Satan's hand. The 1929 riots proved to be the prelude to the countrywide Arab rebellion that began seven years later and pitted Arabs of every class against both the British administration and the Jewish population.

Undoubtedly the government's about-face in MacDonald's letter was a contributing cause of the troubles that began in 1936. But the roots of rebellion lay deeper. The Zionist expectation that economic development would isolate the extremists and win the cooperation of moderate Arabs proved wrong. Just the opposite happened. More Jewish settlements, and the enterprise, confidence, and productivity of their people, led Arabs to fear domination.

The marked increase of Jewish immigration in the 1930s fed those fears. Hitler's rise to power in 1933 led to a major exodus of Jews from Germany and Austria. In one of the more grotesque ironies of Jewish history, the demographic expansion of the Jewish national home in Palestine owes more to Hitler's persecutions than to Britain's policies. Most of the Jewish European refugees headed for the United States, but a substantial number chose Palestine. In 1931 the Jewish population there stood at 200,000. From 1933 to 1936 an average of 40,000 Jews arrived annually, bringing the total Jewish population to about 400,000, or 30 percent of the country's population.[13] The Arabs, who numbered almost 1 million in 1936, saw their share of the total population drop from 90 to 70 percent. The Zionists did not hide their ambitions about immigration. Weizmann thought that as many as 3 million of a diaspora population of 18 million could eventually be brought to Palestine.[14] Jabotinsky spoke more expansively of bringing 8 million Jews to Palestine.

The quarter of a million Jews who entered Palestine between 1919 and 1936 brought with them energy, skills, ideas, and money. Seventy million English pounds sterling flowed into Palestine from 1917 to 1937, fueling an economy that burgeoned in the early 1930s.[15] Employment was full, and wages rose. New houses, roads, and bridges were built. Citrus production for export became the major source of income for the country, creating wealth for both Arabs and Jews. The traditional small-crafts and cottage industries, centered on textiles, soap, and olive oil, yielded to machine-driven industries producing a variety of goods for home consumption. The influx of money led to the founding of banks for both Jewish and Arab communities. More schools were built, which led to advanced education with an increase of engineers, doctors, lawyers, teachers, and other professionals.

Because of the many new immigrants, Jewish land purchases in Palestine increased throughout the 1930s, bringing sharp Arab reaction. Jews sought to purchase contiguous lands, free of Arab tenants. Purchases were concentrated in the largely unsettled and uncultivated areas of the seacoast from Mount Carmel to south of Jaffa, and in the Jezreel Valley and lower Galilee. These areas were drained of swamps, then irrigated, plowed, and planted. By 1936 there were 203 Jewish agricultural settlements, containing 97,000 or a fourth of the country's Jews.

The pattern of settlement in effect divided the land between Arabs and Jews years before any discussion of partitioning Palestine. Arabs were settled in the upper Galilee and in the central hill country from Jenin in the north, south to Nablus, Jerusalem, Bethlehem, Hebron, and the Jordan Valley.

This demographic division of the country was powerfully reinforced by unbridgeable social and cultural differences between the two peoples. We have two vivid accounts of these differences from members of the Royal (Peel) Commission who visited Palestine in 1936.

> Anyone who attended the Toscanini concerts at Jerusalem might have imagined, if he closed his eyes, that he was in Paris, London, or New York. Yet almost within earshot was the old city, the Haram esh-Sharif, and the headquarters of the Arab Higher Committee.

The Daniel Sieff Research Institute at Rehovot [is] watched by chemists all over the world: yet from its windows can be seen the hills inhabited by a backward peasantry who regard it only as the demonstration of a power they hate and fear and who would like no doubt, when their blood is up, to destroy it.[16]

Statistics also tell a remarkable story of Arab population during this same period. In 1919, after the world war, the Arab population stood at 580,000. Ensuing growth was due to a large natural increase and lower infant mortality rates brought about by a general improvement of the country's health, to which both British and Jewish medicine contributed. Other reasons for the Arab gain included greater physical security and new opportunities for employment in construction and citrus production. In just seventeen years Arabs increased their numbers by 67 percent, to 968,000 in 1936, and by 120 percent from 1922 to 1947. In 1947 the Muslim population stood at 1.1 million, Arab Christians numbered 145,000, and Jews about 600,000.[17]

In a terrible paradox, as prosperity came mainly to Arab town dwellers and to Jews, so relationships between them deteriorated. Muslims and Arab Christians could tolerate the presence of the small, older, pious Jewish communities huddled in their quarters in the traditional holy cities of Jerusalem, Hebron, Safed, and Tiberias; the leaders of these communities acted subserviently and posed no economic or political threat. But the new Zionist-led buildup, with its industrious and intelligent young men and women devoted to a secular nationalist ideology, was an expression of strength that directly threatened the assumption that Palestine was a personal Arab possession.

Zionists invariably responded to Arab expressions of resentment by declaring, "We came not to dominate or be dominated." But the goals of a Jewish majority and eventual statehood in Palestine flew directly in the face of the expressed wish not to impose a Jewish will on the Arab peoples. David Ben-Gurion, who became chairman of the Zionist executive in Palestine, had his own federalist scheme for achieving political coexistence: the future Jewish state should be incorporated into a federation of independent Middle Eastern states. Unfortunately few Arabs of any influence were willing to talk and plan with Ben-Gurion for federation.

Certainly most Zionists believed they had immigrated, settled, and worked the land not to dominate the Arab peoples but in some unspecified way to share that land. Yet in contrast to Ben-Gurion's optimism about the future coexistence of Arab and Jewish nationals there was to be found the pessimism of Zev Jabotinsky, who believed that the achievement of Jewish majority status and national independence would inevitably bring armed conflict with the Arabs.

The MacDonald letter of February 1931 proved to be a delayed-action fuse. But Arab militancy had acquired a new resolve even before the troubles of 1936 erupted. In November 1935 a Palestinian delegation drawn from various clans and factions presented to High Commissioner Arthur Wauchope (Chancellor's successor) a set of demands that included election of a national government, cessation of Jewish immigration, and prohibition of land transfers.

As the government mulled over the demands, its attention was shifted to the murder of two Jews by Arab bandits in April 1936, and the reprisal killing by Jews of two Arabs.[18] More blood was spilled when demonstrations on both sides led to assaults. The government imposed a curfew on Jaffa and Tel Aviv. Arab national committees were formed in towns and villages, and on April 20 they declared a general strike. The Higher Arab Committee, newly organized to lead the strike, called for nonpayment of taxes until Jewish immigration was halted. The British government, in a rare show of strength, responded by approving work permits for 4,500 Jewish immigrants to enter the country in the coming six months; though it was only a fraction of what the Zionist leadership had requested.

For the first time rebellion sprang from the people, particularly the peasantry. Taking the lead were Christian Boy Scouts and Muslim youngsters, who mounted anti-Zionist demonstrations. Calling themselves *mujahidun* (warriors of a holy war), armed guerrilla bands, aided by recruits from Syria and Iraq, formed in the mountain villages between Safed, Acre, and Nazareth, and carried out raids against British military and police. Their new slogan: "Zionism is a mere branch of British colonialist domination of Palestine. Cut the tree down and the branch will wither and die." The words were taken literally when guerrillas destroyed Jewish-planted forests and crops in the north of the country. They also damaged rail, telephone, and electrical installations, mined roads, and attacked truck transports. The Iraq-Haifa oil pipeline (so lucrative to the British economy), running through the plain of Esdraelon, was repeatedly cut.

The rise of religiously minded Arab terrorist groups was in part an angry reaction to the ineffectiveness of Arab leaders. After twenty years the older generation, led by Jerusalem's Husayni and Nashashibi clans, had failed to rid the country of Britain and the Jews. Feelings of frustration and militancy were particularly keen among villagers and dislocated peasants in the towns, who had watched the gradual transfer of their land to the Jews as Jewish numbers rapidly increased throughout the 1930s.

The villagers produced their first popular hero and martyr in the person of Sheik Izz al-Din al-Qassam, an *imam* or mosque prayer leader who was the first "to put into practice the idea of armed struggle." Qassam, who was *imam* in Haifa and the lower Galilee area, attracted followers with his fiery sermons, mixing cries of political freedom with the ideals of Islam. Ministering to the illiterate and the poor, he gained a reputation as a saintly figure who effectively turned youth away from "brothels, drink, and gambling, and towards a new life of righteousness in Islam."[19] Qassam's politics flowed from orthodox Islam. To defend the faith, he preached against infidelity, heresy, and the corrupting influences of the West. He condemned popular superstitions involved in the visitation of graves, the worship of saints, indiscriminate repetition of the names of God, and making one's living from the reading of the Koran.

Qassam invoked the Koran against Arabs who sold land to Jews, threatening to brand them as infidels and to deny them religious burial. The loss of land, he charged, had forced peasants to live from hand to mouth. He knew whereof he spoke. According to Pamela Ann Smith's figures, "While each Jewish resident in 1935 had, on average, 28.1 dunams (7 acres) of arable land, there were only 9.4 dunams [slightly more than 2 acres] for each Arab," who had to live well below subsistence level.[20]

Reacting to both the 1929 riot and the MacDonald "black letter," Qassam argued that Palestine would not be freed from British and Zionist domination by sporadic protests, staged demonstrations, or the occasional riot which would soon be forgotten. Palestine could be restored to the Arabs only by an organized and continuous armed struggle to drive out the British and Jewish enemies. To his followers he quoted verses from the Koran referring to *jihad*.

Qassam believed that his was the true revolution, to be distinguished from the mere agitation caused by Mufti Haj Amin al-

Husayni, to whom he was religiously subordinate. Qassam's emphasis on armed struggle repeatedly brought him into conflict with the mufti. For however much Amin agreed in spirit with Qassam's preaching of violence, the mufti was a salaried official of the mandatory government. Concerned to retain office, title, and budget, Amin always sought ways to carry out his own anti-Zionist activities without directly challenging the government. One story has it that in 1933 Qassam asked the mufti to start a rebellion in the south while he, Qassam, would lead one in the north. The mufti's cautious reply was that he was still searching for a "political solution."[21]

The Black Hand was founded by Qassam as a peasant terrorist movement which made a target of moderate Arabs, British officials, and Zionist settlers. The organization established dozens of small terrorist cells of ten to twenty men each in the Arab villages of Nazareth, Nablus, Jenin, and Tulkarm. Guerrilla action was launched against northern Jewish settlements immediately after the 1930 publication of MacDonald's "black letter." Terror was directed against any Arab who sold land to Jews or did business with them, or collaborated with them in any way. Also targeted were members of the Supreme Muslim Council who preached moderation, and Arabs who worked in the British mandatory administration. In 1937 Qassam's followers sent death threats to Mufti Husayni and to Ragheb Bey al-Nashashibi for pursuing policies of nepotism and self-interest.

As the rebellion continued, the prestige of the old urban Arab elite continued to decline in the eyes of the Arab revolutionaries and their peasant supporters. Increasingly Mufti Amin Husayni, for all his rhetorical and financial support of the rebellion, was viewed as a British stooge, an example of the imperial administrative practice of "coopt and conquer." The mufti's archrival, the one-time mayor of Jerusalem, Ragheb Nashashibi, was also despised by the revolutionaries as a puppet who craved foreign respect and money. Qassam understood as had few before him that such Arab leaders might cause trouble for the Jews and the British, but they could never lead a revolution against them.

Nor could the recently established Arab political parties. Instead of setting forth democratic political ideals and goals that might strengthen the people, the parties had formed around the old elite clans. Beyond voicing their opposition to Zionism and a desire for independence, they accomplished little. They could agree only on anti-

Zionist manifestos; otherwise the Husaynis, Nashashibis, and other families were pitted against one another for control of the country. In the mid-1930s clan quarrels led to killing, and power began to shift to the rural hill villages, which provided the peasant recruits for the armed bands that wandered the countryside.

In November 1935 Qassam's luck ran out. British military authorities killed him with several of his followers in their hideout in the Jenin hills. This event adorned the annals of the Arab independence movement in the same way that the mass suicide of the Jewish remnant at Masada became a heroic chapter in ancient Jewish history. Qassam's name is still attached to a military brigade of the Palestine Liberation Organization today. His revolutionary emphasis on youthful militancy was imitated in 1986 by the Palestinian Intifada rebellion. And his stress on Islamic purity is echoed today in the speeches of Hamas revolutionaries.

Virtually overnight, Izz al-Din al-Qassam became the object of a full-fledged cult, and his death provoked further Arab violence. He was the martyr sacrificed for the fatherland. His grave at Balad al-Shakyh became a place of pilgrimage. His embodiment of idealism and terrorism even drew the respectful comment of David Ben-Gurion, who wrote, "These people are not bandits. . . . Mosque preachers, school directors, chairmen of the Young Men's Muslim Association do not engage in banditry. Not a band of thieves but a body of political terrorists has lately confronted the authorities of Palestine."[22]

Britain responded to Arab violence by reinforcing its military and imprisoning Arab strike leaders in what were officially referred to as "concentration camps." And again the government appointed an official investigating body.

The royal commission, headed by Lord Peel, which arrived in Palestine in October 1936, brought a temporary halt to violent activity. Unlike previous commissions, it exercised wide scope in investigating the causes of the troubles and proposing changes. The Peel recommendations were unique in challenging the premises of Britain's mandate to govern Palestine.

The Peel Commission found that in power, durability, and coordination, the Arab rebellion overshadowed all its predecessors. It had aroused the feelings of the Arab world against Zionism—an ominous development that challenged the wisdom of British policymakers in continuing their commitment to the Jewish national home.

Palestine's troubles, the commission found, went deeper than Jewish immigration and Arab violence, to a root political problem: the authentic Arab desire for national independence was blocked by the government's mandate to administer the country in behalf of the Jewish national home. British and Zionist tendencies to dismiss Arab discontent as the work of agitators were judged to be mistakes. The commissioners found that the Zionist belief that "Palestinian society [consisted] of a large illiterate and politically inexperienced population used by political agitators" was no longer true.[23]

For years both Britishers and Zionists mistakenly assumed that Arabs would in time accept the mandate and its Jewish national home provisions once they saw how they materially benefited from Zionist investment and development. But Jewish improvements in agriculture, medicine, and sanitation could not be exchanged for the currency of political coexistence. The Arab attitude was graphically depicted in the commission report which quoted an unnamed Arab source angrily denouncing the economic argument: "You say we are better off: you say my house has been enriched by the strangers who have entered it. But it is *my* house, and I did not invite the strangers in, or ask them to enrich it, and I do not care how poor it is if I am only master of it."[24] Benefits and improvements were viewed by the Arabs as mere palliatives in place of national independence to which British leaders had committed themselves in the promises made to Sharif Husayn in 1915 and repeated in the 1919 Anglo-French Declaration. And national independence meant rule of all Palestine by an Arab majority.

What of the Jews in an Arab Palestine? Mufti Amin was asked by the commissioners about the status of the Jewish minority if national independence were to be realized.

> Q. Does His Eminence think that this country can assimilate and digest the 400,000 Jews now in the country?
> A. No.
> Q. Some of them would have to be removed by a process kindly or painful, as the case may be?
> A. We must leave all this to the future.[25]

The mufti's ominous replies did not go unnoticed by the commissioners, who observed, "We cannot forget what recently happened, despite treaty provisions and explicit assurances, to the Assyrian minority in Iraq; nor can we forget that the hatred of the Arab politician for the [Jewish] National Home has never been concealed and that it has now permeated the Arab population as a whole."[26]

The Peel report further argued that the mandate rested on the crucial premise that both Arabs and Jews would cooperate in the administration of the country. That assumption had been proven wrong by the events of the preceding eighteen years, which had come to a head in the outbreak of countrywide rebellion.

The Peel Commission concluded that the British government, under the conditions of the mandate, could no longer carry out its dual obligation to support the Jewish national home and to protect the rights of Palestine's Arabs. This was a belated but courageous admission that the circle could not be squared.

The commission went on to acknowledge that Britain could not shirk its obligation under the mandate to foster both the Jewish national home and the development of "self-governing institutions," affecting both Arabs and Jews. It noted that past efforts to foster political self-representation through advisory and legislative councils had been unsuccessful chiefly because Arab leaders would not cooperate with their Jewish counterparts. But, the commission admitted, those British-sponsored councils had not provided full and clear assurance that Arab participation in them would lead to national independence.

The Peel report further acknowledged that both the Arab and Jewish peoples of Palestine were just as ready to assume responsibility for national independence as were the peoples of Egypt and Iraq, who now enjoyed it. The commissioners reasoned that the best way for Britain to meet its mandated obligation to provide for self-government in Palestine for both Arabs and Jews was to partition the country, to allow for separate Arab and Jewish political development leading to independence for each people. Therefore, concluded the report, "We feel justified in recommending that Your Majesty's Government should take the appropriate steps for the termination of the present Mandate on the basis of Partition."[27]

The partition plan drawn up by the commission was in fact a realistic recognition of the demographic development that had already been occurring since the time of High Commissioner Samuel. Under this new scheme, Jews would be allotted a small area, about 20 percent of Palestine west of the Jordan River, comprising a northwestern slice of the country, which included the coastal strip, the Esdraelon plain, the Jezreel Valley, and lower Galilee—precisely the areas that Jews were inhabiting. For their proposed area of sovereignty, Arabs were granted 80 percent of the territory west of the Jordan, and, significantly, all of Transjordan.

To solve the problem of the numbers of Arabs and Jews who would find themselves on the lesser half of the territorial division, the commission recommended the transfer of populations, as had occurred with the Greeks and Turks following their 1922 war.

The partition of Palestine did not mean that Britain would leave the country. There were the Christian holy places to consider. The Peel report stated: "The partition of Palestine is subject to the overriding necessity of keeping the sanctity of Jerusalem and Bethlehem inviolate and of ensuring free and safe access to them for all the world." Safeguarding the holy places was considered, in the words of the mandate, "a sacred trust of civilization."[28] Accordingly, the members of the royal commission proposed that Jerusalem, Bethlehem, Nazareth, and the Sea of Galilee (Lake Tiberias) be designated *corpus separatum* and "detached" from the proposed Arab and Jewish states. With a designated road access to the sea, the Christian holy areas would have the status of an enclave under an international administration. For strategic purposes, Britain insisted on continuing its control of the ports of Haifa and Aqaba, and the airfields at Lydda and Ramlah.

The Peel report, it seems, pleased no one. Zionists, disappointed at the modest amount of territory for the proposed Jewish state, refused to endorse the partition plan. Jewish Revisionists rejected the plan because it awarded Transjordan to the Arabs. But the Jewish denial proved to be a major blunder. A Zionist endorsement of partition might have swayed British leaders in favor of an independent Jewish state at a time when, because of German militancy in Europe, the British military sought to retain a strategic hold on Palestine and other places in the Middle East. Seen in retrospect, the existence of an independent, albeit tiny, Jewish state in the late 1930s, with the power to control its own immigration, would have made possible the rescue of thousands of Jews fleeing a Hitler-dominated Europe.

Arab leaders categorically rejected the partition plan because it allowed for a Jewish state on land that justifiably could only be under Arab government. This too proved to be a mistake. For had the mufti and the leaders of the various Arab parties looked beyond their common animosity toward the Zionists, they would have realized that the territorial partition, which included Transjordan, greatly favored them, giving them a solid base for national independence.

What doomed the report, however, were not Arab and Jewish rejections but the mounting tensions in Europe, which persuaded Britain to stay put in Palestine.

Between October 1936, when the Peel Commission began taking testimony, and July 1937, when the report was published, Palestine was characterized by a deceptive calm. The rebellion resumed with greater force after the commissioners returned to England. By the fall of 1937 Arab guerrilla attacks on Jews and on British personnel and facilities increased. As the hostilities resumed, economic depression in the country deepened. Particularly hard hit were Arab peasants, who had begun to benefit materially from the economic boom of the early 1930s and were then devastated by the 1936 general strike.

In September 1937 followers of Sheik Qassam, or the Qassamiyun as they called themselves, murdered Lewis Andrews, acting district commissioner of the Galilee and the most senior British government victim of the conflict. The government now reacted with fury. The Higher Arab Committee and all the village national committees were officially abolished, and many town and village leaders were deported or detained. The Supreme Muslim Council was dismissed, and several of its members were exiled to the Seychelles Islands. Haj Amin was discharged from his offices as mufti of Palestine and president of the Supreme Muslim Council. Fearing arrest, he fled the country for Beirut and other Arab capitals, from which he would direct Arab insurgency in Palestine for the next ten years.

From October 1937 through 1938, Arab guerrilla activity rose. Active guerrilla fighters numbered less than two thousand, but they had the support of thousands of villagers, who supported them and would join their ranks after harvest time. In 1938 the main roads of Palestine were seized by the guerrillas, who took control of several towns, including the old city of Jerusalem, which was seized in October and held for almost a week.[29]

Whatever sense of Arab national unity was forged through the political parties established in the mid-thirties was ruined by increasing inter-Arab terrorism. As the chaos deepened, the Nashashibi faction joined the British army to fight the guerrillas and the Husayni party. Arabs killed Arabs in the hundreds. One historian records, "The reign of terror was so effective that corpses of the murdered were left in the streets for days, their relatives afraid to bury them."[30] Scores of Arab Christian and Muslim families, particularly from Haifa, fled the country, as did many poorer people.

The rebellion also opened an avenue for Jewish extremist groups, led by the Revisionists, to press their political demands and engage in their own terrorist acts against Arabs and the British government. Government buildings were blown up in Jerusalem and Tel Aviv by the Irgun, the fighting arm of the Revisionist party.[31]

As hostilities intensified, the British realized that if they allowed the Arab rebellion to continue, it might turn Palestine to chaos at a time when Britain faced a mounting crisis in Europe. The government thus acted decisively in late 1937, moving substantial numbers of troops and arms to Palestine. Counterattacks soon put the guerrillas on the defensive. In a few weeks, after some killing and many arrests, roads were reopened, towns and villages pacified.

For years Arab leaders in the Middle East had taken notice of the struggle in Palestine. Now they decided to do something in behalf of their Palestinian brothers. At the Bludan Conference, held in Syria in September 1937, Arab leaders from various countries (heeding a plea from one of the most prestigious delegates, Mufti Haj Amin) warned the British government of the consequences of continuing its mandate: "... We must make Britain understand that it must choose between our friendship and the Jews. Britain must change its policy in Palestine, or we shall be at liberty to side with other European powers whose policies are adverse to Britain." The conference was a noticeable success for Jerusalem's mufti, who convinced the three hundred Arab delegates that the Zionists did not wish to control only Palestine but all of the Middle East.[32]

AFTER THE BRITISH put down the rebellion with a quick use of massive force, and to make sure that Palestine would not again divert

British troops at a crucial moment, London decided fundamentally to alter Britain's policy in Palestine. In a new May 1939 White Paper, British leaders showed they were willing to capitulate to Arab demands in order to ensure peace in the country. This White Paper, written over the signature of Colonial Secretary Malcolm MacDonald, son of former Prime Minister Ramsay MacDonald, may be said to have bleached his father's earlier pro-Zionist "black letter."

Where the mandate directed Britain to govern Palestine so as to secure the establishment of the Jewish national home, the new policy held that Britain's objective in Palestine was "self-government" for its resident peoples. Further, it was emphasized that "the British framers of the Mandate in which the Balfour Declaration was embodied could not have intended that Palestine should be converted into a Jewish State against the will of the Arab population of the country." What was intended, as the Churchill White Paper of 1922 made clear, was that "a [Jewish National] Home should be founded *in Palestine.*"

What was the British aim in promoting resident self-government? The White Paper answered that it was the "desire to see established ultimately an independent Palestine State." It would be "a state in which the two peoples of Palestine, Arabs and Jews, share authority in government in such a way that the essential interests of each are secured." Should there be any doubts from either Arabs or Jews about the representation of their interests in the proposed new unitary state, the government was prepared to postpone statehood.

Further stipulations in the White Paper left no doubt that the projected "independent Palestine State," to be established within ten years, would be *de facto* an Arab state, in which Jews would be consigned permanently to the status of a minority.

The government noted that from 1922 to 1939 the Jewish population had risen to 450,000, or nearly a third of the country's total population. In its own judgment, Britain had fulfilled its pledge to secure the establishment of the national home. It was now free to make a new decision affecting the crucial matter of immigration. For the first time Jewish immigration would be guided not chiefly by the "economic absorptive capacity of the country" but by a fixed limit. Fifty thousand Jewish immigrants in the five years after 1939 would be authorized; an additional 25,000 would be allowed immediate entry as refugees from Europe. (This latter concession came after the negative publicity that followed Britain's refusal to allow Palestine's Zionist officials to adopt ten thousand Jewish children after anti-Jewish actions in November 1938 in Nazi-governed Germany and Austria.) After the quota of 75,000 was filled, "no further Jewish immigration will be permitted unless the Arabs of Palestine are prepared to acquiesce in it."

With cool detachment, the government struck back at the Zionists for encouraging illegal Jewish immigration to Palestine from the first days of Hitler's rise to power. The government warned that "the numbers of any Jewish illegal immigrants who . . . may succeed in coming into the country and cannot be deported will be deducted from the yearly quotas."

As to the question of Jewish land purchases, the White Paper found that "owing to the natural growth of the Arab population and the steady sale in recent years of Arab land to Jews, there is now in certain areas no room for further transfers of Arab land. . . ." Expressing its wish to avoid the creation of "a considerable landless Arab population," Britain gave the high commissioner new authority to "prohibit and regulate transfers of land."

The White Paper concluded sanctimoniously with a call to both Arabs and Jews "to practice mutual tolerance, goodwill and co-operation" in a country revered by many "millions of Moslems, Jews and Christians throughout the world who pray for peace in Palestine and for the happiness of her people."

The White Paper was a devastating blow to the Zionists, who correctly read it as a decision to end the British commitment to the Jewish national home. The wisest word on the White Paper came from Viscount Herbert Samuel, who had been Palestine's first high commissioner. He observed somewhat sarcastically that by making continued Jewish immigration conditional on Arab assent, and future Arab sovereignty dependent on Jewish acquiescence, the government of Neville Chamberlain had guaranteed the very opposite of the friendly relations it sought to foster through its new policy.[33]

Evidently with a view to encouraging Arab support, the published White Paper omitted the necessity of Jewish assent to Arab sovereignty.

In issuing the White Paper, the British government, now led by Prime Minister Chamberlain, had once again taken the path of appeasement. In this instance it was not Arab violence but the international situation that prompted the British shift. The Italian-Ethiopian War of 1935 exposed Britain's weakness in the eastern Mediterranean and Red Sea, forcing London to rethink its posture vis-à-vis the Arab East.[34] After the Italian conquest of Ethiopia, Britain found herself increasingly anxious about the deterioration of her position in Europe. She could not afford to allow violent chaos in Palestine to lead to the loss of the support of the Arab Middle East at a time when Hitler's Germany was actively seeking to become the master of Europe and possibly half the world. Britain would hold on to Palestine, even if this meant further deterioration of her relations with the Jews.

IN 1917 BRITAIN, for reasons of security and empire, had issued the Balfour Declaration, pledging support for the Jewish national home and betraying earlier pledges made to Arab clients; in 1939, again for reasons of security and empire, Britain betrayed its pledge to the Jewish national home and extended her hand to Palestine's Arabs.

Yet the Arab rebellion of 1936–1939, which cooled Britain on the Jewish national home, failed to achieve its ostensible goal of national independence for Palestine's Arabs. Militarily the rebellion amounted to sporadic acts of violence by guerrillas who refused a central command, were unable to mount a major offensive, and often turned their arms against each other. Most of the dead (three thousand to five thousand) were victims of inter-Arab fighting. Thus the rebellion also incorporated a civil war, pitting clan against clan, class against class, and village against village. Save for the vague desire to rescue the homeland from foreigners, Arab military action was linked to no clear political objectives. Like their hero Qassam, "many of the rebel leaders came from outside Palestine and seemed to believe, not in any sophisticated notions of political independence, but in vague apocalyptic missions and eschatological futures."[35]

The Arab rebellion was also costly, chiefly to peasants and workers. It provoked massive unemployment in the cities. The economic situation of the peasantry, which had improved in the mid-thirties, collapsed during the years of the rebellion. The important Arab citrus market was ruined by the rebellion and later by war in the Mediterranean which prevented the shipping of fruit.

The internecine conflict within the Arab rebellion forced many Arab Christians and wealthier Muslims to leave the country, particularly from Haifa and Jaffa. It was the beginning of an Arab exodus from Palestine that continued for the next fifty years as events went from bad to worse.

Rebellion cost the Arabs what little leadership they had. The Husayni-Nashashibi factional struggle intensified after the rebellion. It was a destructive rivalry that "blinded them to the larger political, ideological, and moral issues which were then precipitating a new world conflict."[36] Peasants and patricians, villagers and urbanites, sheiks and Bedouins, landowners, merchants, and religious officials—rich and poor alike were consumed by resentments and rivalries. Bloodlettings made chaos of their society. At the end of 1939, on the eve of world war, the Palestinian Arabs might speak of "national independence," but they could do little to bring it about. Uniting under the banner of anti-Britain and anti-Zionism was not enough.

For national unity and the basis of an independent state, Arabs needed precisely those institutions of self-representation which the Zionists had developed over two decades. Repeatedly the Arabs rejected the opportunity to develop alternative institutions of self-government, paralleling those of the Zionists. The Arabs had no Histadrut, or Jewish Agency, or Va'ad Leumi, or Haganah, or Keren Kayemet (the Zionist land purchase and development agency). The various political parties, the Higher Committee, and the Supreme Muslim Council offered a semblance of unity, but in reality they fed factionalism. Finally it was incessant, destructive factionalism which prevented the establishment of a self-government that the Arabs desperately needed in order to prepare for and effectively administer a state of their own.

The 1939 White Paper triggered a shift of power within the Zionist leadership. Chaim Weizmann had established his authority on the dual premise that Britain alone held the key to Jewish independence in Palestine, and that he, as the most influential Anglo-Jewish scientist and Zionist negotiator, could persuade the British government to use that key. The Balfour Declaration had elevated Weizmann's prestige. As president of both the World Zionist Organization and the Zionist Agency, he acted as the principal representative of the Jewish community of Palestine to the government of Britain. Weizmann truly believed that good Anglo-Zionist relations would eventually pay a dividend in an independent Jewish Palestine. To this end he labored to build the national home. His ideas, energy, and personality shaped the Zionist movement in the early positive years of its relationship to the British government. Weizmann was wounded by the 1939 White Paper, which he interpreted as a momentary British expedient that would be overcome in time. But the White Paper in fact put Britain on a collision course with the Zionist movement, and with that Weizmann began to lose power, prestige, and authority.

As Weizmann lost power, David Ben-Gurion, who headed the Zionist Executive in Palestine, gained. Far better than Weizmann, Ben-Gurion understood the White Paper as not merely a diplomatic affront to Zionism but a sea change in policy toward the Jewish national movement. After the White Paper, Ben-Gurion was convinced that if the building of the national home was to continue through immigration, independent statehood was necessary. And for independent statehood, Jews could rely on themselves alone—not only moral suasion and diplomatic skill, as Weizmann had shown for so many years, but also on political power and military force. After the White Paper, the attitudes of defiance and self-defense as expressed by Ben-Gurion prevailed over the attitudes of dependency and patience embodied by Weizmann. From 1939 on, as the focus of Zionist affairs shifted from London to Palestine, Ben-Gurion became the voice of Palestine's Jewish community.

CHAPTER TWELVE

Betrayal and Birth, 1939–1948

> The Arabs are treacherous and untrustworthy, the
> Jews greedy. . . . I am convinced that the Arabs
> cannot be trusted to govern the Jews any more than
> the Jews can be trusted to govern the Arabs.
> —W. G. A. Ormsby-Gore to Neville Chamberlain,
> 1938
>
> The partition of Palestine and the creation of a
> Jewish State would result only in bloodshed and
> unrest throughout the entire Middle East.
> —Hami Bey Franjiyyah, Lebanese foreign minister,
> 1947

When German forces joined Italian in North Africa, Britain was confronted with a major military crisis in the Middle East. Rommel's offense in the western desert was a spectacular success. In the spring of 1942 his tanks reached a point sixty miles short of Alexandria and threatened to drive the British out of Egypt, seize the Suez Canal, and cut Britain's lifeline to India and the Far East.

The widening of the war into North Africa led to an economic boom in Palestine, wiping out her poverty. Money poured into the country when Britain decided to move men and supplies to Palestine as a staging area for its military operations in North Africa and the Middle East. Palestinians were employed building barracks, roads, and air strips, and improving the strategically important harbor facilities at Haifa. By 1942 unparalleled prosperity had come to Palestine.

As British forces engaged both Italy and Germany in North Africa, the call went out to Palestine for Arab and Jewish recruits to the British army. Arabs were told by their leaders to turn a deaf ear. In October 1941 the Mufti Haj Amin had fled Baghdad for Berlin, where Hitler had extended him hospitality. He began to make pro-Axis radio speeches from Berlin, which were beamed to Palestine from a relay station on the Italian coast. Hearing the broadcasts, young Arabs sat home to await the Axis victory and the triumphant return of the mufti to a country liberated from Britain and the Jews.

Despite resentment of the White Paper policy, the Jewish response to Britain's call for recruits was swift and massive. Some 25,000 Jews volunteered to serve in British uniform. From the beginning of the war, Weizmann and Ben-Gurion urged British leaders to allow Jews to serve in their own brigade, under their own commanders, and to fly their own flag, as had been allowed for the French and the Poles. But British leaders did not wish to foster a semi-independent Jewish army which might in the future be used to conquer Palestine. It was only in the last months of World War II that a Jewish army unit was formed to fight far away in Italy and Germany.

The rejection of a Jewish brigade was evidence of Britain's changing strategy in the Middle East during the early crisis years of the war. In the first twenty years of the mandate the British had sought to play one Arab ruler off against another; now London's aim was to promote Arab unity in order to forge a single Anglo-Arab bloc against the common Axis enemy. Thus it was essential for the British to attempt a reconciliation even with the most radical Arab faction, the Husaynis, who had caused them so much trouble during the rebellion.

There was no forgiving the mufti, who had now aligned himself with Hitler. He was forbidden to return to Palestine. But because his capacity to inspire resistance was still feared, no formal charges were brought against him. His cousin, Jamal al-Husayni, was allowed to return from exile, as were many of the rebels in the Husayni-dominated Arab Palestine party. It did not take long for the party to regain its influence in the villages and towns. The Husaynis resumed their practice of intimidating their Arab opposition. Any sign of Arab-Jewish cooperation was punished, as when an Arab dignitary was murdered merely for delivering a welcoming address at a new Jewish village.[1]

British insecurity in the face of the German threat obscured long-term interests. In allowing the Husayni faction to renew its power, the mandatory sacrificed the opportunity to stabilize for the future the Arab political balance. The British action in effect gave the "cold shoulder" to the moderate and compromising Nashashibis, who in the last years of the rebellion had fought with the British against the Husaynis.[2] Certainly the Nashashibis were far more willing than the Husaynis to go along with the government's policy enunciated in the 1939 White Paper.

The Husaynis remained adamantly opposed to the White Paper because it continued to recognize the Jewish national home, failed to halt Jewish immigration, and had no provision for establishing an independent Arab state of Palestine. The National Defense party of the Nashashibis, by contrast, seemed to welcome the White Paper as an important step in limiting Jewish immigration and in recognizing Arab political rights. And the Nashashibis were prepared to support Britain in her war effort. What they demanded in return (and did not receive) was a government commitment to them as Palestine's preeminent leadership, with whom both Britain and the Zionists would negotiate the postwar future of the country.

The Nashashibis' power did not survive the British rebuff. The effectiveness of the National Defense party was ended when its leader, Fakhri Bey al-Nashashibi, was murdered, probably by agents of the mufti, in November 1941 in Baghdad.

THE WHITE PAPER provided for Britain's security at the expense of Palestine's Jewish community. The dilemma for Jews was to fight the White Paper without weakening Britain, whose forces were needed to stop Rommel from seizing Egypt and moving north to Palestine. David Ben-Gurion, secretary of Palestine's Zionist Executive, expressed the delicacy of the Jewish situation by urging his fellow Zionists "to fight with Britain against Hitler as though there were no White Paper and to fight against the White Paper as though there were no war."[3]

The question in Jewish minds of how to fight the White Paper was soon answered. If Arab terrorism had been rewarded by the issuance of the White Paper, in order to force Britain to back away from it, Jews would have to respond in kind. Jewish retaliation during the early war years consisted of defying the British sea blockade by smuggling Jewish refugees into Palestine. Later defiance turned to subversion, sabotage, and terrorism.

Thus, in ways that could not have been seen at the time, Britain had deepened her problems in Palestine. In reempowering the Husaynis, the government gave life to the most uncompromising and divisive of the Arab factions. And in enforcing the anti-immigration provision of the White Paper during what proved to be the most destructive era in Jewish history, Britain unloosed Zionist extremists who were willing to use terrorism not only to defeat the White Paper but to drive Britain out of the country altogether.

Although initially the Zionists were encouraged by the advent in May 1940 of Churchill's coalition cabinet, "which included many outspoken opponents of the White Paper," they would soon be disappointed.[4] Within a year it was clear that for all of Churchill's early support of the Jewish national home, his condemnation of the Nazi treatment of the Jews in Germany and Austria, and his own criticism of the 1939 White Paper policy, he, like Chamberlain before him, was prepared to administer the new policy as an expedient that served British interests during the crisis of world war. And he would do this with the full knowledge that the policy denied Palestine as a haven for Jews fleeing Nazi-dominated Europe.

New restrictions on Jewish immigration and land purchases led to a major change in Zionist thinking about the future of the national home. The Balfour Declaration had been deliberately vague about statehood. In 1917 British leaders had not wished to alienate Arabs nor to make exaggerated promises to the Zionists. The feeling among Lloyd George, Balfour, and their colleagues had been that given Jewish labor, investment, and sound planning, a Jewish state probably would emerge in time, but it would do so by a process of natural political evolution. Jewish immigration to Palestine had to be measured and incremental, not alarming to the Arabs. But the rise of Nazi Germany forced tens of thousands of Jews to Palestine, agitating the Arabs.

Vagueness about Jewish statehood in Palestine had also served Zionist interests during the 1920s, enabling them to develop the Jewish community demographically, economically, and politically without alienating the Arabs. But now in the 1940s, after riots, rebellion, and bloodshed, after the oppressive White Paper, the sea blockade of Palestine, and the first evidence of the Nazi murder of Jews in Europe, the last thing Zionists wanted was vagueness about their future national intentions.

This new attitude infected Weizmann, who in January 1942 wrote with unusual boldness: "[The Arabs must be] clearly told that the Jews will be encouraged to settle in Palestine, and will control their own immigration; that here Jews who so desire will be able to achieve their own freedom and self-government by establishing a state of their own, and ceasing to be a minority dependent on the will and pleasure of other nations."[5]

In May 1942, as Rommel prepared for his big offensive in the western desert, American, European, and Palestinian Zionist leaders met in New York's Biltmore Hotel. With no certainty that the Jewish community of Palestine, much less Europe's Jews, could survive the German onslaught, they proceeded to make an extraordinary announcement. After condemning the White Paper as "a breach and a repudiation of the Balfour Declaration," they resolved "That Palestine be established as a Jewish commonwealth integrated in the structure of the new democratic world," and further that the Jewish Agency (not the British government) be recognized as the instrument for achieving that goal.[6] It was a resolution of hope, courage, and *chutzpah*. Its rationale was that only through statehood could Jews control their own immigration to Palestine at a perilous time in which the survival of European Jewry was at stake.

It was also a defiant and foolish act to declare all of Palestine the site of the future Jewish commonwealth. For it confirmed the Arabs' worst fears about Zionist expansionism, and angered Churchill and other British leaders who did not need aggressive Zionist pronouncements about Palestine at a time when they counted on peaceful relations between Arabs and Jews to see them through the war crisis. It also angered representatives of the American Jewish Committee, who walked out of the conference worried that the establishment of Jewish sovereignty in Palestine would raise the question of dual loyalty for American Jews. And it alienated the small number of Zionists who were members of the Brit Shalom movement, advocating a binational solution to the problem of Palestine. Brit Shalom rejected the idea of a Jewish state as it had earlier rejected partition, viewing both as failing the challenge of Arab-Jewish coexistence. Brit Shalom held out for more talks with Arabs leading to a unitary

Arab-Jewish state, in which both peoples would enjoy political parity.

Did the "Jewish commonwealth" in Palestine extend also to Transjordan? That question was deliberately left unanswered. The General Zionists, led by Ben-Gurion and Weizmann, wished to leave the question of territorial borders open.[7] Once again vagueness served a purpose, for the General Zionists did not wish to lose the support of the Revisionists, who remained uncompromising territorial maximalists. Adhering to Jabotinsky's original vision, most Revisionists were willing to endorse the Biltmore formula and go on fighting for the right of Jews to establish a Jewish commonwealth on both sides of the Jordan River.

The attitude of the binationalists was best expressed by Hayim Kalvaryski, one of the Jewish Agency's "Arab experts." Kalvaryski criticized his fellow Zionists for not accepting a share of blame for their wretched relations with the Arabs. He argued that Jews "bore their share of responsibility for the Arab revolt and the anti-Zionist course of mandatory policy." With Weizmann in mind, he accused the dominant Zionist leaders of miseducating Palestine's Jews "on the conception that it is not necessary to take into account the opposition of the Arabs, that in the solution of the Palestine problem England is the decisive factor." Kalvaryski lamented:

> If only we had invested one-tenth or even one-twentieth of the resources that we have sunk into securing the sympathy of remote nations and individuals . . . into winning the sympathy of the [Arab] nation . . . by creating economic, political, moral, and cultural ties . . . then our present position both in Palestine and in Europe would have been quite different.[8]

Ben-Gurion, who led the Zionist "statists," believed the binationalists lacked realism. Political equality between Arabs and Jews might be acceptable to every right-thinking Jew, but Ben-Gurion doubted the reverse. "I am not quite convinced that the Arabs will agree to such equality, if they have the power to determine the constitution." He argued, moreover, that if Jewish immigration to Palestine depended on Arab consent (as called for by the White Paper), no Jew could expect to be allowed to enter his ancestral homeland. Ben-Gurion concluded, "Our position on this crucial issue [of immigration] should be made unequivocal. Jewish immigration to Palestine needs no consent. We are returning as of right."⁹

THE GERMANS did not prevail in North Africa. Egypt was not conquered. The heroic stand of British forces at El Alamein in November 1942 stopped Rommel's offensive. Combined Anglo-American military action later forced Italy and Germany out of North Africa in less than seven months. The historian Elizabeth Monroe is probably right to argue that British forces were able to hold the line against Rommel in Egypt because the White Paper had served its purpose in keeping the Arab nations on Britain's side.¹⁰ Save for the brief and abortive Iraqi army rebellion of May 1941, no serious trouble in the Middle East required a diversion of troops from the war in North Africa.

After the defeat of German forces, London modified its White Paper policy for Palestine, showing that British leaders were now less anxious about losing the Arab nations to Germany. As the date approached for a complete halt to Jewish immigration (March 31, 1944), as called for by the five-year deadline in the White Paper, London suddenly announced in November 1943 that this deadline was suspended. From April 1, 1944, a new quota of fifteen hundred Jews monthly would be allowed to enter the country. The new policy was an expression of the old expediency. White Paper restrictions on Jewish immigration had kept the Arabs friendly to Britain in the crisis years of war. The sea blockade of Palestine had been effective for three years, 1940–1942, when less than twenty thousand Jews entered Palestine legally and illegally.¹¹ Now, with the passing of the crisis, Britain sought to shore up its relations with the Jews. The British government feared a bad conscience or the public stain of closing Palestine's borders to Jews at a time when news of the Nazi slaughter of Jews had begun to reach Western nations. Nor, more pointedly, did Britain wish to risk antagonizing America's influential Jewish community when Britain was relying increasingly on America for military and financial aid to help fight the war.

AS THE EUROPEAN WAR continued into 1944, with an Allied victory appearing certain, British leaders addressed themselves to the future of Palestine. Churchill, predisposed toward Zionism, wanted a Jewish state in Palestine. He had favored the 1936 Peel Commission recommendation on partition as the only honorable way for Britain to keep its promises to the Zionists without also betraying the Arabs. He had criticized the 1939 White Paper but had enforced its provisions largely because the military and the Foreign Ministry were behind it. Moreover, he had long thought Palestine to be more of a burden than a blessing to Britain. Since Britain's real interest in Palestine was strategic, that need could easily be met by treaties which allowed for the leasing of military bases. In late 1943 Churchill found himself free to act independently regarding Palestine, and so in September he "informed Weizmann of the decision by the British Cabinet Committee on Palestine to grant the Jews full sovereignty in a divided Palestine."[12]

But Churchill's initiative did not result in a divided Palestine. One year later, in November 1944, there occurred one of those unpredictable events (so ugly and yet so common to the Middle East) that changes the course of history and mocks any rational understanding of its tide. Irgun terrorists, paying Britain back for curtailing Jewish immigration during the war, assassinated Lord Moyne, Britain's minister of state for the Middle East in Cairo, and one of Churchill's closest confidants. After the assassination of Moyne, Churchill no longer spoke of a sovereign Jewish state in a divided Palestine, and seemed to wash his hands of the Zionists.[13] His words in Parliament left no doubt about his bitter feelings: "If our dreams for Zionism are to end in the smoke of assassins' pistols and our labors for its future to produce only a new set of gangsters worthy of Nazi Germany, many like myself will have to reconsider the position we have maintained so consistently in the past. . . ."[14]

The Moyne assassination split Zionist ranks. Ben-Gurion, exasperated by costly Irgun terrorist tactics which angered the British and endangered future Jewish independence, ordered the Haganah to assist the British in arresting Irgun extremists, which it did in an operation called *Saison,* the "hunting season," from November 1944 to May 1945.

In early 1945, as the war drew to a close, Britain faced a decision about Palestine. The war had demonstrated the importance of the country as a valuable base for communications with the East. The possible loss of Egypt as a bastion for protection of the Suez Canal enhanced the importance of holding Palestine. The British military thought Palestine's value in protecting the sea and land approaches to

Mesopotamia also increased as British forces left Syria, Lebanon, and Iraq. But a minority, like Churchill, thought the ongoing conflict between Arabs and Jews threatened to draw Britain into a maelstrom.

But all the leaders agreed that in the postwar Middle East the Arab nations, increasingly unified and powerful, could no longer be ordered about or taken for granted. With all the Arab nations Britain now had to maintain excellent relations. If she failed to do so, the diplomatic vacuum might be filled by the United States eyeing the oil market or by an expansionist Soviet Union. At the same time British leaders recognized that the formation of a federation of Arab states, aggressively led by Egypt and Iraq, would only spell trouble for British imperial interests in the Middle East.

Better a league than a federation. So in March 1945 Britain gave her official blessing to the formation of the League of Arab Nations, which would coordinate pan-Arab political policy in the postwar years. The league was formed of seven independent Arab states: Egypt, independent in 1922; Saudi Arabia, whose sovereignty was internationally recognized in 1927, as was that of Transjordan in 1928; Iraq, newly independent in 1932, and Yemen in 1936; and finally Syria, which gained her independence from France in 1943, as did Lebanon in 1946.

A seat in the Arab League was reserved for the representative of Palestine's Arabs, who at the end of the European war were economically strong but without national independence and without the unified political leadership needed to acquire independence. They looked to neighboring Arab nations to secure for them the independence their leaders had for so long failed to gain.

The Arab League was eager to assume the Palestine burden. From the outbreak of the Arab rebellion in Palestine in 1936, neighboring Arab nations had begun to see the Palestine problem as their problem. Fighting for Palestine provided an opportunity to forge that pan-Arab unity so long lacking and so long needed to drive Western imperialists out of the Arab world entirely. But while the turning of the Palestine question over to the Arab League initially bolstered the Arab Palestinians' campaign against Zionism, ultimately it proved detrimental to their cause. For Arab leaders were far less concerned with the Arabs of Palestine than with using the Palestine question to advance their own interests in relations with Britain and other Western nations, and with one another.

August 1944 events in Jerusalem were a portent of coming troubles. Jerusalem's Arab mayor died, precipitating a crisis. The British mandatory government filled the vacancy temporarily with the Jewish deputy mayor, Daniel Auster. Arabs argued that only an Arab could be appointed mayor in a city holy to Muslims and Christians. Jews responded by saying that they were the majority population in the city, paid the most taxes, and deserved to have one of their own appointed mayor because Jerusalem was more sacred to them than it was to Muslims and Christians. High Commissioner Lord Gort, failing to win Arab cooperation on a proposed rotation of the mayor or on an administrative partition of the city, took matters into his own hands by appointing in July 1945 a five-man, all-British commission to govern Jerusalem—which it did until the termination of the mandate, three years later.

At the end of the war Arabs were growing more and more restless that the White Paper had not already produced an Arab state of Palestine. Jews were still finding ways to enter Palestine, and land was changing hands from Arabs to Jews despite legal prohibitions. Jewish legal and illegal immigration during the war years had pushed the Jewish percentage of the total population from one-third (as limited by the White Paper) to one-half. Not without reason were Arabs concerned about Jewish presence and power. In the twenty-five years from 1920 to 1945 the Jewish population had grown almost ninefold, from 66,000 to 554,000. More immigration was expected after the war. Both sides were arming, and in the spring of 1944 terrorism resumed. Many believed a full-scale war between Arabs and Jews was inevitable.

But was it? Not in the opinion of the historian J. C. Hurewitz: "The Jerusalem breakdown," he writes,

> was a forewarning of what lay in store for the entire country, if no remedy were soon found. A combination of the experience of the United Kingdom and the resources of the United States might have been able to salvage the situation. The two allies enjoyed tremendous prestige in the Near East by reason of their victory in Europe, and the presence of determined Anglo-American effort might have been sufficient to hammer out a compromise. Any workable solution would have had to take into consideration the equitable right of Arabs and Jews with their separate ways of life.[15]

Ruling out a unitary, centralized regime as the "least promising," Hurewitz suggests that "a just compromise might have assumed any one of a number of forms— partition, cantonization, or federalism— provided the essentials of democratic self-rule and continued Jewish immigration were expressly included."[16]

Hurewitz's imposed solution assumes the use of force against both Arab and Jewish extremists, and a sufficient number of moderates on both sides to administer a solution imposed by Britain and the United States. He also assumes that Churchill and Roosevelt, who had both the force and experience to resolve the Palestine problem, were prepared to do so. But it seems they were not. Churchill had lost interest after the Moyne assassination, and Roosevelt was caught between his personal advisers, who urged him to back the idea of a Jewish state, and his State Department experts, who argued that any pro-Zionist tilt would cost America valuable political and economic interests in the Arab world. The American president simply could not make up his mind about Palestine.

Whether or not Churchill and Roosevelt could together have solved the Palestine problem continues to be debated. Beyond debate is that with Roosevelt's death in April 1945, and Churchill's election defeat in July of the same year, the fertile moment for settling the Palestine problem passed. Their successors, Prime Minister Clement Attlee and President Harry Truman, had neither the experience nor the will to deal with the Palestine issue. In Hurewitz's opinion, Attlee and Truman "approached the tremendous political problems arising out of the war with the irresolution and timidity of inexperienced statesmen at a time when decisions and boldness were imperative."[17]

In the three years from the appearance of Attlee and Truman to the British withdrawal from Palestine in May 1948, the country was a political football kicked from Britain to America and back again. The Labor party, which had so aggressively championed the Zionist cause against its Conservative party critics, now found itself facing the thorniest questions about Palestine. Zionism and the Middle East looked one way to Labor when it was the opposition party, and a different way once the party was in power. In April 1944 Labor's national executive had "urged the removal of the ban on Jewish immigration" and recommended that "the Arabs be encouraged to move out as the Jews move in. . . . The Arabs have many wide territories of their own: they must not claim to exclude the Jews from this small area of Palestine."[18]

After the war, Prime Minister Attlee and his formidable foreign minister, Ernest Bevin, led a Labor party which won a landslide election victory over Churchill's Conservative party. British voters expected Labor to honor its promises of sweeping economic and social reform. Britain had won the war but lost her wealth. Attlee's challenge was to enact reforms with so few material resources. Since the United States abruptly canceled its lend-lease program for Britain when the war ended, it was vitally important for London to arrange a new loan from Washington to help Britain through her economic crisis. She could no longer afford the military and administrative costs of maintaining a world empire. The chief concern of British strategists was to scale down the cost of empire without at the same time sacrificing vital interests to American and Soviet competitors.

Labor party leaders largely accepted the early Conservative analysis of Britain's stake in the Middle East. The possible loss of bases in Egypt enhanced the importance of Palestine as a strategic center for air, land, and sea communications with the Far East. Just as Conservatives under Chamberlain had executed an Arab turn in order to pacify the empire's Middle Eastern flank during the war, so now Attlee and Bevin felt that to secure Britain's strategic interests in Middle Eastern oil and Far Eastern markets, friendly relations with the Arab nations were essential. The challenge faced by British diplomacy in the first three years of the postwar period was to achieve friendly relations with the Arabs without seeming to repudiate Zionism, betray Palestine's Jews, and alienate the Americans, whose president and Congress had increasingly become advocates of Zionism and the Jews.

The Labor party now took the view that British commitment to the Jewish national home did not mean the transformation of the Jewish home into an independent state. Nor did it mean that Britain must submit to Zionist pressures about increasing Jewish immigration beyond the monthly fifteen-hundred limit already set. Restrictions on immigration would therefore continue, and every means would be used to prevent illegal immigration. But the Labor party could not afford to be seen as an enemy of the national home, which, after all, was an integral part of the mandate. Strong support must be given to Zionist-sponsored economic projects in Palestine. Jewish taxes, after all, were needed to defray the continuing costs of Britain's considerable military presence in the country.

At the end of the war there were about 250,000 Jewish refugees in Europe, most of them anxiously awaiting travel to Palestine. To counter illegal immigration, British authorities announced that illegal immigrants would be subtracted from the authorized quota. But before being admitted to the country, they would be interned for six months. The British army, navy, and air force, which had fought against Hitler, was now put to the task of stopping the survivors of Hitler's genocide from entering their ancestral homeland. Even the most pro-British of Jews felt that for the first time in the history of the mandate, Britain had turned into an enemy. Foreign Minister Bevin was accused of anti-Semitism for declaring that American pressure on Britain to allow the immediate transfer of 100,000 Jews to Palestine was because Americans "did not want too many of them in New York."[19] The Haganah's striking force, the Palmach, responded to Bevin's words by blowing up eight bridges in Palestine.

The Zionist leadership was now determined to make up for the mistake of having earlier rejected the Peel Commission's proposal for Jewish acceptance of partition. Jewish acceptance of partition would have pressed Britain to divide Palestine, thus preventing the anti-Zionist White Paper that followed both Arab and Jewish rejections of partition. Throughout the war years, Zionists suffered regrets that a Jewish state in 1939, however small, would have made possible the survival of thousands of European Jews who perished for want of a haven.

Now the Zionists, despite the fifteen-hundred monthly quota, stepped up their efforts to obtain ships and hire captains who were willing to run a blockade in order to transfer to Palestine the Jews who had survived the Nazi inferno. This illegal immigration was carried out by agents of the Jewish Agency, which now acted in defiance of the very government that had authorized its operations.

In addition to illegal immigration, Jews defied the Labor government's pro-Arab policy by terrorism. Where briefly the Jewish Agency underground army, the Haganah, had helped the British catch Irgun terrorists, from late 1945 through 1946 the Haganah joined forces with the Irgun and an even more terroristic group called the Freedom Fighters in acts of anti-British sabotage. The goal was political: make the British lose stomach for their continuing gov-

ernance of Palestine.[20] Jews blew up railway stations, roads, and telephone lines, and pierced the Iraq petroleum pipeline running overland to Haifa harbor. British police stations were bombed and
policemen shot. In reprisal for Jewish terrorists caught and hanged,
Britishers were killed. In July 1946 Jewish terrorism reached a
crescendo with the bombing of British military headquarters at
Jerusalem's King David Hotel, an incident which left ninety-two
British, Arab, and Jewish dead.

The decision to engage in terrorism pricked the conscience of
many Jews, as in this editorial from *Ha'Aretz,* Palestine's leading
Jewish newspaper.

> There was a time when the overwhelming majority of the Yishuv
> [Jewish settlement] was vigorously opposed to acts of violence. In
> the depths of our hearts we still feel that this path is fraught with
> danger. But it is not up to us alone to prevent grave dangers. If the
> British Government has arrived at a decision that can open a gate
> of hope to the Jewish people—let us hear it.[21]

The editorial was not wasted on Ben-Gurion and other Jewish
Agency leaders, who in October 1946 officially denounced terrorism.
The Jewish Agency reigned in the Haganah, but it had no control
over the Irgun, much less the Freedom Fighters. Jewish terrorism
continued through 1947 and right up to the withdrawal of British
forces from Palestine.

The British reaction to Jewish terrorism was a mixture of rage
and restraint. Britain's high commissioner, Sir Alan Gordon Cunningham, initiated Operation Agatha, which led to the wholesale arrest and imprisonment of major Zionist leaders. Warrants were
issued for the arrest of Ben-Gurion, who was abroad making
arrangements for the training and equipping of the Haganah; for political reasons no warrants were issued for Goldie Myerson (Golda
Meir) or for Chaim Weizmann. The arrest of the moderate Jewish
Agency and National Council leaders removed any check on the
Jewish terrorists, who largely evaded Agatha and intensified their
activities.

With the exception of Agatha, British authorities were reluctant
to use maximum force against terrorism. Behind this decision lay the
unusual wisdom and courage of Cunningham, who proved to be
Britain's last high commissioner in Palestine. Sensitive to political

undercurrents and conscious of his own country's moral reputation, Cunningham was willing to declare martial law briefly but refused to root out terrorism by turning Palestine into a military dictatorship.[22]

AS THE ZIONISTS lost influence with Attlee's Labor government, they turned for support to the United States. The vast majority of American Jews rallied to the Zionist cause. Universal sympathy for the Jewish survivors of the Holocaust helped win American and international support for the establishment of a Jewish state in Palestine. Ben-Gurion and Weizmann had backed off from the overly ambitious Biltmore proposal and were now firm advocates of a Jewish state in a divided Palestine; their only concern was the size that state would be.

Washington was under pressure from both Arab nations and the Zionists. Arab oil was a growing factor in Western thinking about the Middle East. Both the United States and Britain were concerned that any faulty decision might open the door to Soviet penetration of the Middle East. And the Western allies also eyed each other warily. The Americans were rightly suspicious that Britain sought American money and support for her Middle East policy in order to perpetuate strategically important bases in Palestine, Iraq, and Egypt; British leaders grew ever anxious about increasing American domination of Middle East oil resources through U.S.-sponsored exploration and development.

An early source of tensions between London and Washington over Palestine was Truman's effort to persuade Attlee to allow 100,000 European Jewish Holocaust survivors to enter Palestine. He had first broached the issue with Churchill at the Potsdam Conference in July 1945, when he asked the prime minister to ease restrictions for Jewish immigration.[23] Undoubtedly Truman felt sympathy for the Jewish survivors of Hitler's concentration camps, but the president's eye was also on Jewish political support at home.

Attlee was embarrassed by a request that placed him in a delicate position. Eventually he agreed on condition that the United States pay the costs of immigration and station American troops in Palestine to guard against an Arab uprising. Truman, who sought American Jewish support but not at the cost of losing non-Jewish voters, declined. But to the chagrin of Attlee and Bevin, he continued to repeat his request for the 100,000.

Truman's manipulation of the Palestine issue often led him to inconsistencies of attitude. He could be coldly realistic and even cynical, as when he said to his own Middle Eastern ambassadors (who had cautioned against American pro-Zionist policy): "I'm sorry, gentlemen, but I have to answer to hundreds of thousands who are anxious for the success of Zionism; I do not have hundreds of thousands of Arabs among my constituents."[24] But when Zionist pressures got the best of him, he could blurt out about the Jews, "Jesus Christ couldn't please them when he was here on earth, so how could anyone expect that I would have any luck."[25] For the most part, Truman continued Roosevelt's inconsistent and often contradictory "nonpolicy" in the Middle East: support the Zionist cause, but reassure Arab leaders that nothing would be done in Palestine to harm Arab interests.

Zionists had considerable success with American political parties and the Congress. Both the Democratic and Republican parties adopted pro-Zionist planks in their 1944 and 1948 platforms. In late March 1944, on the eve of the official halt by Britain to Jewish immigration to Palestine, Congress passed resolutions urging the government to "take appropriate measures" to oppose the British White Paper and establish Palestine as a Jewish state. The resolutions were shelved under pressure from the State Department and the secretary of war, both viewing a Jewish state as detrimental to American-Arab relations.[26]

Arab reaction to the American pro-Zionist declarations was predictable. In one voice the Arabs said that if Americans were sincere in their concern for Jewish refugees, they should admit them to their own country. They welcomed Jews, Arabs maintained, but they rejected political Zionism, which had no other goal than to steal land and to create through immigration a majority that would establish a state to dominate the Arab society of Palestine. They believed that Zionist-sponsored economic projects had created an industrial and agricultural power which posed a major threat to Middle Eastern Arab markets. Hurewitz writes that "The Egyptians were urged by one Cairo daily to oppose the establishment of a Jewish state in order 'to prevent the transfer of the economic and financial capital of the Near East from Cairo to Tel-Aviv.'"[27] Yet after the war Palestine had rapidly become an Arab concern, as evidenced by the demonstrations and riots that occurred in every capital on the anniversary of the Balfour Declaration. On these occasions Jews, and their shops and synagogues, were often attacked.

BY THE END of 1946 Britain was sinking in the financial quagmire of Palestine. Staying on was costing Britain a million pounds sterling daily; at home Britishers were still on bread rationing. Arab and Jewish subversion of British installations continued, as did the shootings, kidnapings, and killings of British personnel. Mandatory authorities had grown sick of the country. Without exactly deciding to leave, British leaders were looking for a way out.

Labor party leaders looked to American support to solve the Palestine problem. Two joint committees of inquiry were set up in 1946, and both proved failures. The first was the Anglo-American Committee, formed in January 1946; its findings were published May 1, 1946. The committee emphatically endorsed the binationalist position, which envisaged setting up an independent, democratic government based on equal rather than proportional representation. Failing cooperation from Arabs and Jews, the committee recommended that the mandate be converted into a UN trusteeship, with the aim of preparing the peoples for binationalism. The committee further recommended resettling 100,000 Jewish refugees, consonant with President Truman's wish. The Anglo-American Committee report did not mince words. It declared Britain's limitations on immigration and land purchase to be discriminatory against Jews, just as the Jewish National Fund's policy to employ only Jews, and not Arabs, was discriminatory.[28] For different reasons, both Arabs and Jews rejected the report.

The second failed effort at joint diplomacy was the Morrison-Grady Commission of May 1946, which recommended provincial autonomy and offered Arabs the bulk of Palestine's territory. This proposal too was rejected by Arabs because it allowed for continued Jewish immigration.

All subsequent proposals from the Zionists, the Arabs, and from Foreign Minister Bevin himself failed to gain general acceptance. The Labor government was unable to obtain Arab consent even to the generous conditions of Bevin's plan for an independent, unitary Palestine state at the end of five years. The Arabs insisted on a formal British repudiation of the Balfour Declaration, to be followed immediately by an independent Arab state. And they would not agree to proposals that included the opening of Palestine to 100,000 Jews, as Truman wanted.

In this they misjudged the curiously principled character of British hypocrisy. Britain might eviscerate the Balfour Declaration by imposing restrictions on Jewish immigration and land sales, and then rationalize her actions on the ground that the aims of the Balfour Declaration had been fulfilled; but an official renunciation of the Balfour Declaration she could only view as unethical.

BRITISH AUTHORITIES took the organization of illegal Jewish immigration as a test of their resolve to enforce the fifteen-hundred monthly limit. Most of the immigrant ships were intercepted by an effective British naval blockade, land routes were blocked by Arab states. But the Jewish Agency's secret organization, Mosad, met with some success in smuggling Jews illegally into Palestine. Between 1945 and 1948 almost seventy thousand Jews were shipped to Palestine; of these about fifty thousand were caught and placed in transit camps by British authorities.[29] There they were held for months until they were "subtracted" from the monthly quota of immigration certificates.

But the illegals kept mounting, the transit camp at Atlit on the coast filled up, and the decision was made in August 1946 to deport the illegals to newly constructed centers on the island of Cyprus. By April 1, 1947, almost twelve thousand Jews were living in Cyprus camps. It was a sorry spectacle for many at the time who contemplated the moral irony of recent British history. The liberators of Jewish survivors of Hitler's concentration camps were now putting Jews behind barbed wire in British detention camps.

More questions were raised worldwide about Britain's prevention of Jewish immigration in the notorious incident involving the ferryboat *Exodus 1947*. In August 1947 the ship, bearing 4,550 Jewish refugees, was intercepted off the coast of Palestine. Instead of sending the refugees to Cyprus, the British government decided to experiment with a new policy of sending refugees back to the country from which their ship had originally sailed, in this case France. To prevent this, the refugees fought the British on the high seas. They were forcibly removed from the *Exodus* in Palestine, transferred to three British vessels, and shipped back to France, where they refused to leave the ship. French authorities refused to cooperate with the British in forcibly disembarking them. The decision was then made to ship the Jews to the British zone in Germany, where there were adequate housing facilities. This entire drama, lasting weeks, was covered by the world press, which portrayed Britain as heartless in its refusal to allow the Jews to enter their ancestral homeland and cruel in sending them back to the country of their persecutors.[30]

REACTING TO mounting Jewish terrorism, in 1946 Palestine's Arabs formed a new Higher Committee, a coalition of Husayni's Palestine party and the Istiqlal party, the only one of the six major Arab parties not based on a family clan.[31] The presidency of the new organization was left open for the mufti, who continued to remain outside the country. The Higher Committee, recognized by the Arab League and also by the British government of Palestine, proved woefully ineffective in countering Jewish terrorism. The problem was lack of unity, the old bane of Arab nationalism in Palestine. Even when the Arab League offered money to the Higher Committee, the personal squabbles of local politicians made the distribution and proper use of the funds impossible.

At the end of May 1946, at a meeting of the Arab League in Bludan, Syria, Haj Amin al-Husayni made a sudden dramatic appearance. To arrive there he had traveled a twisted road. In May 1945, with the collapse of Nazi Germany, he had left Berlin for Switzerland, where he was denied asylum and forced to France, where he was put under "residential surveillance."[32] In early 1946 he stole away from Paris on an American plane bound for Cairo. From Cairo and later from Beirut he would continue his anti-Zionist crusade until his death in 1974.

It did not take the mufti long to resume control of the Arab nationalist movement. At the Bludan conference in early June 1946 the Anglo-American Committee report was formally rejected, and secret protocols were agreed on to secure an independent Arab Palestine, by military means if necessary. Jerusalem's mufti played a key role in this fateful decision. Under his leadership a Palestine Arab army began to be recruited in anticipation of the coming confrontation.

Yet another indication that the Palestine problem would not be resolved by moderate, diplomatic means was the failure in late 1946 of Chaim Weizmann to win reelection as president of the World Zionist Organization.

By early 1947 the effort to contain mounting disorders had forced the British government to deploy eighty thousand troops in Palestine. The country had become an armed camp. Wives and children of British personnel were sent home, and men locked themselves in barbed-wire compounds to avoid kidnapings and killings. Jewish anti-British terrorism continued unabated; Arabs, when not attacking Jews, were battling each other in newly formed paramilitary units.

Britain still clung to Palestine but now looked for a way to ease the burden of government whose daily cost in blood, money, and prestige mounted. Truman, sensitive to the Zionists, refused to bail the British out of Palestine. But British leaders took heart at the comprehensive American military security arrangement for Greece and the eastern Mediterranean, announced in March 1947 as the Truman Doctrine. This extension of American power in the region encouraged Attlee and Bevin to think that Britain could safely consider reducing its own military involvement in Palestine without resigning the mandate. Just a month earlier Britain had asked the United Nations to reconsider the conditions of the mandate for Palestine. As the colonial secretary declared in Parliament: "We are not going to the United Nations to surrender the Mandate. We are going to the United Nations setting out the problem and asking their advice as to how the Mandate can be administered. If the Mandate cannot be administered in its present form, we are asking how it can be amended."[33]

In April 1947 the UN Special Committee on Palestine (UNSCOP) was formed to deal with the question of Palestine's future. As UNSCOP was doing its work, in October Britain unexpectedly announced its decision to relinquish the mandate. In the period between February, when Britain turned to the UN for help, and October, when she decided to quit the mandate, Britain's mind was decisively changed about the wisdom of continuing to govern the country. More than anything else, what caused the change, according to Elizabeth Monroe, was the Irgun reprisal kidnaping in July of two British soldiers, their execution by hanging, and the booby-trapping of their bodies which caused still more death. The incident caused a

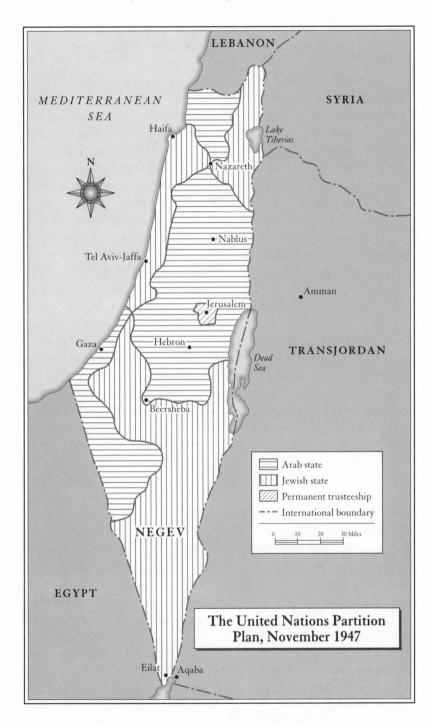

The United Nations Partition
Plan, November 1947

revulsion in England and forced the Labor government to the drastic decision to withdraw entirely from Palestine, with or without the UN's blessing.

In October UNSCOP completed its work and recommended partition of the country to allow for the creation of both Arab and Jewish states. The recommendation was put before the General Assembly, which after much lobbying by Arab opposition and Zionist support, on November 30, 1947, recommended partition. The recommendation, following the lines of the Peel Commission formula on partition, set aside Jerusalem and Bethlehem as a *corpus separatum,* to be governed by an international regime.

The UN's decision was self-defeating. Since Britain had already decided to leave Palestine, and since no other military power was stepping into the vacuum created by Britain's departure, it was unclear who would enforce the UN resolution on partition. And without enforcement it was a certainty that the violence already occurring in Palestine would escalate into countrywide war.

Not surprisingly, the UN recommendation on Palestine prompted an immediate increase of violence, sparked by the entry of some two thousand Syrian volunteers. Here was the start of the first Arab-Jewish war, which intensified following Britain's formal departure from Palestine on May 14, 1948, and the Zionist declaration of the State of Israel one day later.

In mid-May the combined forces of six neighboring Arab nations and the irregular Arab Palestinian soldiers succeeded in capturing territory in the Judean hills around Jerusalem. But the fighting also forced more than 200,000 Arabs from the country. Jews, who had nowhere to go, were concerned not to lose control of the western part of Jerusalem, where 100,000 Jews—16 percent of their population—lived. Jerusalem, a salient in Arab-held territory, was the scene of ferocious fighting. Jewish forces regrouped under David Ben-Gurion, now defense minister as well as prime minister, and began receiving arms and supplies from abroad. As the fighting progressed, Jewish forces seized control of the coastal plain and eastern Galilee, and successfully defended western Jerusalem's new city.

The conclusion of the war did not bring about an Arab Palestinian government in those parts of mandated Palestine not controlled by the Jews. The ambitions and army of Transjordan's Emir

Abdullah saw to that. After first failing in secret diplomacy to convince the Zionists to accept him as a kind of lord over an Arab-Jewish federal state of Palestine and Transjordan, he decided on his own military solution. Emir Abdullah saw an opportunity to expand his emirate, and with Britain's tacit blessing sent his British-trained Arab Legion across the Jordan River with the aim of fulfilling a part of the territorial dream he had shared with his father and brother. Thus the Husayni party lost out to the Hashemites, whose expansion into Palestine was opposed by neighboring Arab states. Other Arab nations invaded Palestine as much to thwart Abdullah's expansionist plans as to defeat the Zionists. Here, as often in the past, the Arab war waged against the Zionists contained a divisive rivalry that weakened the struggle.

A last desperate effort to avert Hashemite domination—by establishing in September 1948 a Husayni-led Arab government of all Palestine, with a capital in Gaza—failed. In December 1948 Abdullah was acclaimed king of a united Palestine and Transjordan by anti-Husayni Palestinian Arabs, a move approved by the Transjordan parliament. But the mufti would have his revenge against Abdullah in 1950, when agents of the mufti assassinated Abdullah in Jerusalem as he was about to enter Al Aksa mosque for Friday prayers.

In mid-November 1948 the war came to a halt with Israel controlling the coastal plain, including Jaffa, both western and eastern Galilee, and west Jerusalem. The Transjordanian army occupied all the central hill country on the western bank of the Jordan River, from Jenin in the north to Hebron and Jericho in the south, and Arab-populated east Jerusalem, including the old city. To the tragedy of several hundred thousand Arab Palestinian refugees fleeing their homeland was later added the dislocation of Jews who had lived for generations in Arabic-speaking countries. The new exodus would dramatically increase Israel's population from 650,000 to 1 million within two years.

A POLITICAL QUESTION and a moral question arise from the struggle between Arabs and Jews for control of Palestine during three decades of British rule. The political question focuses on ambitions and opportunities. We should ask why the Zionists in great part realized their nationalistic ambitions and the Arabs of Palestine failed. The question points to the complex reality we know as modern nationalism.

The Zionist success had much to do with the opportunities they were given. The Balfour Declaration opened the door to Jewish immigration, and the support of the mandatory government throughout the 1920s and 1930s made Jewish national development possible. The Zionists made good use of their opportunities during those years. They planned, planted, and built. They raised vast sums of money abroad for support of their communities in Palestine. The refugee immigrants who arrived in the country from 1933 on brought with them money and talent that contributed to a growing, educated, and skilled population.

The White Paper of 1939 did not impede the growth of the Jewish national home. Seen in retrospect, it was a blessing in disguise. For in severely curtailing immigration, the new policy was an alarm bell to Zionists: Britain's willingness to sacrifice the Zionist project in order to improve relations with the Arabs showed the Jews that the transformation of their national home into statehood would come about only by defying, not by cooperating with, Britain.

The Jewish awakening in 1939 led to the recruitment, training, and equipping of a modern army, the Haganah. It was a farsighted decision. For without the Haganah, Jews could not have later defended themselves against the combined attacks of the Arab nations.

The shifting of power from the moderate Weizmann to the aggressive Ben-Gurion provided the Zionists just the kind of leadership they needed in the crisis of the postwar period. Better than anyone, Ben-Gurion understood the essentials: the need for a large, unified Jewish fighting force; the need to defy Britain; and the need for the overly ambitious Biltmore program of a Jewish commonwealth in all Palestine to give way to the more realizable formula of a small Jewish state in a partitioned Palestine.

The Zionists had plans, energy, money, and great quantities of will and foresight. In acting with restraint, even in anti-British actions, the main Zionist leadership did not alienate the British mandatory leadership, without whose cooperation a Jewish state could not have been realized. For had the Jewish Agency under Ben-Gurion imitated the terrorist tactics of the Irgun and the Freedom Fighters, the British authorities would have felt constrained to use their full police and military powers—with disastrous consequences for the Zionist goal of statehood.

While the Zionists succeeded in establishing a sovereign Jewish state in Palestine, they utterly failed in gaining Arab consent to their presence. The reasons for that failure cannot be found simply in Arab rejectionism. As Hayim Kalvaryski and many of the binationalists understood, the dominant Jewish leadership made few attempts to gain Arab support for the Zionist project. The attitude of Chaim Weizmann was endemic to Zionist thinking: not the Arabs but the British were the key to Jewish independence in Palestine.

Weizmann and many Zionists also suffered from the patronizing attitude that Jewish money could buy Arab goodwill. By contrast, one of the clearest, wisest Zionist voices on the Arabs was the father of "cultural Zionism," Ahad Ha'Am, a close colleague of Weizmann's, who in 1891 had written:

> The Arabs, especially the townsmen, see through our activities in their country, and our aims, but they keep silence and make no sign, because for the present they anticipate no danger to their own future from what we are about. But if the time should ever come when our people have so far developed their life in Palestine that the indigenous population should feel more or less cramped, then they will not readily make way for us. . . .[34]

In stark contrast to the Zionists, Arabs ignored and cast aside crucial opportunities that would have led to a self-governing Arab state of Palestine, in which Jews would have held minority status. To fully understand why these opportunities were missed, one should remember that from the last years of Ottoman rule in the Middle East, a pan-Arab nationalism was developing in Beirut and Damascus, initially among Arab Christian cultural and literary circles. Yet a specific sense of Arab Palestinian nationalism did not arise until after 1922, and then only after Price Faysal was evicted from Damascus and only after Zionist-sponsored immigration had begun to mount. From the beginning, the Arabs were so preoccupied with stopping Jewish immigration and driving out the Zionists, as to give scant meaning to the idea of an Arab state of Palestine. This proved a costly mistake.

More than anywhere else, the mistake can be traced to the stratification and inequalities of Arab society in Palestine. Unlike Zionism, Arab nationalism in Palestine was never truly a popular political movement, reaching into villages and towns, mobilizing peasants and workers. Where Zionism could credibly convince Jews that returning to Eretz Yisrael was fulfillment of historic religious hopes, Arab nationalists could make no similar connection between Islam and Palestine. For where Islam was the supremely unifying religious energy, no similar value could be attached to such an abstract political entity as "Palestine." If the word *watan* (homeland) meant anything to an Arab, it meant first his own town or village, only vaguely the larger country.

From the beginning, leaders of the Arab Palestinian nationalist movement said little about what they stood for as nationalists and much about what they were against, namely Zionist immigration and land purchases. In the mid-1930s Sheik Izz al-Din al-Qassam ignited the Muslim peasantry not with a nationalist rallying cry of Palestine but under the religious banner of Islam. He was persuasive in branding Britishers and Zionists as infidels, whose presence was desecrating the land made holy by the visit of the Prophet. What was to be done with that land once rid of the infidel was left unclear.

Mufti Haj Amin al-Husayni also used Islam against the Zionists, especially after the 1929 riots. But his influence divided as much as it unified Palestine's Arabs. Together with all the Muslim and Arab Christian city-dwelling elite, the mufti formed an oligarchy which largely scorned the Arab peasantry until political needs made them reach out. Husayni failed at the ultimate challenge of leadership, which was to unite the peasantry and the urban elite not only against Zionism but in behalf of a national program. Political impulses were so overwhelmingly directed against Zionism that there remained little interest in or energy for unifying and preparing the Arabs of Palestine for national independence. The various Arab political parties established in the early 1930s were pale imitations of Western democratically based parties. They took the shape of the powerful family clans. Party members were not registered or allowed to vote on issues or run for party office.[35]

The Arab elite, as typified by the Husayni and Nashashibi clans, assumed without question that the land belonged to them, that the Arab peasants and workers served them, and that Jewish immigrants were an illegitimate presence. This attitude, reinforced by centuries of traditional teaching of the religious and social superior-

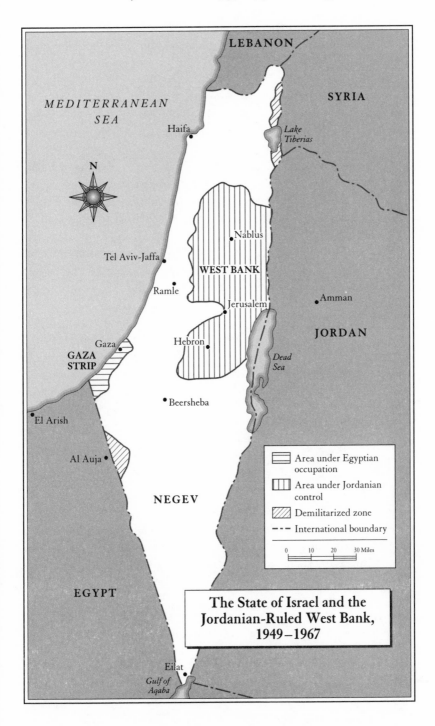

The State of Israel and the
Jordanian-Ruled West Bank,
1949–1967

ity of the Muslim to the Jew and the Christian, ensured that the Zionist immigration was rarely seen by Muslims as a political challenge to be seriously confronted by political, pragmatic, and rational means. Rather than deal with Zionism that way, the Arab elite assumed they could crush it through inflammatory rhetoric and mob violence. When this failed, rather than enter on the path of negotiation and compromise, the elite turned to the neighboring Arab nations, with fateful consequences.

The golden opportunity for establishing an Arab state of Palestine came with the 1939 White Paper. Officially the Arabs, led by the mufti and the Husayni party, rejected the White Paper, but unofficially they approved of it and expected the British to honor all its specifications. And Britain did. But instead of raising up new leaders to replace the exiled mufti, the elite fell to quarreling among themselves. Worse, they yielded the Palestine problem to the newly formed Arab League, which had no solution other than war with the Zionists.

While the Arab elite of Palestine was intent on defeating Zionism, it was actively destroying itself, as evidenced in the fratricidal war between the Husaynis and Nashashibis. Family power, pride, and arrogance blinded the Arabs to their own political self-interest. Nothing better illustrates this than the story credited to Musa Alami, one of the principal Arab leaders originally allied to the Husaynis, but who later opposed them. Alami reported that in 1947 the mufti, who had rejected earlier partition plans, was ready to accept the UN General Assembly's resolution on partition only if he were named head of the new small Arab state of Palestine.[36] When he was not named, he urged his supporters to reject the resolution.

The moral question that rises from the Arab-Jewish struggle for Palestine concerns Britain. One could justifiably blame both Zionists and Arabs for insufficient sensitivity to each other and for proceeding with their respective political agendas in willful disregard of the other. But this touches only the surface of the moral problem that Palestine posed.

In 1920 Britain accepted the mandate to govern Palestine as custodian of an international trust. Her charge was to encourage political maturity through institutions of self-government for both Arabs and Jews, and eventually to turn the country over to them. The League of Nations did not establish criteria by which political maturity was to be judged, nor did it set a timetable for Britain's withdrawal from Palestine.

In fact Britain for thirty years governed Palestine not as a trust but as one of its many crown colonies, administered through the Ministry of Colonial Affairs. And not without reason. From the out-set Britain's overriding interest in Palestine was strategic and eco-nomic. Historians can still argue the sincerity of Britain's commitment to the Jews under the Balfour Declaration. But we owe to the research of Leonard Stein and Mayir Vereté a powerfully rea-soned argument that the Balfour Declaration served Britain's larger strategic goals by initially convincing the League to grant Britain the mandate for Palestine.[37]

Few today can read the mandate document and look back over the history of the land that is now called both Israel and Palestine without feeling that Britain not only accepted contradictory obliga-tions to Arabs and Jews but knew that she was doing so. After Her-bert Samuel's failed efforts in the early 1920s to establish Arab and Jewish joint legislative and advisory bodies, the British largely gave up trying to find ways to achieve Arab-Jewish cooperation in the government of Palestine. Britain's heart was never fully committed to encouraging political maturity among Arabs and Jews and to erecting a framework for shared government.

On the contrary, the practice of the British mandatory author-ity, from Samuel's time on, was that of conqueror and colonialist. The mandatory encouraged the Zionist projects of immigration and land purchase because the Zionists were influential and served Britain's imperial objectives. At the same time the mandatory threw its support to the Husaynis and their allies—who were the most ex-treme, least compromising of the Arab political factions—under the ruler's principle of divide and conquer. Unfortunately the Husaynis, beginning with the mufti, led their people to ruin. In supporting the Husaynis, the mandatory's mind was not on Arab-Jewish coexis-tence, much less on a framework for binational government in Pales-tine. Its shrewd deals with Arabs and Jews were designed to minimize tensions and stabilize British rule in the country. The strat-egy worked in the early years, but from the Arab rebellion of 1936 on, it proved more and more faulty.

Ultimately Britain's self-centered policy in Palestine was a moral failure, apparent in the last months of mandatory government.

Having succeeded in shoving the Palestine burden onto the United Nations, Britain, in deference to her Arab clients, used diplomacy to try to undermine UNSCOP's recommendation of partition. Failing in this effort, Britain then took her time withdrawing from Palestine while first arming and training Arab forces both in Palestine and in Transjordan. The British government officially ceased functioning on May 15, 1948, effectively clearing the way for war between Israel and the Arab states. That conflict would lead in the succeeding fifty years to continuing warfare between Arabs and Jews to the present day, with a just and durable peace nowhere in sight.

The history of the land from Bonaparte's invasion of the Arab East to the establishment of the Jewish state offers no confidence that peace can be achieved. The contradiction rooted in the country was seen centuries before by the Hebrew scriptural writer we know as the Deuteronomist, who cautioned the Israelites about to enter Canaan: "And when the Lord your God brings you into the Land which you are entering to take possession of it, you shall [know] both blessing and curse."

Notes

Chapter One: Land Weathered by Miracles

1. Yehoshua Ben-Arieh, *Jerusalem in the 19th Century: The Old City* (New York, 1984), 105.

2. See the article "Filastin," in B. Lewis, Ch. Pellat, and J. Schact, eds., *The Encyclopedia of Islam*, Vol. 2 (Leiden, 1965), 910–914.

3. Kenneth W. Stein, *The Land Question in Palestine, 1917–1939* (Chapel Hill, 1984), 3.

4. For a powerful but extreme critique of the Western perception of Arab peoples and culture, see Edward W. Said, *Orientalism* (New York, 1979).

5. See Naomi Shepherd, *The Zealous Intruders: The Western Rediscovery of Palestine* (San Francisco, 1987).

6. C. F. Volney, *Travels Through Egypt and Syria* (New York, 1978).

7. *Ibid.*, 283.

8. Fred M. Gottheil, "Money and Product Flows in Mid-19th Century Palestine: The Physiocratic Model Applied," in David Kushner, ed., *Palestine in the Late Ottoman Period: Political, Social and Economic Transformation* (Jerusalem, 1986), 103.

9. Raphael Mahler, *A History of Modern Jewry* (New York, 1971), 103.

10. *Ibid.*

11. Jacob de Haas, *History of Palestine: The Last Two Thousand Years* (New York, 1934), 362.

12. Volney, *Travels*, 256.

13. Mahler, *History*, 605.

14. Sherman Lieber, *Mystics and Missionaries: The Jews in Palestine, 1799–1804* (Salt Lake City, 1992), 29.

15. Archie Bell, *The Spell of the Holy Land* (Boston, 1915), 151.

16. Volney, *Travels*, 231.

17. Lieber, *Mystics*, 292–317; also see Uziel O. Schmelz, "Some Demographic Peculiarities of the Jews of Jerusalem in the Nineteenth Century," in Moshe Ma'oz, *Studies on Palestine During the Ottoman Period* (Jerusalem, 1975), 119–141.

18. Alexander Kinglake, *Eothen*, 4th ed. (London, 1845), 220.

19. Volney, *Travels*, 238.

20. *Ibid.*, 186–187.

21. *Ibid.*, 235.

22. *Ibid.*

23. *Ibid.*, 288.

24. Chateaubriand quoted from *Famous Travelers to the Holy Land*, compiled by Linda Osband (London, 1989), 32–33.

25. François René de Chateaubriand, *Travels to Jerusalem and the Holy Land through Egypt*, translated from the French by Frederick Shobert, 3rd ed., Vol. 1 (London, 1835), 342.
26. Alex Carmel, "The Activities of the European Powers in Palestine, 1799–1914," *Asian and African Studies*, 19 (1985), 89.
27. B. Walker, *The Future of Palestine as a Problem of International Policy and in Connection with the Requirements of Christianity and the Expectations of the Jews* (London, 1881). Quoted from Alexander Schölch, *Palestine in Transformation, 1856–1882* (Washington, D.C., 1993), 63.
28. Cited in Ben-Arieh, *Jerusalem*, 139.

Chapter Two: Conquerors, Explorers, Mapmakers, Artists

1. Christopher J. Herold, *The Age of Napoleon* (New York, 1963), 68.
2. *Ibid.*
3. Walter Zander, *Israel and the Holy Places of Christendom* (New York, 1971), 27.
4. *Ibid.*, 34–35.
5. De Haas, *History of Palestine*, 380.
6. Herold, *Napoleon*, 78.
7. *Ibid.*
8. Christopher J. Herold, *Bonaparte in Egypt* (New York, 1962), 307.
9. De Haas, *History of Palestine*, 381.
10. Ben-Arieh, *Jerusalem*, 21.
11. Israel Finestein, "British Opinion and the Holy Land in the Nineteenth Century: Personalities and Further Times," in Moshe Davis and Yehoshua Ben-Arieh, eds., *With Eyes Toward Zion: III, Western Societies and the Holy Land* (New York, 1991), 231.
12. Neil Asher Silberman, *Digging for God and Country: Exploration, Archaeology, and the Secret Struggle for the Holy Land, 1799–1917* (New York, 1982), 19.
13. *Ibid.*
14. *Ibid.*, 51.
15. U. J. Seetzen's book, yet untranslated from German, is *Reisen durch Syrien, Palastina, Phonicien,* 4 vols. (Berlin, 1854–1859).
16. Silberman, *Digging*, 22.
17. Shepherd, *Zealous Intruders*, 54.
18. Kathryn Tidrich, *Heart Beguiling Araby* (New York, 1981), 26.
19. Yehoshua Ben-Arieh, *The Rediscovery of the Holy Land in the Nineteenth Century* (Jerusalem, 1979), 129.
20. See MaryAnne Stevens, "Western Art and Its Encounter with the Islamic World, 1798–1914," in MaryAnne Stevens, ed., *The Orientalists: Delacroix to Matisse: European Painters in North Africa and the Near East* (London, 1984). For a sharp critique of Western "orientalist" art, see Linda Nochlin, "The Imaginary Past," *Art in America,* May 1983.
21. Stevens, "Western Art," 18–19.
22. Malcolm Warner, "The Question of Faith: Orientalism, Christianity and Islam," in Stevens, *Orientalists,* 37–38.

23. David Roberts, R.A., *The Holy Land: 123 Colored Facsimile Lithographs and the Journal from his Visit to the Holy Land* (London, 1982), 1–21.

24. Warner, "Question of Faith," 32–39.

25. Caroline Bugler, "'Innocents Abroad': Nineteenth-Century Artists and Travellers in the Near East and North Africa," in Stevens, *Orientalists,* 27.

26. Yehoshua Ben-Arieh, *Painting the Holy Land* (Jerusalem, 1997), 118.

Chapter Three: A Taste of Equality

1. Herold, *Napoleon,* 79–80.

2. M. S. Anderson writes: "The Sublime [or Noble] Porte (Bab Ali) was the grandiloquent title given to the palace inhabited by the Grand Vizier, the chief minister of the Sultan, from 1654 onwards. During the eighteenth and nineteenth centuries it was widely used in western Europe, by extension, as a synonym for the Turkish central government as a whole." *The Eastern Question, 1774–1923* (New York, 1966), xii.

3. For an informative study of M. Ali, see Henry Dodwell, *The Founder of Modern Egypt: A Study of Muhammad Ali* (Cambridge, England, 1967, reprinted from the 1931 edition); also Shafik Ghorbal, *The Beginnings of the Egyptian Question and the Rise of Mehemet Ali* (London, 1928).

4. See M. S. Anderson, *Eastern Question.*

5. Dodwell, *Founder,* 251.

6. Shimon Shamir, "Egyptian Rule (1832–1840) and the Beginning of the Modern Period in the History of Palestine," in Amnon Cohen and Gabriel Baer, eds., *Egypt and Palestine: A Millennium of Association, 868–1948* (Jerusalem, 1984), 225.

7. In response to Edward Said's "anti-orientalist" thesis about Western domination of the Middle East in the nineteenth century, it should be noted that Muhammad Ali and many other Muslim leaders welcomed Western financial, military, and political aid. Edward W. Said, *Orientalism* (New York, 1978).

8. Mordechai Abir, "Local Leadership and Early Reforms in Palestine, 1800–1834," in Moshe Ma'oz, ed., *Studies on Palestine,* 305. Also see Yitzhak Hofman, "The Administration of Syria and Palestine Under Egyptian Rule (1831–1840)," in Ma'oz, *Studies on Palestine.*

9. Dodwell, *Founder,* 56–157.

10. De Haas, *History of Palestine,* 392.

11. Anderson, *Eastern Question,* 103.

12. Dates cited from Mordechai Eliav, *Britain and the Holy Land, 1838–1914* (Jerusalem, 1997), 15.

13. *Ibid.*

14. See Mayir Vereté, "Why Was a British Consulate Established in Jerusalem?" in Norman Rose, ed., *From Palmerston to Balfour: Collected Essays of Mayir Vereté* (London, 1992).

15. Lieber, *Mystics,* 381.

16. Barbara W. Tuchman, *Bible and Sword: England and Palestine from the Bronze Age to Balfour* (New York, 1956), 191.

17. Lieber, *Mystics,* 327.

18. Cited from Eliav, *Britain and the Holy Land,* 65.

19. Moshe Ma'oz, *Ottoman Reform in Syria and Palestine, 1840–1861* (Oxford, 1968), 30–74.
20. *Ibid.*, 198.
21. *Ibid.*, 179.
22. *Ibid.*, 202.

Chapter Four: Ascending to the Land of Israel

1. Mahler, *History,* 624.
2. Lieber, *Mystics,* 51.
3. Mahler, *History,* 625.
4. Lieber, *Mystics,* 255.
5. *Ibid.*, 53.
6. Zalman Abramov, *Perpetual Dilemma: Jewish Religion in the Jewish State* (Rutherford, N.J., 1976), 33.
7. Lieber, *Mystics,* 69.
8. *Ibid.*, 75.
9. *Ibid.*, 175.
10. *Ibid.*, 78.
11. *Ibid.*, 79.
12. *Ibid.*, 175.
13. *Ibid.*, 238.
14. *Ibid.*
15. *Ibid.*, 240.
16. *Ibid.*, 241.
17. *Ibid.*, 176.
18. Tudor Parfitt, *The Jews in Palestine, 1800–1882* (Woodbridge, England, 1987), 31.
19. *Ibid.*, 33.
20. Lieber, *Mystics,* 333–366.

Chapter Five: Millenarian Missionaries

1. Mayir Vereté, "The Idea of the Restoration of the Jews in English Protestant Thought," in Rose, *Palmerston to Balfour,* 133, note 12.
2. See Lieber, *Mystics,* for a detailed account of the career of this Christian missionary among Palestine's Jews.
3. *Ibid.*, 161.
4. *Ibid.*, 164.
5. *Ibid.*, 168.
6. *Ibid.*, 171.
7. *Ibid.*, 309.
8. *Ibid.*, 295.
9. *Ibid.*, 306.
10. *Ibid.*, 313.
11. *Ibid.*, 314.
12. A. L. Tibawi, *British Interests in Palestine, 1800–1901* (Oxford, 1961), 36.
13. *Ibid.*, 50.

14. Osband, *Famous Travelers,* 47.
15. Tibawi, *British Interests,* 89.
16. *Ibid.,* 94.
17. *Ibid.,* 108.

Chapter Six: Building the New Jerusalem

1. The Slavophiles were nineteenth-century Russian intellectuals who championed native Slav or Russian values and ways of living. They reacted sharply to Tsar Peter the Great's efforts at Westernization by denouncing Western culture as an inappropriate model for Russian imitation. Slavophiles believed that it was Russia's divine mission to save the West by infusing it with the philosophical and religious idealism native to Russia. That sense of divine mission also extended to the Muslim-dominated East, where the liberation of the holy city of Constantinople from Turkish rule was also predicted.

2. In the first half of the eighteenth century a great many Orthodox Christians in Syria and Lebanon became dissatisfied with Greek church authority and formed a separatist movement, which resulted in union with the Catholic church. These separatist Greek Catholic Melkite churches worship according to Byzantine rites, allow for a married clergy, but also recognize the authority of the pope. See Saul P. Colbi, *A History of the Christian Presence in the Holy Land* (Lanham, Md., 1988), 127–130, 159–161, 215–220, 306–308, 310.

3. Cited in Derek Hopwood, *The Russian Presence in Syria and Palestine, 1843–1914* (Oxford, 1969), 101.

4. *Ibid.,* 32.

5. *Ibid.,* 30.

6. *Ibid.,* 37–38.

7. Alex Carmel, "Russian Activity in Palestine in the Nineteenth Century," in Richard I. Cohen, ed., *Vision and Conflict in the Holy Land* (New York, 1985), 50.

8. See Derek Hopwood, "'The Resurrection of Our Eastern Brethren' (Ignatev): Russian and Orthodox Arab Nationalism," in Ma'oz, *Studies on Palestine,* 394–407.

9. Celebrated for centuries, the Greek Orthodox "Holy Fire" ritual is held in Jerusalem annually on Saturday afternoon during Easter week. The ritual involves the Greek Orthodox patriarch of Jerusalem who enters the tomb of Christ with an unlit candle which miraculously catches fire, thus signaling to the faithful that the Almighty is pleased with their devotions. The miracle of the Holy Fire is taken to be further evidence of the miracle of Christ's Resurrection, whose celebration is held that night at a midnight service. For a vivid account of the ritual during late Ottoman times, see Robert Curzon, *Visits to the Monasteries in the Levant* (London, 1844); also see my own account of the ritual as performed today, "Holy Fire in Jerusalem," *Christian Century,* April, 7, 1982. More on the Holy Fire may be found in Chapter 7.

10. Rachel Simon, "The Struggle Over the Christian Holy Places During the Ottoman Period," in Cohen, *Vision and Conflict,* 30.

11. See Alex Carmel, "The Activities of the European Powers in Palestine, 1799–1914," *Asian and African Studies,* 19 (1985), 43–91.

12. Simon, "Struggle," 31.

13. *Ibid.*, 36.

14. Carmel, "Activities of the European Powers," 51.

15. *Ibid.*, 15.

16. *Ibid.*, 50.

17. See Alex Carmel, "The German Settlers in Palestine and Their Relations with the Local Arab Population and the Jewish Community," in Ma'oz, *Studies on Palestine*, 442–465.

18. *Ibid.*, 445.

19. *Ibid.*, 452.

20. *Ibid.*, 447.

21. *Ibid.*, 448.

22. *Ibid.*, 450.

23. Arnold Blumberg, *Zion Before Zionism, 1838–1880* (Syracuse, 1985), 69.

24. Ma'oz, *Ottoman Reform*, 217.

25. *Ibid.*, 217, 219, 225, 227.

26. *Ibid.*, 226–227.

27. *Ibid.*, 231.

28. *Ibid.*, 238.

29. *Ibid.*, 232.

30. *Ibid.*, 242.

31. *Ibid.*, 243.

32. See Gad G. Gilbar, "The Growing Economic Involvement of Palestine with the West, 1865–1914," in Kushner, *Palestine in the Late Ottoman Period*.

33. *Ibid.*, 188.

34. Alexander Scholch, *Palestine in Transformation, 1856–1882* (Washington, D. C., 1993), 29.

35. Haim Gerber, "The Population of Syria and Palestine in the Nineteenth Century," *Asian and African Studies*, 13 (1979), 58–80.

36. Scholch, *Palestine*, 284.

37. See Alexander Schölch, "The Demographic Development of Palestine, 1850–1882," *Journal of Middle East Studies*, 17 (1985), 485–505.

Chapter Seven: Dream and Reality

1. Vivian D. Lipman, "Britain and the Holy Land: 1830–1914," in Davis and Ben-Arieh, *Eyes Toward Zion*, 195.

2. Thomas Hummel, "English Protestant Pilgrims of the Nineteenth Century," in Anthony O'Mahony with Goran Gunner and Kevork Hintlian, eds., *The Christian Heritage in the Holy Land* (London, 1995), 170.

3. *Ibid.*, 174.

4. John Kelman, *The Holy Land* (London, 1904), 233. Cited in Hummel, "English Protestant Pilgrims," 177.

5. Hummel, "English Protestant Pilgrims," 177.

6. Mark Twain, *The Innocents Abroad, or The New Pilgrim's Progress* (New York, 1899), II, 243.

7. Mary Eliza Rogers, *Domestic Life in Palestine* (London, 1989, first published in 1862), 3.

8. *Ibid.*, 9.

9. *Ibid.*, 16–17.
10. *Ibid.*, 18.
11. *Ibid.*, 26–27.
12. *Ibid.*, 33.
13. *Ibid.*
14. *Ibid.*, 95.
15. *Ibid.*, 97.
16. *Ibid.*, 98.
17. *Ibid.*, 100.
18. *Ibid.*, 100–101.
19. *Ibid.*, 154.
20. *Ibid.*, 232.
21. *Ibid.*, 253.
22. For a vivid account of the trampling to death of scores of worshipers at the doorway of the Church of the Holy Sepulchre, while Ibrahim Pasha was in attendance, see Curzon, *Monasteries*.
23. Rogers, *Domestic Life*, 300.
24. *Ibid.*
25. *Ibid.*, 303.
26. *Ibid.*, 305.
27. *Ibid.*
28. *Ibid.*, 306.
29. For an excellent analysis of Twain's sardonic view of the Holy Land, see Franklin Walker, *Irreverent Pilgrims: Melville, Browne, and Mark Twain in the Holy Land* (Seattle, 1974).
30. Twain, *Innocents Abroad*, 262.
31. *Ibid.*, 263.
32. *Ibid.*, 265.
33. *Ibid.*, 295.
34. Walker, *Pilgrims*, 213. Cited from William C. Prime, *Tent Life in the Holy Land* (New York, 1865), 142.
35. Walker, *Pilgrims*, 187.
36. *Ibid.*, 345.
37. *Ibid.*, 185. Cited from *Mark Twain's Notebooks and Journals* (New York, 1935), 368.
38. Walker, *Pilgrims*, 385.
39. Twain, *Innocents Abroad*, 329.
40. Walker, *Pilgrims*, 192.
41. Cited in *ibid.*, 221.
42. Hummel, "English Protestant Pilgrims," 163.

Chapter Eight: Palestinians and Zionists

1. James Finn cited by Alexander Schölch, "European Penetration and the Economic Development of Palestine, 1856–82," in Roger Owen, ed., *Studies in the Economic and Social History of Palestine in the Nineteenth and Twentieth Centuries* (Oxford, 1982), 19.

2. Kenneth Stein, *The Land Question in Palestine, 1917–1939* (Chapel Hill, 1984), 19.

3. *Ibid.*, 19.

4. See Doreen Warriner's article "Land Tenure Problems in the Fertile Crescent in the Nineteenth and Twentieth Centuries," in Charles Issawi, ed., *The Economic History of the Middle East, 1800–1914* (Chicago, 1966), 71–78; also Gabriel Baer, "Land Tenure in Egypt and Fertile Crescent, 1800–1950," *ibid.*, 79–90.

5. Scholch, "European Penetration," 23. Cf. Rashid Khalidi, *Palestinian Identity: The Construction of Modern National Consciousness* (New York, 1997), 89–117.

6. The alienation of the peasant from the land during the late Ottoman period is well researched. See Abraham Granott (Granovsky), *The Land Issue in Palestine* (New York, 1940) and *The Land System in Palestine: History and Structures* (London, 1952). Also Stein, *Land Question,* 3–34, and Joel S. Migdal, "The Effects of Regime Policies on Social Cohesion and Fragmentation," in Joel S. Migdal, ed., *Palestinian Society and Politics* (Princeton, 1980), 9–17.

7. Ma'oz, *Ottoman Reform,* 92–93.

8. Stein, *Land Question,* 10. Cf. Ma'oz, *Ottoman Reform,* 92–93.

9. Fred M. Gottheil, "Money and Product Flows in Mid-19th Century Palestine: The Physiocratic Model Applied," in Kushner, *Palestine in the Late Ottoman Period,* 225.

10. See Albert Hourani, "Ottoman Reform and the Politics of Notables," in William R. Polk and Richard L. Chambers, eds., *Beginnings of Modernization in the Middle East: The Nineteenth Century* (Chicago, 1968), 54.

11. Stein, *Land Question,* 5.

12. *Ibid.*, 8; also see Roderick H. Davison, *Reform in the Ottoman Empire, 1856–1876* (Princeton, 1963), 148, and Miriam Hoexter, "The Role of the Qays and Yaman Factions in Local Political Divisions: Jabal Nablus Compared with the Judean Hills in the First Half of the Nineteenth Century," *Asian and African Studies,* 10 (1974), 285.

13. Arab reactions to Ottoman decline are explained in Hisham Sharabi, *Arab Intellectuals and the West: The Formative Years, 1875–1914* (Baltimore, 1970); Muhammad Y. Muslih, *The Origins of Palestinian Nationalism* (New York, 1988); C. Ernest Dawn, *From Ottomanism to Arabism: Essays on the Origins of Arab Nationalism* (Urbana, Ill., 1973); Rashid Khalidi, "Arab Nationalism in Syria: The Formative Years, 1908–1914," in William W. Haddad and William Ochsenwald, eds., *Nationalism in a Non-National State: The Dissolution of the Ottoman Empire* (Columbus, Ohio, 1977); and Albert Hourani, *Arabic Thought in the Liberal Age, 1798–1939* (Oxford, 1962).

14. Dawn, *Ottomanism to Arabism,* 134.

15. *Ibid.*, 137.

16. *Ibid.*, 138.

17. *Ibid.*, 146.

18. *Ibid.*, 143.

19. Sharabi, *Arab Intellectuals,* 55.

20. Dawn, *Ottomanism to Arabism,* 149–150.

21. *Ibid.*, 151ff.

22. Sharabi, *Arab Intellectuals,* 106.

23. George Antonius, *The Arab Awakening: The Story of the Arab National Movement* (New York, 1965), 107, 121.

24. The story of this planned rebellion is complex and extends to the relations between Arab revolutionaries and both Sharif Husayn of Mecca and Lord Kitchener. The story is well told by Dawn, *Ottomanism to Arabism*, 1–68.

25. Rashid Khalidi provides a comprehensive and fascinating account of the Arab fear of Zionist expansion by surveying the Arab press of the times, in *Palestinian Identity*, 119–144.

26. Russian westward expansion in the last quarter of the eighteenth century led to the transfer of more than 1.25 million Jews from Polish to Russian sovereignty and created a "Jewish Problem" for tsarist Russia. "The Russians," according to the historian Martin Gilbert, "prevented the spread of Jews from this area by turning it into a 'Pale of Jewish Settlement.'" By 1885 more than 4 million Jews lived in the Pale, which extended southward from the Baltic Sea to the Black Sea, and westward to the border of Germany. Martin Gilbert, *Jewish Historical Atlas* (London, 1969), 67, 68.

27. Dan Giladi, "The Agronomic Development of the Old Colonies in Palestine, 1882–1914," in Ma'oz, *Studies on Palestine*, 157.

28. For a simplified account of the role of the Alliance in the early stage of Jewish immigration to Palestine, see Israel Pocket Library, *Immigration and Settlement* (Jerusalem, 1973), 13–17.

29. See Giladi, "Agronomic Development," 175–189.

30. Abramov, *Perpetual Dilemma*, 62.

31. Khalidi, *Palestinian Identity*, 93–94. Also see Yaacov Ro'i, "The Zionist Attitude to the Arabs, 1908–1914," *Middle Eastern Studies*, 4 (1968), 198–242.

32. Giladi, "Agronomic Development," 180.

33. Neville J. Mandel, "Ottoman Practice as Regards Jewish Settlement in Palestine, 1881–1908," *Middle Eastern Studies*, 11 (1975), 38.

34. Israel Kolatt, "The Organization of the Jewish Population of Palestine and the Development of Its Political Consciousness Before World War II," in Ma'oz, *Studies on Palestine*, 211.

35. *Ibid.*, 219. Also see Abramov's account in *Perpetual Dilemma*.

36. Kolatt, "Organization."

37. David Farhi, "Documents on the Attitude of the Ottoman Government Toward the Jewish Settlement in Palestine After the Revolution of Young Turks, 1908–1909," in Ma'oz *Studies on Palestine*, 190, 204. Also see Kolatt, "Organization."

38. Neville J. Mandel, "Ottoman Policy and Restrictions on Jewish Settlement in Palestine, 1881–1908, Part One," *Middle Eastern Studies*, 10 (1974), 316–317.

39. Cited in Farhi, "Documents," 195.

40. Yehoshua Porath, "The Political Awakening of the Palestinian Arabs and Their Leadership Towards the End of the Ottoman Period," in Ma'oz, *Studies on Palestine*, 375.

41. See Khalidi, *Palestinian Identity*, 63–88. Also Porath, "Political Awakening," 372ff.

42. See Khalidi, *Palestinian Identity*, and Porath, "Political Awakening."

43. Excerpted from Azoury's book *Le reveil de la Nation Arabe dans l'Asie Turque* (Paris, 1905) and cited in original French in Albert Hourani, *Arabic*

Thought in the Liberal Age (London, 1962), 279. An English translation of Azoury's statement appears in Porath, "Political Awakening," 376.

44. See Porath, "Political Awakening," 360.
45. *Ibid.*, 377.
46. *Ibid.*, 378.
47. *Ibid.*, 379.
48. *Ibid.*
49. Alex Carmel, "The Activities of the European Powers in Palestine, 1799–1914," *Asian and African Studies*, 19 (1985), 61.

Chapter Nine: Allenby at Jerusalem's Gate

1. See Tuchman, *Bible and Sword.*
2. John Gray, *A History of Jerusalem* (London, 1969), 289.
3. See Mayir Vereté, "The Balfour Declaration and Its Makers," in Rose, *Palmerston to Balfour,* 1–38.
4. Jon Kimche, *The Unromantics: The Great Powers and the Balfour Declaration* (London, 1968), 34.
5. Vereté, "Balfour Declaration," 10.
6. Yehuda Reinharz, *Chaim Weizmann: The Making of a Statesman* (New York, 1993), 4.
7. Lieber, *Mystics,* 382.
8. Cited from Reinharz, *Weizmann,* 204.
9. *Ibid.*, 220.
10. Kimche, *Unromantics,* 29.
11. See Michael J. Cohen, *The Origins and Evolution of the Arab-Zionist Conflict* (Berkeley, 1987), 14–28.
12. See the discussion in Chapter 8.
13. A. L. Tibawi, *A Modern History of Syria, Including Lebanon and Palestine* (New York, 1969), 219.
14. Cited from Cohen, *Arab-Zionist Conflict,* 19.
15. *Ibid.*
16. Yaacov Herzog and Michael Cohen seem to suggest that the Arab "misunderstanding" was contrived to gain political advantage from Britain's dual territorial promises to the Zionists and to the Hashemites. See Yaacov Herzog, "Israel in the Middle East: An Introduction," *Jerusalem Papers on Peace Problems,* Leonard Davis Institute for International Relations, Jerusalem, February 1975, 59ff. Cohen, *Arab-Zionist Conflict,* 18ff.
17. Cohen, *Arab-Zionist Conflict,* 22.
18. Tibawi, *Modern History of Syria,* 244.
19. Yehoshua Porath, *The Emergence of the Palestinian-Arab National Movement, 1918–1929* (London, 1974), 40.
20. William Basil Worsfold, *Palestine of the Mandate* (London, 1925), 6.
21. *Ibid.*, 4.
22. Elizabeth Monroe, *Britain's Moment in the Middle East, 1914–1971* (Baltimore, 1981), 82.
23. *Ibid.*

24. Kimche, *Unromantics,* 64. A. L. Tibawi takes the view that Joyce's report of Faysal's remarks was a fabrication. Tibawi, *Modern History of Syria,* 287.

25. Reinharz, *Weizmann,* 232.

26. *Ibid.,* 256.

27. *Ibid.,* 236.

28. *Ibid.,* 218.

29. Cited from Antonius, *Arab Awakening.* The Anglo-French declaration of November 7, 1918, appears as Appendix E, 435–436.

30. Reinharz, *Weizmann,* 273ff.

31. Tibawi, *Modern History of Syria,* 291.

32. Reinharz, *Weizmann,* 294.

33. *Ibid.,* 295.

34. Tibawi, *Modern History of Syria,* 296–298.

35. Reinharz, *Weizmann,* 274.

36. Porath, *Emergence,* 89.

37. Cited in *ibid.,* 43.

38. Bernard Wasserstein, *The British in Palestine: The Mandatory Government and the Arab-Jewish Conflict, 1917–1929* (London, 1991, 2nd ed.), 22.

39. *Ibid.,* 24.

40. *Ibid.*

41. *Ibid.,* 34.

Chapter Ten: Herbert Samuel Changes His Mind

1. The Hill of Evil Counsel, which dominates Jerusalem from the south, is the site where, according to early church tradition, Judas received his payment of thirty pieces of silver, and where the governor's mansion of the British mandate was built.

2. Wasserstein, *British in Palestine,* 79.

3. *Ibid.,* 199.

4. *Ibid.,* 101.

5. *Ibid.*

6. *Ibid.,* 105.

7. Neil Caplan, "The Yishuv, Sir Herbert Samuel, and the Arab Question in Palestine, 1921–25," in Elie Kedourie and Sylvia G. Haim, eds., *Zionism and Arabism in Palestine and Israel* (London, 1982), 19.

8. Wasserstein, *British in Palestine,* 77.

9. *Ibid.,* 109.

10. *Ibid.,* 108.

11. Reinharz, *Weizmann,* 22.

12. Wasserstein, *British in Palestine,* 113.

13. *Ibid.,* 110.

14. Porath, *Emergence,* 17.

15. Wasserstein, *British in Palestine,* 141.

16. Israel Kolatt, "The Zionist Movement and the Arabs," in Shmuel Almog, ed., *Zionism and the Arabs: Essays* (Jerusalem, 1983), 14.

17. *Ibid.,* 5–6.

18. Michael J. Cohen, *Palestine and the Great Powers, 1945–1948* (Princeton, 1982), 6.

19. Wasserstein, *British in Palestine,* 108.

20. The Zionist need for land to accommodate a burgeoning population is well documented in Stein, *Land Question.*

21. *Ibid.,* 214.

22. *Ibid.,* 39.

23. *Ibid.,* 69.

24. Cohen, *Arab-Zionist Conflict,* 73.

25. Stein, *Land Question,* 71.

26. Pamela Smith, *Palestine and the Palestinians, 1876–1983* (New York, 1984), 59.

27. Esco Foundation, *Palestine: A Study of Jewish, Arab, and British Policies* (New Haven, 1947), 718.

28. See Stein's account of the dislocation of Arab peasants in the Wadi Harith area, south of Haifa. *Land Question,* 76–79.

29. Ylana Miller, *Government and Society in Rural Palestine, 1920–1948* (Austin, Tex., 1985), 86.

30. Stein, *Land Question,* xvi.

31. Cohen, *Arab-Zionist Conflict,* 73.

32. *Ibid.,* 76.

33. Miller, *Rural Palestine,* 159.

34. *Ibid.,* 160.

35. *Ibid.,* 158.

36. *Ibid.,* 117.

37. *Ibid.,* 115.

38. *Ibid.,* 89.

Chapter Eleven: Nobody Wants a Palestinian Flag

1. See Martin Kolinsky, "Premeditation in the Palestine Disturbances of August, 1929?" *Middle Eastern Studies,* 26 (1990). Cf. Pinhas Ofer, "The Commission on the Palestine Disturbances of August, 1929: Appointment, Terms of Reference, Procedure and Report," *Middle Eastern Studies,* 21 (1985); Yaacov Goldstein, "The 1929 Disturbances and Their Impact on the Formulation of Zionist Positions Concerning the Palestine Problem," *Asian and African Studies,* 24 (1990), 231–265. For a contrary view of the Mufti Amin's role in the disturbances, see Philip Mattar, "The Role of the Mufti in the Political Struggle over the Western Wall, 1928–29," *Middle Eastern Studies,* 19 (1983).

2. Kolinsky, "Premeditation," 28.

3. Norman Kotker, *The Earthly Jerusalem* (New York, 1969), 147.

4. See Philip Mattar, *The Mufti of Jerusalem: Al-Hajj Amin and the Palestinian National Movement* (New York, 1988). For a different appraisal, see Zvi Elpeleg, *The Grand Mufti: Haj Amin al-Hussaini, Founder of the Palestinian National Movement* (London, 1993).

5. Porath, *Emergence,* 258–273.

6. *Ibid.,* 262ff.

7. Cited in *ibid.,* 270.

8. Esco Foundation, *Palestine,* 620.
9. Cited from the Shaw Report by Kolinsky, "Premeditation," 22.
10. *Palestine Royal Commission Report* (London, July 1937), 72.
11. *Ibid.,* 75.
12. Stein, *Land Question,* 82.
13. J. C. Hurewitz, *The Struggle for Palestine* (New York, 1976; first published 1950), 28, 29.
14. Kolinsky, "Premeditation," 31.
15. Hurewitz, *Struggle,* 27–28; Esco Foundation, *Palestine,* 662.
16. *Palestine Royal Commission Report,* 117.
17. Hurewitz, *Struggle,* 28.
18. *Ibid.,* 96.
19. Shai Lachman, "Arab Rebellion and Terrorism in Palestine, 1929–39: The Case of Sheikh Izz al-Din al-Qassam and His Movement," in Kedourie and Haim, *Zionism and Arabism,* 60.
20. *Ibid.,* 52.
21. Joseph Nevo, "Palestinian Arab Violence During the 1930s," in Michael J. Cohen and Martin Kolinsky, eds., *Britain and the Middle East in the 1930s* (London, 1992), 175.
22. Lachman, "Arab Rebellion," 72.
23. Yehohada Haim, "Zionist Policies and Attitudes Towards the Arabs on the Eve of the Arab Revolt, 1936," *Middle Eastern Studies,* 14 (1978), 213.
24. *Palestine Royal Commission Report,* 131.
25. *Ibid.,* 141.
26. *Ibid.*
27. *Ibid.,* 380.
28. *Ibid.,* 381.
29. Nevo, "Arab Violence," 179, 183.
30. *Ibid.,* 183.
31. Hurewitz, *Struggle,* 108.
32. *Ibid.,* 89.
33. *Ibid.,* 105.
34. See Haim, "Zionist Policies."
35. Tom Bowden, "The Politics of the Arab Rebellion in Palestine, 1936–39," *Middle Eastern Studies,* 11 (1975), 149.
36. Hurewitz, *Struggle,* 113.

Chapter Twelve: Betrayal and Birth, 1939–1948

1. Hurewitz, *Struggle,* 294.
2. *Ibid.,* 182–194.
3. Ben Halperin, *The Idea of the Jewish State* (Cambridge, Mass., 1961), 358.
4. Hurweitz, *Struggle,* 138.
5. Chaim Weizmann, "Palestine's Role in the Solution of the Jewish Problem," *Foreign Affairs,* 20 (1942), 337.
6. Hurewitz, *Struggle,* 150.
7. See Halperin, *Jewish State.*
8. Hurewitz, *Struggle,* 160.

9. *Ibid.*, 164.

10. Monroe, *Britain's Moment,* 89.

11. Israel Pocket Library, *Zionism* (Jerusalem, 1973), 111.

12. Hurewitz, *Struggle,* 204.

13. Cohen, *Palestine and the Great Powers,* 9.

14. Michael J. Cohen, *Palestine: Retreat from the Mandate* (London, 1978), 179.

15. Hurewitz, *Struggle,* 223.

16. *Ibid.*

17. *Ibid.*, 226.

18. *Ibid.*, 215.

19. *Ibid.*, 253.

20. *Ibid.*, 233.

21. *Ibid.*

22. Cohen, *Palestine and the Great Powers,* 230.

23. *Ibid.*, 55.

24. *Ibid.*, 51.

25. *Ibid.*, 130.

26. Hurewitz, *Struggle,* 213.

27. *Ibid.*, 219.

28. *Ibid.*, 245.

29. Cohen, *Palestine and the Great Powers,* 250.

30. *Ibid.*, 250–259.

31. Hurewitz, *Struggle,* 239.

32. Mattar, *Mufti of Jerusalem,* 108.

33. Israel Pocket Library, *Zionism,* 120.

34. Cited in Don Peretz, *The Middle East Today* (New York, 1965), 251.

35. See Joseph Nevo, "The Palestine Arab Party, 1944–1946," *Asian and African Studies,* 14 (1980), 99–115.

36. Cohen, *Palestine and the Great Powers,* 267.

37. Leonard Stein, *The Balfour Declaration* (New York, 1961); Rose, *Palmerston to Balfour.*

A Note on Sources

LIKE A TREE LIMB, this book grew from a previous study, *Jerusalem Blessed, Jerusalem Cursed* (now in paperback as simply *Jerusalem*). When I finished it, I wanted to learn more about the extraordinary outpouring of ideals and zealotry, of patriotism, politics, and passion that drove the Western nations toward Palestine in the last century, beginning with Bonaparte's invasion of the Middle East in 1798. What I came to find was a deeply rooted enmity between Easterner and Westerner, between Muslim and Christian, between Arab and Jew, and now between Israeli and Palestinian. The roots of these conflicts go back at least to Bonaparte's time and perhaps earlier—to the medieval Crusader invasion of the Muslim East. Born of interreligious jealousy, rivalry, and triumphalism, these antagonisms mock the shared vision of a common God.

But this is not the whole story of Palestine from Bonaparte to Ben-Gurion. There were also ideals, vision, energy, and sacrifice which transformed this country, ridding it of disease, poverty, ignorance, and oppression. The record of that transformation is a complicated one which involves both the Christian and Jewish rediscovery of the Holy Land. Had it not been for Christian and Jewish involvement in this land, Palestine might have remained in the Ottoman Empire, languishing, ignored, remembered only in prayer, merely a destination for pilgrims. It was the Western involvement—and that alone— that provoked Muslims, "awakening" them (to borrow Antonius's metaphor) to Palestine, its possible loss to the West, its worth to Arabs, its meaning to Islam.

I relied on a great many sources in trying to achieve an accurate, comprehensive, balanced, and critically sound understanding of this country in the time of its transformation.

I began my study of nineteenth-century Palestine through the diaries and memoirs of travelers. The most interesting of these were C. F. Volney, *Travels Through Egypt and Syria in the Years 1783, 1784, and 1785* (New York, 1798); Viscount de Chateaubriand, *Travels to Jerusalem and the Holy Land Through Egypt* (London, 1835); and Alphonse de Lamartine's three-volume work, *A Pilgrimage to the Holy Land* (London, 1837).

The first truly scientific studies of nineteenth-century Palestine begin with the writings of F. D. Clarke, *Travels in Various Countries of Europe, Asia, and Africa,* 6 vols. (Cambridge, England, 1810–1823); Ulrich Seetzen, *Reisen durch Syrien, Palastina, Phonicien,* 4 vols. (Berlin, 1854–1859); J.-L. Burckhardt, *Travels in Syria and the Holy Land* (London, 1822); J. S. Buckingham, *Travels Among the Arab Tribes* (London, 1825); and W. F. Lynch, *Narrative of the United States Expedition to the River Jordan and the Dead Sea* (Philadelphia, 1849).

The pioneering work of Edward Robinson is contained in several volumes that make wonderful reading: *Biblical Researches in Palestine* (London, 1841); *Later Biblical Researches* (London, 1856); and *Physical Geography of the Holy Land* (London, 1865).

My study of nineteenth-century Palestine was aided by the pictures of W. H. Bartlett and David Roberts, and by the books of C. R. Conder and Laurence Oliphant.

There are few book-length studies of Ottoman Palestine in the nineteenth century. Among the best are Moshe Ma'oz, *Ottoman Reform in Syria and Palestine, 1840–1861* (Oxford, 1968); Sherman Lieber, *Mystics and Missionaries: The Jews in Palestine, 1799–1840* (Salt Lake City, 1992); and Neil Asher Silberman, *Digging for God and Country: Exploration, Archaeology, and the Secret Struggle for the Holy Land, 1799–1917* (New York, 1982). Also see A. L. Tibawi, *British Interests in Palestine, 1800–1901* (Oxford, 1961); Mordechai Eliav, *Britain and the Holy Land, 1838–1914: Selected Documents from the British Consulate in Jerusalem* (Jerusalem, 1997); Derek Hopwood, *The Russian Presence in Syria and Palestine, 1843–1914* (Oxford, 1969); and Isaiah Friedman, *Germany, Turkey, and Zionism, 1897–1918* (Oxford, 1977).

Particularly valuable are Yehoshua Ben-Arieh's two-volume *Jerusalem in the 19th Century,* covering both *The Old City* (1984) and *The New City* (1986), and his popular and useful survey, *The Rediscovery of the Holy Land in the Nineteenth Century* (Jerusalem, 1979). Ben-Arieh's recently published *Painting the Holy Land in the Nineteenth Century* (Jerusalem, 1997) should also be consulted. Of special interest is Y. Nir's splendid *The Bible and the Image: The History of Photography in the Holy Land, 1839–1899* (Philadelphia, 1985). For an intimate glimpse of Palestine in the early 1820s and 1830s, see the valuable document of S. N. Spyridon, "Annals of Palestine, 1821–1841," *Journal of Palestine Oriental Society,* 18 (1938).

Among general studies of Palestine is the readable but dated book of Jacob de Haas, *History of Palestine: The Last Two Thousand Years* (New York, 1934); also readable and somewhat dated is the modern history of Palestine by A. L. Tibawi (New York, 1969). Sarah Searight's *The British in the Middle East* offers insights into the sensibilities of the imperialist adventurers (New York, 1970), as does Barbara W. Tuchman, *Bible and Sword: England and Palestine from the Bronze Age to Balfour* (New York, 1956). Also of note is Sari J. Nasir, *The Arabs and the English* (London, 1976); Kathryn Tidwell, *Heart Beguiling Araby* (New York, 1981); and R. Blake, *Disraeli's Grand Tour: Benjamin Disraeli and the Holy Land, 1830–1831* (London, 1982). Arnold Blumberg's *Zion Before Zionism* is a useful introduction to mid-nineteenth-century Palestine (Syracuse, 1985); Ruth Kark's detailed *Jaffa: A City in Evolution, 1799–1917* (Jerusalem,

1990) provides an in-depth treatment of one of historic Palestine's central cities in the context of the land's social history.

My treatment of Palestine under Muhammad Ali and Ibrahim Pasha was influenced by Henry Dodwell's *The Founder of Modern Egypt* (Cambridge, England, 1939), and Shafik Ghorbal, *The Beginnings of the Egyptian Question and the Rise of Mehemet Ali* (London, 1928). Essays by Mordechai Abir, Yitzhak Hofman, and Shimon Shamir, cited in the Notes, were lucid and informative.

There are many excellent studies on the Christian rediscovery of the Holy Land. I began my research with the diaries and memoirs of pilgrims and travelers. Among these are Alexander Kinglake, *Eothen, or Traces of Travel* (London, 1845); Bayard Taylor, *The Land of the Saracens* (New York, 1856); Sarah Barclay Johnson, *Hadji in Syria* (Philadelphia, 1858); Mary Eliza Rogers, *Domestic Life in Palestine* (London, 1862); Isabel Burton, *The Inner Life of Syria, Palestine and the Holy Land* (London, 1875); W. M. Thomson, *The Land and the Book* (London, 1893); H. B. Tristram, *Eastern Custom in Bible Lands* (New York, 1894); A. Goodrich-Freer, *Inner Jerusalem* (New York, 1904); and G. Robinson Lees, *Village Life in Palestine* (London, 1905).

Add to these works the important observations on Palestine of Mark Twain, contained in his travel journal, *The Innocents Abroad, or the New Pilgrim's Progress. Excursion to Europe and the Holy Land* (New York, 1899). On the Holy Land experiences of famous American writers, I found it a delight to read Franklin D. Walker's *Irreverent Pilgrims: Melville, Browne, and Mark Twain in the Holy Land* (Seattle, 1974).

Of primary interest to any student of nineteenth-century Palestine are the publications of British diplomat James Finn and his wife, Ann. Among the most important of these are *Byways in Palestine* (London, 1868) and *Stirring Times*, 2 vols. (London, 1878) by James Finn. Ann Finn's books include *Palestine Peasantry* (London, 1923) and *Reminiscences* (London, 1929).

Our knowledge of nineteenth-century Christian feeling about Palestine has been greatly advanced by the American–Holy Land Project carried out under the editorial leadership of Moshe Davis at Hebrew University's Institute for Contemporary Jewry. I am particularly indebted to this project for the reprinting of the writings of many American travelers to the Holy Land, and for the scholarly essays collected in *With Eyes Toward Zion-III* (New York, 1991).

Single-volume studies of American Christian pilgrimage to the Holy Land include Lester Irwin Vogel, "Zion as Place and Past: An American Myth: Ottoman Palestine in the American Mind Perceived Through Protestant Consciousness and Experience," Ph.D. dissertation, George Washington University, 1984; David Klatzker, "American Christian Travelers to the Holy Land, 1821–1939," Ph.D. dissertation, Temple University, 1987; Gershon Greenberg, *The Holy Land in American Religious Thought, 1620–1948*, (Lanham, Md., 1984); Moshe Sharon, ed., *The Holy Land in History and Thought* (Leiden, 1988);

and Anthony O'Mahony with Goran Gunner and Kevork Hintlian, *The Christian Heritage in the Holy Land* (London, 1995).

Of particular interest in assessing the American involvement in Palestine is Ruth Kark, *American Consuls in the Holy Land, 1832–1914* (Jerusalem, 1994).

Alex Carmel has produced superb scholarship on nineteenth-century Christian Palestine, in particular his essays "The Activities of the European Powers in Palestine, 1799–1914," *Asian and African Studies,* 19 (1955), and "Russian Activity in Palestine in the Nineteenth Century" in *Vision and Conflict in the Holy Land*, ed. Richard I. Cohen (Jerusalem, 1985). Carmel's exacting standards of scholarship are upheld in the writings of Rachel Simon and Daphne Tsimhoni, which I consulted.

I found that shorter, specialized studies, taken as a whole, provided a rich and reliable picture of Ottoman Palestine. Many of these are to be found in the anthologies superbly edited by Moshe Ma'oz, *Studies on Palestine During the Ottoman Period* (Jerusalem, 1975), and *Palestinian-Arab Politics* (Jerusalem, 1975); Amnon Cohen and Gabriel Baer, *Egypt and Palestine: A Millennium of Association, 868–1948* (Jerusalem, 1984); Richard I. Cohen, *Vision and Conflict in the Holy Land* (Jerusalem, 1985); Gad G. Gibar *Ottoman Palestine, 1800–1914: Studies in Economic and Social History* (Leiden, 1990); and Ruth Kark, *The Land that Became Israel: Studies in Historical Geography* (New Haven, 1990).

We are all in the debt of the late Alexander Schölch for his essays explaining the economic and the geopolitical significance of events in nineteenth-century Palestine. These essays may be found in Roger Owen, ed., *Studies in the Economic and Social History of Palestine in the Nineteenth and Twentieth Centuries* (Oxford, 1982), and in Scholch's own book-length monograph, *Palestine in Transformation, 1856–1882* (Washington, D.C., 1993). Also see "The Demographic Development of Palestine, 1850–1882," *International Journal of Middle East Studies,* 17 (1985), 485–505.

Additional essays of value on economics are by Doreen Warriner, "Land-Tenure Problems in the Fertile Crescent in the Nineteenth and Twentieth Centuries," and Gabriel Baer, "Land Tenure in Egypt and the Fertile Crescent, 1800–1950," both in Charles Issawi, ed., *The Economic History of the Middle East, 1800–1914* (Chicago, 1966).

Reinforcing our knowledge of the socioeconomic conditions of Palestine in the last century are the essays in William R. Polk and Richard I. Chambers, eds., *Beginnings of Modernization in the Middle East* (Chicago, 1968), particularly the influential essay of Albert Hourani, "Ottoman Reform and the Politics of Notables." Other works of Hourani's that I found of particular value were *A Vision of History* (Beirut, 1961); *Arabic Thought in the Liberal Age, 1798–1939* (London, 1962); *Europe and the Middle East* (Berkeley, 1980); *The Emergence of the Modern Middle East* (Berkeley, 1981); and "The Political and Social Background in the Eighteenth Century," in Issawi, *Economic History of the Middle East.*

For specific and useful studies of economic issues affecting Palestine in the last century, see Amnon Cohen's "Local Trade, International Trade and Government Involvement in Jerusalem During the Early Ottoman Period," *Asian and African Studies,* 12 (1978), and Kais M. Firro, "The Impact of European Imports on Handicrafts in Syria and Palestine in the Nineteenth Century," *Asian and African Studies,* 25 (1991). Also see Haim Gerber "The Ottoman Administration of the Sanjaq of Jerusalem, 1890–1908," *Asian and African Studies,* 12 (1978); Gabriel Baer, "The Dismemberment of AWQAF in Early 19th Century Jerusalem," *Asian and African Studies,* 13 (1979); and Ruth Kark, "The Jerusalem Municipality at the End of Ottoman Rule," *Asian and African Studies,* 14 (1980).

A useful anthology, *The Syrian Land in the 18th and 19th Centuries,* edited by Thomas Phillipp (Stuttgart, 1992), contains essays by Itamar Rabinovich, "Syria and the Syrian Land: The 19th Century Roots of 20th Century Developments"; Adel Manna, "Continuity and Change in the Socio-Political Elite in Palestine During the Late Ottoman Period"; and Khairieh Kasmieh, "Ruhi al-Khalidi 1864–1913: A Symbol of the Cultural Movement Towards the End of the Ottoman Period."

My general knowledge of Ottoman imperial history and its policies affecting Syria and Palestine during the nineteenth century was gained from a reading of Moshe Ma'oz's book on the Tanzimat, mentioned above. This was supplemented by Bernard Lewis, *The Emergence of Modern Turkey* (Oxford, 1961), and writings by P. M. Holt and Roderick H. Davison. Of particular use was Davison's book, *Reform in the Ottoman Empire, 1856–1876* (Princeton, 1963), and his essay, "The Millets as Agents of Change in the Nineteenth-Century Ottoman Empire," in Benjamin Braude and Bernard Lewis, eds., *Christians and Jews in the Ottoman Empire: The Functioning of a Plural Society,* 2 vols. (New York, 1982). For specific study of the diplomatic history surrounding the Eastern Question, I turned to M. S. Anderson, *The Eastern Question, 1774–1923* (New York, 1966).

For the Crimean War and its impact on the Middle East, I relied on David Wetzel, *The Crimean War: A Diplomatic History* (New York, 1985) and Ann Pottinger Saab, *The Origins of the Crimean Alliance* (Charlottesville, Va., 1977).

My study of the Jewish community of Palestine during the nineteenth century utilized several outstanding works. I have already noted the studies of Raphael Mahler and Sherman Lieber, upon which I relied heavily, and Tudor Parfitt's marvelous book *The Jews in Palestine, 1800–1882* (Woodbridge, England, 1987). Also of use were Jeff Halper, *Between Redemption and Revival: The Jewish Yishuv of Jerusalem in the Nineteenth Century* (Boulder, Colo., 1986), and Joseph B. Glass and Ruth Kark, *Sephardi Entrepreneurs in Eretz Israel: The Amzalak Family, 1816–1918* (Jerusalem, 1981). Also see Thomas Phillipp, "The Farhi Family and the Changing Position of the Jews in Syria, 1750–1860," *Middle Eastern Studies,* 20 (1984). For knowledge of Sir Moses Montefiore and his wife, Lady Judith, I relied on their own words: Moses's *Diary and Letters from*

Voyages: Palestine in the 1830s (Jerusalem, 1974), and Lady Judith's *Notes from a Private Journal of a Visit to Egypt and Palestine, 1839* (London, 1844). Also see P. Goodman, *Moses Montefiore* (Philadelphia, 1925), and V. D. Lipman, *Sir Moses Montefiore: A Symposium* (Oxford, 1982).

The rise of Zionism and Arab Palestinian nationalism are complex events, easily misunderstood and hastily judged. I have tried to gain a clear understanding of both movements by using works that I consider well researched, measured, and lacking in partisan polemics. My knowledge of Zionism was gained from two masterful studies: Walter Laqueur, *A History of Zionism* (London, 1972), and David Vital, *Zionism: The Crucial Phase* (Oxford, 1987).

Foremost among scholarly books on the rise of Arab Palestinian nationalism is the magisterial two-volume study by Yehoshua Porath, *The Emergence of the Palestinian-Arab National Movement, 1918–1929* (London, 1974), and *The Palestinian Arab National Movement: From Riots to Rebellion* (London, 1977). In addition one should consult Porath's third volume in this series, *In Search of Arab Unity, 1930–1945* (London, 1986). Other essays of Porath's bearing on the rise of Arab Palestinian nationalism are "The Political Awakening of the Palestinian Arabs and Their Leadership Towards the End of the Ottoman Period," in Moshe Ma'oz, ed., *Studies on Palestine During the Ottoman Period* (Jerusalem, 1975), and "The Political Organization of the Palestinian Arabs Under the British Mandate," in Ma'oz, ed., *Palestinian Arab Politics* (Jerusalem, 1975).

In addition to Porath, I found the most informative studies of the origins of Arab Palestinian nationalism to be those by Rashid Khalidi, particularly his recently published book, *Palestinian Identity: The Construction of Modern National Consciousness* (New York, 1997). Also see his essays: "Arab Nationalism: Historical Problems in the Literature," *American Historical Review*, 95 (December 1991); "Ottomanism and Arabism in Syria Before 1914: A Reassessment," in Khalidi, *et al.* eds., *The Origins of Arab Nationalism* (New York, 1991); "Society and Ideology in Late Ottoman Syria: Class, Education, Profession and Confession," in J. Spagnolo, ed., *Problems of the Middle East in Historical Perspective: Essays in Honor of Albert Hourani* (Reading, England, 1992); and "Arab Nationalism in Syria: The Formative Years, 1908–1914," in William W. Haddad and William Ochsenwald, eds., *Nationalism in a Non-National State: The Dissolution of the Ottoman Empire* (Columbus, Ohio, 1977).

For other reliable accounts of the origins of Arab nationalism, see C. Ernest Dawn, *From Ottomanism to Arabism* (Urbana, Ill., 1973); Hisham Sharabi, *Arab Intellectuals and the West: The Formative Years, 1875–1914* (Baltimore, 1970); Anne M. Lesch, *Arab Politics in Palestine, 1917–1939* (Ithaca, 1979); Neville Mandel, *The Arabs and Zionism Before World War I* (Berkeley, 1976); Muhammad Muslih, *The Origins of Palestinian Nationalism* (New York, 1990); Rosemary Sayigh, *Palestinians: From Peasants to Revolutionaries* (London, 1979); A. L. Tibawi, *Anglo-Arab Relations and the Question of Palestine* (London, 1977); and Donna Robinson Divine, *Politics and Society in Ottoman Palestine* (Boulder, Colo., 1994).

The following anthologies proved useful: Ibrahim Abu-Lugdhod, ed., *The Transformation of Palestine: Essays on the Origins and Development of the Arab-Israeli Conflict* (Evanston, Ill., 1971); Walid Khalidi, ed., *From Haven to Conquest: Readings in Zionism and the Palestine Problem Until 1948* (Beirut, 1971), and *Palestine Reborn* (London, 1992); and Richard P. Stevens, ed., *Zionism and Palestine Before the Mandate: A Phase of Western Imperialism* (Beirut, 1972). Also see the useful summary by Roger Owen, "Economic Development in Mandatory Palestine: 1918–1948," in George T. Abed, ed., *The Palestinian Economy* (London, 1988). A fine group of essays appeared under the editorship of Gabriel Ben-Dor, *The Palestinians and the Middle East Conflict* (Ramat Gan and London, 1979). Also see Joel S. Migdal, ed., *Palestinian Society and Politics* (Princeton, 1980), and Baruch Kimmerling and Joel S. Migdal, eds., *Palestinians: The Making of a People* (Cambridge, Mass., 1993).

A fascinating specialized study is Beshara Doumani, *Rediscovering Palestine: Merchants and Peasants in Jabal Nablus, 1700–1900* (Berkeley, 1995). Two works of note are Said K. Aburish, *Children of Bethany: The Story of a Palestinian Family* (London, 1988), and Aref El-Aref, *Bedouin Love, Law and Legend* (Jerusalem, 1944).

My understanding of the government of Palestine during the period of the League of Nations mandate was enhanced by reading several basic texts: Bernard Wasserstein, *The British in Palestine: The Mandatory Government and the Arab-Jewish Conflict, 1917–1929*, 2nd ed. (Oxford, 1991); J. C. Hurewitz, *The Struggle for Palestine* (New York, 1976); A. W. Kayyali, *Palestine: A Modern History* (London, 1978); Pamela Ann Smith, *Palestine and the Palestinians, 1876–1983* (New York, 1984); Albert M. Hyamson, *Palestine Under the Mandate* (Westport, Conn., 1976); and H. Edward Knox, *The Making of a New Eastern Question: British Palestine Policy and the Origins of Israel, 1917–1925* (Washington, D.C., 1981). I found the writings of Norman Bentwich to be useful: *Fulfillment in the Promised Land, 1917–1937* (London, 1938), and his *England in Palestine* (London, 1932). Also see Herbert Sidebotham, *British Interests in Palestine* (London, 1934), and Richard Crossman, *A Nation Reborn: The Israel of Weizmann, Bevin and Ben-Gurion* (London, 1960).

No one can write on British policy in the Middle East without consulting Elizabeth Monroe's *Britain's Moment in the Middle East* (Baltimore, 1981), whether or not one agrees with her judgments. The same is true of Jukka Nevakivi's *Britain, France and the Arab Middle East, 1914–1920* (London, 1969).

I also studied British government policy papers and the two-volume study carried out by the Esco Foundation: *Palestine: A Study of Jewish, Arab, and British Policies* (New Haven, 1947).

For an appreciation of the cultural atmosphere of Palestine under the mandate, see Fannie Fern Andrews, *The Holy Land Under Mandate*, 2 vols. (Boston, 1931). Also see, in the same regard, Bertha Spafford Vester, *Our Jerusalem: An American Family in the Holy City, 1881–1949* (Jerusalem, 1988). I derived both pleasure and profit from reading David Fromkin, *A Peace to End*

All Peace: The Fall of the Ottoman Empire and the Creation of the Modern Middle East (New York, 1989); Connor Cruise O'Brien, *The Siege: The Saga of Israel and Zionism* (New York, 1986); and Ronald Sanders, *The High Walls of Jerusalem: A History of the Balfour Declaration and the Birth of the British Mandate for Palestine* (New York, 1983).

As previously noted, the best treatment of the causes behind Britain's issuance of the Balfour Declaration is Leonard Stein, *The Balfour Declaration* (New York, 1961), and the extension of Stein's analysis by the late Israeli historian Mayir Vereté. See in particular Vereté's "The Balfour Declaration and Its Makers," in Norman Rose, ed., *From Palmerston to Balfour: Collected Essays of Mayir Vereté* (London, 1992). Both Stein and Vereté take the position that while Chaim Weizmann certainly played a role in bringing about the Balfour Declaration, it was just that—a role, not the *cause* of the declaration, as others have argued. Among those who give Weizmann greater credit for influencing British policy vis-à-vis Jewish immigration and statehood are Yehuda Reinharz, whose splendid *Chaim Weizmann: The Making of a Statesman* (New York, 1993) I found of great use. So too the interesting essay of Jon Kimche, *The Unromantics: The Great Powers and the Balfour Declaration* (London, 1968). See also Erik Goldstein, "British Peace Aims and the Eastern Question: The Political Intelligence Department and the Eastern Committee, 1918," *Middle Eastern Studies*, 23 (1987).

To extend my knowledge of the Arab-Zionist conflict as it developed during the mandate, I relied on a number of works: Elie Kedourie and Sylvia G. Haim, eds., *Zionism and Arabism in Palestine and Israel* (London, 1982), and *Palestine and Israel in the 19th and 20th Centuries* (London, 1982). Elie Kedourie's own research proved invaluable for understanding the problems of British-Arab-Jewish relations. Among his most important works are *The Chatham House Version and Other Middle-Eastern Studies* (London, 1939), and *In the Anglo-Arab Labyrinth* (Cambridge, England, 1976).

The essays collected under the title *Zionism and the Arabs* (Jerusalem, 1983), ed. Shmuel Almog, were valuable in shaping my thinking.

For the diplomatic history surrounding the Arab-Zionist conflict, I turned to the works of Neil Caplan, *Palestine Jewry and the Arab Question, 1917–1925* (London, 1978), and Michael J. Cohen, *Palestine: Retreat from the Mandate: The Making of British Policy, 1936–45* (London, 1978); *Palestine to Israel: From Mandate to Independence* (London, 1988); *Palestine and the Great Powers, 1945–1948* (Princeton, 1982); and *The Origins and Evolution of the Arab-Zionist Conflict* (Berkeley, 1987). For a readable account of Palestine in the period of accelerated Jewish immigration from Europe after 1935, see Nicholas Bethell, *The Palestine Triangle: The Struggle Between the British, the Jews, and the Arabs, 1935–48* (London, 1979).

For specific analysis of the career and character of Palestine's grand mufti, Haj Amin al-Husayni, I relied on Philip Mattar, *The Mufti of Jerusalem: Al-Haj Amin Al-Husayni* (New York, 1988); also Zvi Elpeleg, *The Grand Mufti:*

Haj Amin al-Hussaini, Founder of the Palestinian National Movement (London, 1993). For a discussion of the mufti's role in the 1929 disturbances, see the accounts of Philip Mattar, "The Role of the Mufti of Jerusalem in the Political Struggle over the Western Wall, 1928–29," *Middle Eastern Studies,* 19 (1983); Pinhas Ofer, "The Commission on the Palestine Disturbances of August, 1929: Appointment, Terms of Reference, Procedure and Report," *Middle Eastern Studies,* 21 (1985); Yaacov Goldstein, "The 1929 Disturbances and Their Impact on the Formulation of Zionist Problems Concerning the Palestine Problem," *Asian and African Studies,* 24 (1990); Martin Kolinsky, "Premeditation in the Palestine Disturbances of August 1929?" *Middle Eastern Studies,* 16 (1990); and Uri M. Kupperschmidt, *The Supreme Muslim Council: Islam Under the British Mandate for Palestine* (Leiden, 1987).

Among the several accounts of the Arab rebellion of 1936–1939, I found instructive Tom Bowden's "The Politics of the Arab Rebellion in Palestine, 1936–39," *Middle Eastern Studies,* 11 (1975); Yehohada Haim, "Zionist Policies and Attitudes Towards the Arabs on the Eve of the Arab Revolt, 1936," *Middle Eastern Studies,* 14 (1978); and Israel Gershoni, "The Muslim Brothers and the Arab Revolt in Palestine, 1936–39," *Middle Eastern Studies,* 22 (1986).

On the later development of Arab politics, the articles of Joseph Nevo proved particularly useful: "The Arabs of Palestine 1947–48: Military and Political Activity," *Middle Eastern Studies,* 23 (1987); "The Palestine Arab Party, 1944–1946," *Asian and African Studies,* 14 (1980); "Palestinian-Arab Violent Activity During the 1930s," in Michael J. Cohen and Martin Kolinsky, eds., *Britain and the Middle East in the 1930s* (London, 1992); "Al-Hajj Amin and the British in World War II," *Middle Eastern Studies,* 20 (1984); and "The Renewal of Palestinian Activity, 1943–1945," in Ben-Dor, *Palestinians and the Middle East Conflict.*

Also see Haim Levenberg, "Abdullah and Cunningham: Palestine 1945–48," *Middle Eastern Studies,* 27 (1991); G. Sheffer, "British Colonial Policy-Making Towards Palestine (1929–1939)," *Middle Eastern Studies,* 14 (1978). On interpreting the role of Ben-Gurion, I turned to Ronald W. Zweig, ed., *David Ben-Gurion: Politics and Leadership in Israel* (Jerusalem, 1991); Shabtai Teveth, *Ben-Gurion: The Burning Ground, 1886–1948* (Boston, 1987); and Yaacov Goldstein, "David Ben-Gurion and the Bi-national Idea in Palestine," *Middle Eastern Studies,* 24 (1988). I found valuable Yehohada Haim's book-length essay, *Abandonment of Illusions: Zionist Political Attitudes Toward Palestinian Arab Nationalism, 1936–1939* (Boulder, Colo., 1983).

On the specific question of land acquisition, development, and dislocation, I relied mainly on the books of Abraham Granott (Granovsky) and Kenneth Stein. In addition one should see Stein's "The Jewish National Fund: Land Purchase Method and Priorities, 1924–1939," *Middle Eastern Studies,* 20 (1984). See also Arieh L. Avneri, *The Claim of Dispossession* (New Brunswick, N.J., 1984), and Charles S. Kamen, *Little Common Ground: Arab Agriculture and Jewish Settlement in Palestine, 1920–1948* (Pittsburgh, 1991); and Y. Porath,

"The Land Problem as a Factor in Relations Among Arabs, Jews and the Mandatory Government," in Ben-Dor, *Palestinians and the Middle East Conflict.*

For the problems affecting education of the Arab peasantry during the mandate, I utilized Ylana N. Miller's fine study, *Government and Society in Rural Palestine, 1920–1948* (Austin, Tex., 1985).

There are several interesting works on Arab women of Palestine, beginning with the memoirs of Fannie Fern Andrews, cited above. See *The Arab Woman and the Palestine Problem* by Mrs. Matiel E. T. Mogannam (London, 1937), and Sylvia G. Haim, "The Situation of the Arab Woman in the Mirror of Literature," *Middle Eastern Studies*, 17 (1981).

Index

A NOTE ON THE AUTHOR

Thomas A. Idinopulos grew up in Portland, Oregon, and studied at Reed College, Duke University, the University of Athens, and the University of Chicago, where he received both an M.A. and a Ph.D. He has written widely on the political and religious history of the Middle East, including award-winning articles in the *Christian Century,* the *Middle East Review, Midstream, Worldview,* the *Journal of Religion, USA Today,* and other periodicals. His books include *Jerusalem* and *The Erosion of Faith.* Mr. Idinopulos has been a resident scholar at the Ecumenical Institute for Advanced Theological Studies in Israel; a guest scholar at Mishkenot Sha'ananim, the "Dwellings of Tranquility" of the Jerusalem Foundation; and a fellow to the Patriarchal Institute for Patristic Studies at the Vlatadon Monastery, Thessaloniki, Greece. He is professor of religious studies at Miami University in Oxford, Ohio, and is married with two sons.